The Organic
HOME GARDEN

The Organic HOME GARDEN

HOW TO GROW VEGETABLES
& FRUITS NATURALLY

Patrick Lima

Photography by John Scanlan

Good Luck
Patrick Lima
John Scanlan
Thanksgiving
'06

KEY PORTER BOOKS

This book is dedicated to our mothers, Anne Marie Scanlan and Katie Lima, for their support and encouragement; and to all organic gardeners, novice or seasoned, who understand the need to take care of the land for both the present and the future.

National Library of Canada Cataloguing in Publication

Lima, Patrick
The organic home garden : how to grow vegetables and fruits naturally / Patrick Lima ; photography by John Scanlan.

Includes index.
Originally published as: The kitchen garden. Toronto : Key Porter, 1992.

ISBN 1-55263-305-5

1. Vegetable gardening. 2. Fruit-culture. 3. Organic gardening.I. Scanlan, John II. Title.

SB324.3.L55 2004   635'.0484   C2003-905744-5

The publisher gratefully acknowledges the support of the Canada Council for the Arts and the Ontario Arts Council for its publishing program.

We acknowledge the support of the Government of Ontario through the Ontario Media Development Corporation's Ontario Book Initiative.

We acknowledge the financial support of the Government of Canada through the Book Publishing Industry Development Program (BPIDP) for our publishing activities.

Page i:
A sampling of the garden's seasonal abundance.

Frontispiece:
Lovely to look at and delightful to eat, French lettuces, such as 'Canasta' and 'Victoria,' can be cut at the leafy stage or left to form dense, compact heads.

Portions of this book appeared in *The Kitchen Garden*.

Design: Peter Maher
Typesetting: Jean Lightfoot Peters
Printed and bound in China

Key Porter Books Limited
70 The Esplanade
Toronto, Ontario
Canada M5E 1R2

03 04 05 06 07 5 4 3 2 1

Contents

Breaking New Ground

FIRST GARDEN

Almost from the moment I set trowel to earth I knew I had found something I loved to do. Suddenly a world of wonders opened up. It was 1973. My friend John Scanlan and I had access to the garden of a rented city house. Like many other people then—and now—we were concerned about the array of pesticides routinely used on food plants. A small yard meant that we could grow at least some of our own food free from chemical residues. From the start, it never occurred to us to garden any way other than organically. We knew that freshly picked vegetables and fruits are at their nutritional best, and we soon learned how delicious they could be: vine-ripened tomatoes, peas fresh from the pod, a crisp head of cabbage or lettuce mere minutes from garden to salad bowl. We also discovered the simple pleasure and satisfaction that come from working with the soil, sowing seeds, tending a garden, bringing in the harvest.

The soil in our first city garden was dense and full of cinders, probably the dumping ground for years' worth of coal ashes. But optimistically we dug and planted. Results were mixed. Tomatoes spread into a wild tangle, half their fruit lost under leaves; zucchinis swelled overnight, apparently blown up by some unseen squash fairy. Marigolds bloomed among the vegetables and morning glories crawled over everything. Unwittingly we spread fungus on the Swiss chard by watering every evening. Not knowing better, we transplanted small pea vines from the shade to the sunnier front yard; the peas, not knowing that they "resent transplanting," attached themselves to strings and began to climb. Cucumbers soon joined them to veil the front porch in green vines hung with fruit. Squirrels helped themselves. It was not

a completely successful garden, but in a season we were smitten. And we had learned the gardener's perennial refrain: "Next year. . . ."

Our homesteading instincts were roused. That winter we pored over copies of *Organic Gardening* magazine in preparation for some "real" gardening next spring. Seeds arrived in the mail. From bits of scrap wood, we knocked together shallow boxes for seedlings that sprouted under a bank of florescent lights in the basement. Gardening articles had convinced us that the key to good growth lay in adding quantities of organic matter—manure, compost, rotted leaves and such—to the soil. Dutifully, we looked around for sources.

As it happened, this was shortly after the downtown zoo had closed. One day, while walking through the deserted grounds, we saw a heap of manure on the other side of a high chain-link fence. The sign on the fence read "Yak," but there was no yak (or any other creature) in sight. Longingly, we looked through the fence. "If we could get in there," John said, "with buckets or bags and a shovel . . ."

Early next morning we were back, with two burlap potato sacks and a spade in hand. Up and over the fence we climbed, and in no time had two bags full—and heavy. With considerable effort we hoisted the bags over the fence and dragged them to the boulevard. It was going to be a long haul home. There had to be a better way. And there it was, coming down the street. We were soon settled comfortably on the streetcar with our bags of soggy yak dung—and no one the wiser. It was the first of several excursions to collect what is now sensibly composted and sold as Zoo Poo.

Eager to experiment that second season,

OPPOSITE:
Larkwhistle, our garden, grew out of a flat, sandy hayfield thick with twitch grass and weeds. Seasons of organic care and cultivation have transformed the field into a lush and productive home garden.

we grew a little of almost everything. Adding organic matter to the garden made a noticeable difference. Spaghetti squash trailed along a wire fence, dangling yellow fruit on both sides. Brilliant Scarlet Runner beans coiled up a tropical looking sumac tree. Cabbages and romaine folded into proper heads, while yellow crookneck squash cascaded down a hill of compost. Tomatoes, staked and trained by the book, grew red in the sun. To our delight, the small city yard provided us with almost all the fresh vegetables we needed through the summer and into fall.

To use the yard to the fullest, we laid the garden out in beds (rather than rows) and planted the beds intensively so that every square foot of earth was growing vegetables, herbs or flowers. Even today, with room to spare in a country garden, we continue to grow vegetables and fruit in beds tended with basic hand tools.

The chapter called By Design (page 23) details how to design, build and plant intensive beds that make the best use of any space. Throughout the book, photos show small, easily maintained beds of odd shapes and dimensions filled with lettuces, beans, carrots, even corn. To get the most from small space, tomatoes are staked and anything that can climb—cucumbers, peas, beans, squash—is directed upward on strings, wire, netting or trellises. For most home gardeners some variation on intensive gardening is the most efficient way to grow—planting a little of this and that in whatever space you have, back yard or front, along a walkway, up a fence or porch. Food plants take their place beautifully in any landscape.

GOING TO THE COUNTRY

In July of 1975, just as our second city garden was overflowing with growth and color, notice came: the house was to be sold and we would have to be out by the end of August. Confirmed city slickers until then, it had never occurred to us to search for a place in the country. We had no car. Where would we work? What was out there anyway? And yet, when a friend told us about land four hours north, we decided to investigate. The land, she said, belonged to a couple, university professors who lived in town and had bought property to preserve it. In a spirit of experimentation, the professors had allowed some of their students to build a geodesic dome on the property, and try their hand at "homesteading." A succession of students had lived in the dome and done some gardening; but all had pulled up stakes, usually after the first winter. The dome now stood empty, our friend said, and assured us that the professors, almost second family to her, would not mind if we moved in and gardened a half-acre corner of the 300-acre parcel.

We had a rough map, a few lines and an X penciled on a scrap of paper. One Saturday morning, we boarded a northbound Greyhound, got off three hours later and reboarded a yellow school bus that traveled on from there on summer weekends. The driver opened her doors for us at a gravel sideroad. Laden with back-packs and tent, rake and shovel over our shoulders, we hitchhiked and walked the remaining six miles in—looking for a place to garden.

Turning the last corner, we saw a flat field waist-high in swaying grass. A giant dead elm, gray and barkless, spread its twisted arms against the sky. A leaning barn, sided with weathered wooden shingles, sheltered a flock of swallows. Toppling fence posts, looped with rusty barbed wire, outlined what may once have been a garden. Half-hidden in the grass, a rusty iron hand-pump stood beside a shoulder of exposed rock. The field was broken here and there by piles of rock, old apple trees and banks of lilacs. Later we came to recognize the signs that tell a story: here a family cleared land; piled stones by hand; joined with neighbors to build shelters; planted shrubs, an orchard, daylilies, daffodils, a vegetable garden; perhaps suffered a fire; rebuilt down the road or moved away.

After pitching our tent by the well, we were eager to find out what lay under the grass. Digging through the thatch of roots, we came up with handfuls of earth so dry it flowed through our fingers like sand in an hourglass. This was not the dark loam we were hoping for, but it was late July of a dry year—and better sand than brick-hard clay. And weren't the magazines filled with tales of unpromising ground transformed into fertile soil?

Back in the woods, and the end of a rutted track, a quarter-mile from field and well, stood the dome, bug-eyed and silver, like an alien craft landed by accident among the maples, a pod-like assembly of 2x4's and canvas covered in something resembling sponge-toffee. The curious cabin was uninhabited, cluttered, dirty, and filled with flotsam from previous occupants—snowshoes, oil-lamps, buckets and basins, an old oak dining table, over-stuffed chairs and a massive wood-burning cookstove—not, at first glance, unlivable, but not obviously inviting either. If we made the move this would be our home—no indoor plumbing, no electricity, water source a quarter mile away—at least for a while.

What to do? Nothing in our experience had prepared us for this. The change from city life to living on the land would be drastic and complete. We had no vehicle—once here, we'd be here. Winter would present special challenges—firewood to cut, water to haul, the outdoor privy. There would be no easy way to run out to a store; we'd be totally isolated. On the other hand, we could garden to our heart's content, without a hiatus of who knew how long, saving tips from waitering jobs, looking for a place, going into debt. The land was not for sale, but it was available. The price was risking change. We could simply start.

It is my experience that at life's inevitable crossroads—times of difficult decisions—there is often a wise voice of guidance, either from within or without—an intuition, a friend's counsel, a twist of fate. Was it a coincidence, then, that on the bus going home we happened to sit next to a woman who said exactly what we needed to hear to tip the balance? As we told her what we were contemplating, she asked a few simple questions: "Is there anything keeping you in the city?" (Not really—no family obligations and restaurant jobs are not hard to find.) "Why not give yourselves a year, try it out, see how you like living in the country? You're not burning any bridges—you can always go back."

Looking at it that way, we were able to see the whole implausible scheme as experiment and adventure. Two weeks later, my brother-in-law hauled us (and three cats) back to the land, trucking our few possessions, a second-hand tiller, and heavy sacks of rice, grains and beans—enough food to see us through winter, mere months away. After helping us move in, he pulled away with a wave and the encouraging parting words: "You'll never make it here." John tells me that at that moment he made up his mind to meet the challenges presented in this new phase and see them through. A line from the I Ching had stayed with him: "Perseverance brings good fortune."

Not that we knew where "here" was for a year or more. So focused were we on gardening, so tired from hauling water from pump to cabin and flats of seedlings the other way, we had no idea that beautiful blue Georgian Bay was just over the hill until one Sunday we went for a longer-than-usual walk.

DIGGING IN

We had come to garden. Taking a clue about where to start from the line of leaning fence posts in the field, we began to clear space. Sputtering with effort, the second-hand tiller chewed into the wiry grass roots. This was no tame lawn. We soon learned to identify quackgrass and bindweed, no friends to gardeners. Or were they? As we tilled, it occurred to us that this sandy soil would have been gone with the wind long ago without the closely woven roots protecting it from erosion. In a few days we had opened up a long narrow strip of earth.

Curious to test the soil's potential, we seeded a row of 'Purple-Top White Globe' turnips. Over the next weeks, until snow flurries called time-out, we continued to dig, clear, rake and shape beds for spring. It was an ideal fall for turnips—warm, wet and

At mid-growth, many vegetable plants benefit from a palmful of blood meal or balanced natural fertilizer sprinkled in a circular band around them and worked gently into the ground with shallow cultivation.

drawn out. Despite the mid-August planting date, the roots turnips grew fat and round, and by late October we had two bushels of turnips—our first harvest. We ate a lot of turnips with our rice and beans that winter—curried turnip, stir-fried and mashed turnip, shredded turnip salad—and, good as they were, we haven't planted them since.

WINTER WONDER

How to describe that first winter? The landscape painted in swaths of simple color: black-and-white birch trunks, shadowy green cedars, the purple-gray haze of the leafless forest. Above the encrusted snow, crackling stalks and seedheads of last summer's wildflowers stood stiff under a sky brilliant blue for a spell, then drained of all color for days on end, even the sun coldly pale behind a veil of icy flakes.

Indigo night skies glittered with more stars than we'd ever seen; moonlit shadows lay across the blue-white snow. I remember the silence, nights so still that at first the silence made us as uneasy as the occasional creak of branches and the howling wolves. What was out there in the dark? Gradually we began to feel safe; to realize that we were in a benign place inhabited by a few industrious squirrels and chipmunks, some brave and lively winter birds—and little else. During the first raging blizzard we realized how much shelter the trees gave. Moving from open field back into the woods, buck-

ets of water bouncing on a toboggan, was like closing a door on the gale; it was always warmer and calmer in the forest. Chickadees, swooping down to take sunflower seeds from our hands, welcomed us.

It was a winter of new experiences. Priorities were pared to life's basics, first among them keeping warm. Lacking cut and dried wood, we burned what a neighbor called "gopher wood—you need 'er, you go fur 'er." Cutting dead elm trees with ax and Swede saw, we discovered that wood does indeed warm you twice.

HOMEWORK

At one o'clock, every day but Sunday, John or I would trudge down to the road, park ourselves in a seat cut in the snowbank, and wait for the mailman's station wagon, often the only car to pass all day. The mail brought gardening books from the library and seed catalogs from all over. In those winter weeks we took a crash course in food-growing. Seed and nursery orders reflected not only a curiosity that now had room to grow, but also a wish to raise enough food to feed ourselves all summer and fall with plenty left over to store for winter.

By early March, as the days grew mercifully longer, seedlings began to sprout in pots and flats by the windows. Salvaged lumber and old storm windows became two cold frames that were set outside the moment the snow subsided. More scrap lumber and a pair of old bicycle wheels were transformed into a wobbly version of those expensive two-wheeled garden carts pictured in gardening magazines. We'd be making many trips with tools and plants from cabin to garden and back.

Never was spring more welcome, a stirring reveille after the long spell of sleep. Wet moss shone with emerald vibrancy against glistening snow remnants; spreading junipers shook off winter's weight and sprang back to growth. Ravens heralded the change. As the snow curtain receded from our patch of cleared earth, moist dark beds full of potential came to light. In the woods, white patches still lay in hollows and in the shadow of boulders, but the warming sun roused us to action. It was time to put away the books, roll out the wobbly cart and load it with tools, stakes and string, packets of peas, spinach seeds and onion sets—the first seeds of our first full season on the land. A new garden beckoned.

For two seasons we concentrated on developing a big organic vegetable garden—we needed something beside turnips to jazz up those rice and beans—mining a dense accretion of sheep manure from the tumbling barn to nourish new beds. In standard organic fashion, bug-repellent marigolds and nasturtiums, vivid yellow, orange and scarlet, grew among the vegetables. We were caught. There had to be more color, something for spring at least. In our simple idealism, we took to heart the old saying: If you have two dollars, spend one on bread and one on daffodils: feed body, feed soul. Spending our next-to-last twenty on daffodils and crocuses, we tucked them into the earth before hitching (cats and all) back to the city to sort Christmas mail and wait on tables for a few months. What can I say: we were young; we loved to garden.

FOR INSPIRATION

Times change. One trial year on the land has become many seasons of making and caring for a garden, putting down roots in a place that is now home. The old dome collapsed one winter under a weighty burden of snow—luckily, no one was in it. Suddenly our small tool shed by the garden had to be enlarged, insulated, and turned into proper living quarters. The old iron hand-pump, first powered with a solar motor, and now operated electrically, continues to supply all the water for home and garden. Gradually our horticultural horizons expanded to include herbs, fruit trees and the lovely realm of perennial flowers. Our garden acquired a name: Larkwhistle.

Our purpose in this book is not to provide hard-and-fast rules, but rather to share how we meet the challenges of our site, soil, and climate. Local variations, as specific as the microclimate in your own back yard, need local solutions. Planting times also vary widely from north to south. The tomato plants which we put into our garden in late May might go into the ground in April down south, in June further north. The chapters that follow are organized according to the sequence of the food grower's year. The specific timing of seeding and transplanting changes from one part of the country to another, but the sequence remains the same: plant lettuce, whether early or late, in the cool of the year, and set out your peppers when there is no danger of frost. The calendar and charts on pages 34–35 can be customized to suit your area once you know the approximate date of the last frost in spring and the first frost in fall.

Measuring less than one-quarter of an acre, our kitchen garden yields something good to eat from May until the following March, if you count what is stored, and the hardy roots that stay in the ground all winter. The entire one-acre garden, including a number of flower beds, is nearly full-time work for the two of us, with occasional helpers. All the work is done by hand, except for some spring and fall tilling. Larkwhistle is a big country garden, but the food beds are small, almost intimate, and the techniques we use can be translated to any yard. Whether you wish to grow a summer's supply of salad greens, a few tomatoes and peppers or a full season harvest of all your family's favorites, we hope you'll find both inspiration and information aplenty in these pages. On any scale, an organically tended kitchen garden provides the best-tasting and healthiest food you can find. The natural gardener leaves the soil in good condition, a valuable legacy for future generations.

Earth Care
Creating and Sustaining Lively Soil

The roots of the words garden, yard and orchard all spring from the same source, an old word meaning an enclosed or protected place. As gardeners we are reminded of our responsibility to do our best by the piece of land we tend; to protect—and restore if necessary—the fragment of Earth in our care. Some people treat earth like dead old dirt, but it is actually vibrant with life. How else could it give rise to such a constant wonder of growth and beauty? The layer of soil, from a fraction of an inch to several feet deep, that mantles the planet's surface, gives birth and sustenance to all that lives on it and then, in a miracle of recycling, takes back what has died and transforms it into nourishment for new life. The natural gardener looks to the earth itself for soil-building lessons.

LIVELY EARTH

Soil scientists confirm that earth teems with living creatures. In a single teaspoon of fertile soil, they say, live 4 billion bacteria, up to 325 feet (100 m) of mold or fungus filaments, 144 million actinomycetes (one of the infinitely small, and unpronounceable, organisms responsible for changing organic matter into nutrients for plants), as well as countless other microorganisms such as algae and yeasts. That's a lot of life in a teaspoon.

The goal of organic gardening is to nourish and maintain life in the soil, for the simple reason that lively earth gives rise to vigorous, healthy plants that are less susceptible to diseases and, curiously, less appealing to insects. I find the notion of 4 billion bacteria as hard to grasp as that of the infinity of stars in space, but I know that gardening organically helps me to feel actively connected to Earth's eternal cycles—the turning seasons, the process of growth, decay and new growth. I like the sense of cooperating with nature, rather than opposing. By now we know the devastating consequences of forgetting our vital links with the Earth—the damage we are capable of inflicting on water, soil, air, other creatures and, ultimately, ourselves. Organic gardening is good medicine, a positive step toward mending our relationship with the world around us.

SOIL SCIENCE

Over the years we have seen Larkwhistle's original soil—pale, dry and sandy in the extreme—grow darker, richer and more productive with each application of compost, leaf mold, manure and other organic matter. Nurturing the soil first means much less time spent later on solving problems that could have been prevented—and much more time enjoying the garden.

The first step toward a flourishing food garden is to find out what type of soil you have. Gardeners are often advised to have a soil test done. The process involves digging trowelfuls of earth from various parts of the garden, mixing them up and sending a sample to your local department of agriculture for testing. You can also buy soil-testing kits, some more sophisticated than others, that let you play chemist in your own backyard.

In large cities, or if you are planning a food garden close to an older house that has been shedding paint flakes for years, it is wise to have the soil tested for lead, arsenic and other toxins. In contaminated soils, many food plants can accumulate toxins at unhealthy levels. The solution is to dig out the poisoned soil and replace it with good, clean earth.

When my partner and I first moved to the country, we sent off a vial of sandy soil to the nearest agricultural college. In a few weeks

OPPOSITE: To improve the texture and fertility of any soil, spread a generous layer of fine-textured organic matter and turn it under.

the results were back, and we were left scratching our heads. The test assumed we were going to apply artificial fertilizers and the results were a perplexing mix of chemistry and mathematics. For someone who has trouble decoding instructions for mixing liquid fertilizer, some of the recommendations might as well have been hieroglyphics.

As we were mulling over the numbers, a neighbor stopped by. After glancing at the page for a few seconds, he handed it back, as baffled as we were. "Haven't a clue what that means," he said, leaning on a fence post, "but I know this place. It's good land. Just sock the shit to it and it'll grow anything." Here was advice we could understand. Not that we completely ignored the information on the soil test. Results showed that the pH hovered around neutral, but the earth was deficient in phosphorus, a nutrient essential for strong roots, fruit development and improved disease resistance. With that in mind, we have made a habit of applying crushed phosphate rock and bone meal over the past twenty-five years. And, of course, we keep socking not only the manure to the land, but also compost, decayed leaves, soggy old hay and such—a well balanced soil-food diet. Soil tests have changed over the years. Now some labs specialize in tests for organic gardeners. Test results suggest corrective doses of natural fertilizers and even tell you how much manure to use.

Generous and consistent applications of organic matter are the surest way to enhance the life of any soil. That may be all you need to know to grow a perfectly wonderful garden. It makes sense: you can't expect a splendid harvest year after year without giving something back to the earth in return.

SWEET AND SOUR SOIL

When it comes to earth care, an organic gardener sets out to accomplish several things: improve soil texture, boost and balance fertility, and sometimes alter pH, a measurement of the soil's degree of acidity or alkalinity on a scale of 0 to 14. The lower the number, the more acidic the soil, with 0 being the most sour and 14 the most alkaline. Typically, soils range from 4.5— quite acidic ground suitable for blueberries and cranberries and found mainly in cold, damp areas—to a slightly alkaline 7.5. Once again, the middle ground is best, with most food plants thriving in a pH hovering around neutral (6 to 6.8). In the old days, farmers would taste their soil to see if it was sour (low pH), bitter (too alkaline) or nice and middling sweet, but if you're averse to eating dirt, a soil test will tell you.

Given the typical pH range, you are more likely to have to raise rather than lower the pH. Ground limestone, otherwise known as horticultural lime, is like a sugar for the soil and, like sugar, it is better to add too little than too much. You can always spread more, but you'll never remove it. To raise the pH of sandy loam by one point, use 3 pounds (1.4 kg) of lime spread evenly over 100 square feet (9 m²) and dig in, either in fall or in early spring. On clay loam use 5 pounds (2.25 kg) per 100 square feet. One application should be sufficient for three to five years. Hold the lime in an area planned for berries or potatoes.

However, if the soil test indicated that the earth has too much lime, then powdered sulfur moves the pH toward neutral. Typical applications: 3 pounds (1.4 kg) of sulfur per 100 square feet (9 m²) to change the pH from 8.0 to 6.5; 2 pounds (0.9 kg) per 100 square feet moves the needle from 7.5 to 6.5, or 7.0 to 6.0. To dramatically alter the pH from 7.0 to 5.5, apply 3 ½ pounds (1.6 kg) of sulfur per 100 square feet.

Lime and sulfur help balance extremes, but if the soil holds a generous measure of organic matter, many plants will grow well despite a less-than-perfect pH. Our garden grows most of the common vegetables and some exotics; a raft of herbs, berries and tree fruit; over 500 different flowering perennials and numerous shrubs and ornamental trees. Except for that first soil test, we couldn't tell you what the pH is. We seldom apply lime, and the only plant that gets an annual dose of sulfur is a clump of acid-loving Japanese iris, and even it seems to care more about water than soil.

An array of natural soil amendments (from left to right): homemade compost, peat moss, bone meal, a balanced natural fertilizer and kelp meal.

HANDS IN

Garden soil is composed of sand, silt (micro-scopic rock pieces) and clay in various proportions, with an admixture of small or large stones. Bringing these inert particles to life is that magical ingredient—organic mat-ter, with all its attendant creatures.

"Feed the soil, not the plants" is another tenet of organic gardening. But before we look at food for the soil, we had better get our hands into the soil itself—literally. One of the best ways to find out if you have sandy or clay soil is to feel it. Both extremes make for difficult growing.

Rub fairly dry soil between thumb and fingers. Sand particles feel coarse and gritty; very silty soil has the floury texture of tal-cum powder; dry clay is hard and chunky. If the soil is moist, squeeze a handful into a ball. Clay-based soil feels sticky and may ooze water when squeezed; open your hand and a ball of clay soil will hold together and probably show your fingerprints. Sandy soil, in contrast, tends to fall apart as you open your hand, whereas loam may adhere into a ball, but will crumble when prodded. Loam,

lovely loam, is a balanced blend of sand, silt and clay, with a good amount of organic matter. As such, it is usually darker than very sandy or clay soil. Depending on what particles predominate, you may have coarse sandy loam, fine sandy loam, clay loam of various densities and so on. Sandy soil warms up quickly in spring, dries quicker and is a pleasure to dig and weed. The gar-den's state after a downpour also tells you something about its soil. If water sits in pud-dles for some time and the soil sticks to shoes and shovel, you have clay or clay loam. If rain drains away and you can tread the paths afterward without getting bogged down, you are walking on sandy loam.

What happens in a dry spell? Clay-based soil holds moisture longer than sandy ground, but if clay is unmulched or unculti-vated it dries to a hard surface often criss-crossed with cracks. Sandy ground retains less water at first and dries more quickly, turning to gritty dust that may whip away in the wind. As water drains through sandy land, it takes soluble nutrients out of the reach of roots. Loam, that happy medium, holds moisture well but lets super-fluous water drain through; as it dries, it turns fluffy and crumbly, rather than hard or dusty.

Fortunately for gardeners, most soils are in the loam category—although you may not think so as you shovel lumps of unyielding clay, or struggle to keep sandy soil even vaguely damp in July. Most hover within a few degrees of neutral on the pH scale. The rest of the good news is that, sweet or sour, clay or sand or anything in-between, all soils respond favorably to similar care and feeding.

Soil Food

A good way to find out how to enhance texture and fertility of soil is to take a hike, and observe what is happening in woods or meadows at ground level. Leaves slowly moldering on the forest floor are composting; dead meadow grasses seared by winter's frost are being broken down by the damp earth beneath. Turn over a mat of leaves under a lilac bush (if you haven't swept them all away), and chances are you'll see earthworms beating a fast retreat into the ground and sow bugs scurrying away. These are but two of the creatures that work incessantly to turn fallen leaves, dead trees, frosted tomato vines, corn stalks—all spent vegetation—into soil food and, eventually, nutrients for plant growth.

The perfect food for soil and its inhabitants is organic matter. This includes plant residues such as old hay, grass clippings, leaves, coffee grounds, fruit and vegetable scraps, even sawdust, woodchips and newsprint. Animal manure of any kind is good—and only becomes a threat to water supplies when it is spread in staggeringly large quantities in liquid form, something a home gardener never does. Other animal by-products such as ground bone and dried blood also benefit the soil. Over time, soil life literally digests organic matter, transforming it into smaller and smaller bits that hold together as humus, a dark, porous, sticky substance that wonderfully improves both the texture and the fertility of any earth.

COMPOST
Piles and Pits

The terms "humus" and "organic matter" are often used interchangeably, but organic matter is the raw material you put into the compost heap, and humus is the rich, dark, crumbly finished product. If you can identify it, it's still organic matter. Humus is what organic matter becomes when it is completely broken down.

It is a mark of nature's efficiency that returning lots of organic matter to the earth works, over time, to bring both sandy and clay soil toward a loamy middle ground. Because humus is bulky and fibrous, it breaks up dense, fine-grained clay, allowing air (an important free fertilizer) to enter and water to drain better. Since it is also somewhat spongy, humus helps to bind sandy soil's coarse, loose particles and to hold moisture that might otherwise run through. Organic matter also tends to correct the soil pH, bringing both extremes toward a favorable neutral range.

On the subject of compost, garden writers wax eloquent: "brown gold," "recycled sunlight," "the key to soil fertility," "a great healer and buffer, and the gentle way to restore soil health," "in the dank and moldy pile the wheel of life is turning." And it's true. Compost is the heart of an organic garden, a symbol of nature's eternal effort to re-create healthy soil and the gardener's willingness to cooperate. Nature has all the time in the world to turn forest leaves into fertilizer, but a well-built compost accelerates the process, allowing a gardener to significantly improve the soil each season.

Garden books are filled with recipes for turning out perfect compost in fourteen days, a task that involves shredding ingredients, building precise layers of green stuff and manure and turning the works over and over. The result is rich chocolate-cakey compost that plants all but thank you for.

I don't think we've ever succeeded in achieving that result. What we usually settle for is less-than-perfect compost in about fourteen months. All through the season, our one-acre garden generates compostable

When we clean up in the fall, we build a large compost heap, a "layer cake" composed of manure and garden refuse chopped into smaller pieces with a machete. Topped with soil and left unturned, the heap cooks for fourteen months.

material, but literally tons of stuff becomes available in September and October during the fall cleanup when we build "the big pile."

Our fall composting process goes something like this:

1. Haul wheelbarrow-loads of green stuff to the growing heap, and dump enough plant residues to make a fluffy layer about 1 foot (30 cm) deep.
2. Jump onto the pile, machete in hand, and whack away at the leaves and stalks to chop them into smaller pieces, trampling the heap to about half the original size in the process.
3. Spread a 2- to 3-inch (5- to 8-cm) layer of manure, fresh if possible, over the green layer.
4. Keep building the heap in layers of green stuff and manure over the next days and weeks until it grows to about 4 feet (1.2 m) high.
5. Top the finished pile with a few inches of soil or a thatch of hay.

You might call this the haul-dump-jump-whack-tread-spread-top-and-wait method.

Once built, the heap is left to slow-cook through the fall, all winter (very slow indeed) and over the next summer.

But the compost is not merely taking up space over those months. The fact that compost heaps routinely sprout tomato, cucumber, and squash seedlings (not to mention weeds) tells us there is growth potential there. In the spring, we plant winter-squash vines on top of the heap; the vines seem not to mind the rough texture—and surely appreciate the manure—and their roots may help aerate and break down the pile.

Turning such a pile by hand is more than we are prepared to do; patience saves the back. By fall, the compost should be ready for use. Because fine-textured compost is easier to turn into the garden, we usually sift out lumps and chunks by shaking the compost into a wheelbarrow through a screen of ¾-inch mesh fastened to a wooden frame.

Over the summer, we make another compost using kitchen scraps, spent pea vines, seedy lettuces, coarse cabbage leaves, dead-head flowers, out-of-favor plants, weeds before they've gone to seed, manure,

In the compost pile, raw ingredients (foreground) are transformed into the best all-round fertilizer and texturizer you can find. Sifting reduces the compost into rich, dark crumbs that are a pleasure to work into the soil or spread as mulch.

and the like. Grass clippings are left where they fall to fertilize the lawn.

Such large-scale composting is appropriate in a big country garden where there is a ready supply of manure and few neighbors to object to the growing pile of "debris" and the occasionally whiffy dung heap. Last fall, when pressed for space, we built a big oval compost, enclosed by snow fencing, outside the garden, a few feet from the road, something that would probably raise cries of protest in suburbia. Personally I think composting ought to be encouraged wherever and however it happens, but many gardeners want to find a tidy, odorless way.

CITY COMPOST

Tidy compost means enclosed compost, and there are a number of ways to do it. Easiest of all is a ready-made commercial composter, usually some variation on a perforated black plastic drum or barrel. One model sits on the ground, which is a good feature because it invites earthworms. Another, suspended horizontally in a metal frame, can be spun around (like those drums full of lottery tickets) to tumble and mix the compost. Though not quite the humus factories they claim to be, commercial composters do keep

everything out of sight; they also fill up rather quickly unless you have a very small garden.

Homemade compost bins also do the trick of hiding and containing. Bins should be at least 3 feet (90 cm) square, and situated on bare earth, in some shade if possible. If they are easily accessible, so much the better. Two compost bins are better than one, and one is better than none. Triple bins, side by side, allow you to build one compost pile, let it simmer while you make a second pile and then turn the first pile into the empty third bin and the second pile into the first bin. Bins may be made of boards (scrap lumber, if you have it) on three sides, with or without removable front slats or a hinged front door.

Alternatively, use some type of metal mesh—fine-mesh chicken wire, hardware cloth, wire fencing—stapled or nailed to two-by-fours; a hinged front door makes for easy loading and holds the compost in place. Wire mesh may deter rodents, especially if it is sunk a few inches into the ground.

A cylinder of snow fence, a meter or more in diameter, makes a movable enclosure; two or three can fit inconspicuously in most yards. Snow fence can also be used to contain your yard's output of tree leaves, which, if added to the "regular" compost, will tend to mat down and slow the process. The leaves will eventually decay into leaf mold, a valuable fertilizer and conditioner. Shredding leaves will turn them into leaf mold much faster. Indeed, leaves are one of the finest sources of organic matter you can get—free, mineral-rich and abundant.

NATURAL FERTILIZERS
Soil contains three major plant foods: nitrogen (N), phosphorus (P) and potassium (K). Lesser amounts of magnesium, calcium, sulfur and various trace minerals also contribute to healthy growth.

I wouldn't recognize nitrogen if it jumped up and bit me, but I do know that a row of spinach perks up amazingly when watered with fish emulsion, a fertilizer high in nitrogen; and tomato seedlings that are looking a little peaked and purplish—a sign of low phosphorus—turn green again after a dose of bone meal.

Synthetic fertilizers are scientifically (and conveniently) formulated to contain a certain percentage of each major nutrient. The three numbers on the box tell you how much: 5-10-5 simply means that this fertilizer contains 5 percent nitrogen (N), 10 percent phosphorus (P) and 5 percent potassium (K).

CHEMICAL FIX

So, why not pour on the chemicals? First, chemicals contribute nothing to the earth's store of organic matter. In fact, rather than improving soil texture, harsh chemical fertilizers can dissolve the organic ties that help create nice loamy ground. With this soil "glue" weakened, the earth tends to disintegrate. Chemicals used in the absence of humus can spoil a soil's texture.

Used alone, chemical fertilizers gradually starve and deplete soil life, including all-important earthworms. Synthetics provide a quick fix of concentrated nutrients—an overdose will burn or kill plants—but their effect is short-lived as the water-soluble chemicals leach out of reach of roots. Curiously, chemically fed plants tend to be more vulnerable to insect damage and diseases, giving rise to yet more chemicals in the form of pesticides, resulting in a dependency. You can grow anything in a bath of chemicals and water; but, in time, chemically treated soil can indeed become nothing more than dead old dirt.

NATURAL ALTERNATIVES

Organic gardeners must ensure that the soil contains enough nitrogen, phosphorus and potassium. Your own homemade compost and leaf mold, as well as decayed animal manures, are the best all-round, slow-release fertilizers and texturizers you can use—and may be all you need. But the timely use of store-bought natural fertilizers will help to boost and balance nutrients. Garden centers and mail-order sources stock alternatives to chemicals. Some, such as rock phosphate

and sulphate of potash, come directly from the earth; others, such as kelp meal and greensand, are harvested from the sea; and still others, such as bone meal and blood meal, are animal byproducts.

Each of the natural fertilizers contains a concentrated amount of one of the major plant nutrients. Nitrogen promotes lush leaves and greener greens. Phosphorus goes in part into increased fruit set and earlier ripening, brighter flowers, and enhanced disease resistance. Often described as the "root" nutrient, potash also strengthens disease resistance, gives better flavor and color to vegetables and fruit, and may help plants through times of drought.

• **NITROGEN:** Blood meal contains 10 to 14 percent nitrogen in a concentrated, volatile form. To avoid the risk of burning plants, some experts suggest introducing it into the soil by way of the compost heap. Sprinkling blood meal through the layers lets this expensive powder do double duty as both compost catalyst and fertilizer. The recommended soil dose is 2 cups (500 mL) sprinkled over 100 square feet (9 m²) before spring digging. For direct garden application, look for a balanced natural fertilizer that contains blood meal as one of its ingredients.

• **PHOSPORUS:** Bone meal, or ground-up bone, has been the organic gardener's standard source of phosphorus (10 to 15 percent) for decades. Its value was first recognized in England centuries ago. To fertilize 100 square feet (9 m²), dust on 2 cups (500 mL) of bone meal if a soil test shows that the ground is already fairly high in phosphorus; for fair to low levels, double or triple the dose. Symptoms of low phosphorus are a reddish-purple tinge to leaves that ought to be green, and tomatoes and peppers that grow lush and leafy but set relatively few fruit. Spread the fine white powder when there is no wind or you'll be breathing bone or watching it blow away.

Ground phosphate rock contains up to 30 percent phosphorus and some minerals, released slowly into the soil. To correct a moderate deficiency, spread about 4 pounds (2 kg) of rock phosphate over 100 square feet of garden, an application that will do for up to five years. For plants to benefit from this fertilizer, it has to be in their root zone; and since it doesn't move much in the soil, you'll have to dig it in.

• **POTASSIUM:** Kelp meal, a green, mineral-rich fertilizer from the seas, is fairly high in potassium (4 percent). As an added benefit, the presence of kelp meal helps release nutrients that might otherwise remain locked in the soil. Be sure not to add more than 1 pound (0.5 kg) per 100 square feet (9 m²) because an overdose can adversely affect growth.

Sulfate of potash magnesium is another name for langbeinite, a mineral mined in the American southwest. Packaged as Sul-Po-Mag, it provides a concentrated (22 percent) but slowly released measure of potassium, as well as decent levels of sulfur and magnesium. Use 2 cups (500 mL) per 100 square feet.

Greensand, like kelp meal, comes from the sea and contains much of the oceans' wealth of trace elements and minerals. An ideal soil builder, it provides a ready source of available potash and helps unlock other nutrients already in the soil. It also absorbs and holds water for plant use. Spread an application of 3 pounds (1.4 kg) per 100 square feet before spring digging or sprinkle greensand around growing vegetables; there is no danger of injuring surface roots.

High in potash, stove and fireplace ashes have always been dumped on the garden. But be warned, large amounts of caustic ash can injure and kill germinating seeds and small plants. The best plan is to spread ashes very thinly, and dig it in along with compost or manure in the fall or very early in spring so that the ash has time to mellow before seeds go in. You will lose some nutrients to leaching, but better that than burned roots. Always store ashes under cover or their potash will be gone with the rain. Like limestone, wood ash tends to sweeten soil; it has

no place in a berry patch or around acid-loving azaleas, Japanese irises, heathers, and the like. Also hold the ashes, or add them in thin layers to the compost, if your garden pH is higher than 6.8.

In recent years, in response to growing numbers of organic gardeners, fertilizer makers have come out with various blends of all-purpose natural fertilizers. Effective and easy to use (once you decipher the mathematical puzzle of dosage), such fertilizers keep a food garden lush and productive when used in conjuction with annual applications of compost and other organic matter.

There are four principal ways to get the goodness of natural fertilizers into the ground: (1) broadcasting, (2) spot enrichment, (3) side- or top-dressing and (4) via compost. The method depends on the time of year, the needs of plants and the state of your soil. At Larkwhistle, we do all of the above, using the fertilizers we have on hand in ways that seem best at the time.

• **BROADCASTING:** Gardeners who routinely turn over vegetable beds in fall or early spring might opt to broadcast fertilizers before digging and raking. This method works especially well in intensive beds—an area of ground, from 2 to 5 feet (60 to 150 cm) wide, planted fairly thickly with edibles—because nutrients are distributed evenly throughout the root zone. Broadcasting is most appropriate with the less expensive, slow-released fertilizers, such as rock phosphate. You'd go broke spreading blood meal around like grass seed.

• **SPOT ENRICHMENT:** If fertilizer is in short supply and you have a number of transplants to set out, it's wise to concentrate nutrients under each plant. By stirring a handful of bone meal into the transplanting hole for each tomato, for example, you create a zone of fertility that will boost growth all season. If you can mix store-bought powders with old manure or sifted compost, so much the better. This kind of spot enrichment works wonders in a new plot

To create a localized zone of fertility for leeks over the whole season, we sprinkle kelp meal (or other natural fertilizer) into the bottom of the furrows and stir it in.

where the soil is not up to par, but it is appropriate only for larger vegetables—such as lettuce, cabbages, broccoli, peppers and eggplant—that are going into the ground as individual transplants set at least 8 inches (20 cm) apart.

Clearly you can't spot-enrich radishes or carrots. Instead, sprinkle fertilizer into the furrow before you plant the seeds, or spread it in a band about 3 to 4 inches (8 to 10 cm) wide along the length of the row and then scuffle it in with a hoe.

• **SIDE-DRESSING:** Plants in active growth take in a lot of food and water. Side-dressing is the practice of spreading fairly fast-acting fertilizer on the ground around each broccoli or cabbage plant, or along either side of a row of beans—a special treat for hard-working plants. Blood meal gives a quick dose of nitrogen for leafy crops, but a dressing of kelp would be more useful to beans just starting to flower.

It's remarkable how quickly plants respond to side-dressing. We routinely spread a layer of very old manure or compost, several inches thick, around tomatoes, peppers or cabbages in mid-growth. Clearly, the plants know that it's there, for within days they are sending thin new roots out into the dark humus to draw in nutrients.

• **VIA COMPOST:** Blood meal stimulates a compost heap, but (as one expert notes) "adding rock powders, such as rock phosphate and greensand, to the compost is a sterling idea." In the composting stewpot, the minerals are changed into a form that plants can easily take up—and the compost itself, applied when and where you can, always benefits the soil texture and fertility.

By Design
A Kitchen Garden Layout

Our kitchen garden—in some ways the heart of Larkwhistle—is a constant source of interest and pleasure. I love to see the peas run up their wire fence, to have a hand in the progress of lettuces from seeds to heads. A ripe melon is cause for a small celebration. Whenever I pick a red pepper or pull a bunch of carrots, I take a moment to admire their forms and colors. The whole process of growing food is full of wonder and satisfaction. I often linger in the kitchen garden in the early morning (after splashing my face in the chilly water of one of the garden pools) or at twilight, just watching the garden grow. The Chinese have a saying: "The best fertilizer is the gardener's shadow." Shadows are longest at dawn and dusk.

OF ROWS AND BEDS

Vegetables were traditionally grown in an open rectangle of land. The organizing principle was simple: long, straight, single rows. Row planting has one distinct advantage: weeding may be done mechanically, by running a tiller or small tractor up and down the aisles. In a big country garden, this could be the factor that dictates design. But one look at a conventional row garden—thin lines of green in an expanse of bare ground—tells you that this is the least efficient use of space. A row garden may be made much more productive simply by doubling or tripling the rows. If beans, for example, typically stand 8 inches (20 cm) apart in their row, there is no reason why you cannot plant another parallel row, or two, the same distance away. Why have skinny rows of carrots separated by an unproductive path when you can get the equivalent of three rows in a single 8-inch-wide (20-cm-wide) band? For most gardeners, rows waste far too much space;

only a fraction of available ground is growing what you want, while the rest is wide open to weeds. Monotonously straight and narrow, long rows offer little to delight the eye. But put that band of carrots right next to a double row of beans, and you begin to see the potential for beds of vegetables, an arrangement that every flower grower uses all the time.

Gardeners who have gone to the considerable work and expense of landscaping a property may wonder if vegetables fit in. I would say emphatically, yes. Mixing edibles and ornamentals is a time-honored style. Sometimes referred to as cottage gardening, the method was adopted by British cottage dwellers of the past centuries, who loved flowers and wanted food, and grew both in an eclectic mix, integrating vegetables and herbs in the over-all landscape. This was in contrast to the practice followed on grand estates where edibles were kept out of sight behind a wall or hedge, tended by the gardener and harvested for the masters by kitchen staff.

Every garden has room for vegetables, and the most appealing and workable setup for growing them is a series of permanent beds harmoniously placed in relation to the rest of the garden. At Larkwhistle, some of the kitchen-garden beds are 4 feet (1.2 m) wide and 25 feet (7.5 m) long. Others are odd-sized triangles, curving trapezoids and half-moon patches arranged around two water-lily pools and four semidwarf apple trees. Paths weave and criss-cross throughout. Some beds are fairly big, others quite small. The odd assortment of shapes and sizes lets us plant just a little Swiss chard here, a long band of carrots there, a little triangle of radishes or full bed of corn. The design is an attempt to balance practical

OPPOSITE: Diversity is the hallmark of a healthy natural garden. Sun-loving perennials—blue-flowered anchusa, chives and peonies—flank beans, lettuces and peas. Besides attracting bees and butterflies, herbs and flowers add to the bug-baffling mix.

During a heavy rain, the fluffy raised beds absorb water more quickly than the compacted pathways. Given an indoor start and protection in a cold frame, tomatoes may be flowering at tulip time; lettuce is ready to eat.

needs—getting around with wheelbarrow and watering can—with a wish to harmonize the food beds with the flower borders, and make the kitchen garden as ornamental as it is practical.

If "a long row to hoe" feels like a recipe for backache and boredom, beds sound cozier somehow, more intimate. And they are. A bed is an area of soil from 2 to 5 feet (60 to 150 cm) wide, with a path all around it. Length varies, depending on the scope of a garden. If beds are longer than 30 feet (9 m) or so, a bisecting path midway saves steps. You putter around a bed, tending the plants by hand, reaching in to weed or spread mulch. Beds make a big garden more manageable. Our kitchen garden measures about a quarter of an acre, and I would balk at the thought of digging the entire space by hand. But one bed at a time is not so overwhelming. It takes less than a half-hour to turn over the soil in a typical 4-foot by 25-foot bed (1.2-m by 7.5-m), and it leaves you with a sense of completion, a job done.

From an ecological stand-point, bed gardening is good for the earth. How so? First, you walk and wheel your barrow around a bed, not over it. The paths become hard, compact and, mercifully, less hospitable to weeds. But the beds themselves remain light, fluffy and full of air. Beds also save your back:

Because the earth is not compacted by traffic, the earth turns over easily. On sandy soils, beds may not need digging every year, unless you are turning in compost or manure. Sometimes, we simply scuffle and loosen the top few inches with a hefty hoe, perhaps stirring in a dressing of natural fertilizer as we go. A quick rake and we are ready to plant. Digging, though, is generally good for the ground, especially clay soils. Where soil insects such as earwigs are a menace, fall digging helps keep them in check.

Beds allow you to concentrate your soil-building efforts. Since compost is always in short supply, why fritter it away on unproductive pathways? A better plan is to concentrate both compost and those expensive commercial fertilizers in permanent beds that will grow richer each season.

First-time food growers may discover, as we did, that their enthusiasm is not matched by muscle, that their interest exceeds their time. The first rules for new gardeners should be: (1) Start small; (2) Concentrate your efforts; (3) Open up only the amount of garden space you feel you can tend; (4) Branch out as you become more experienced. Small can, indeed, be beautiful. I have an impression that a lot of people don't grow vegetables because they remember the hot hours spent hacking away at weeds or picking a never-ending line of beans in their parents' big row garden. But a few scaled-down vegetable beds, nicely placed in the landscape and carefully tended, may be every bit as productive as a neglected larger plot—and a lot more satisfying.

SOD OFF

But before beds can be shaped, there may be some ground-breaking to do. Lawns are shrinking all over as people realize that the effort they put into watering, weed-and-feeding and cutting the grass could yield a much more interesting return of colorful flowers, aromatic herbs, and organic food. Our garden evolved from a field of quack grass, not tame lawn. Compared to an over-grown field, sod-breaking in a town lot may be less strenuous, but the approach is the same.

"Skim off the turf," one book blithely instructs—as if turf were like cream floating on milk. I wish. Converting a stretch of lawn or field into new kitchen garden beds may make everything that follows feel like "jes potterin." Here are the steps:

1. With stakes and string, mark out the perimeter of the new site.
2. Using a sharp, square-bladed spade, first slice a line through the sod around the edges, then slice the enclosed turf into a grid of chunks no bigger than you can lift—the size of a floor tile is about right. Push the spade all the way through roots and as deeply into the ground as it will go.
3. Using a spading fork, pry loose a flap of sod, flip it earth-side up, and whack away at the roots to loosen the precious topsoil. Then spear the chunk, lift it, shake it, knock it around, drop it hard on the ground a few times—all in an effort to release as much soil as possible. If the earth is soggy, invert all the pieces, exposing them to the elements to dry for a few hours, but not so long that the ground bakes to an unyielding crust.
4. Once the grass is gone, dig the patch over with spade or fork, removing more roots, missed bits of sod and any rocks bigger

At Larkwhistle, eggplant are protected in a simple glass frame. Hay mulch keeps the ground cool and moist for onions and cabbage and, in a triangular bed, snap beans grow close enough to crowd out weeds.

than your fist. Small stones actually bene-fit plants and soil by improving the flow of water and air, an important considera-tion in clay ground. Stones gradually release minerals and, in a dry spell, each one harbors a little reservoir of moisture underneath.
5. Finally, rake the earth to break up clods of soil and catch stray roots, rocks, and rubbish.

Good-quality sods can be used, if need be, to patch bald spots in the lawn. Other-wise, pile them by themselves grass-side down, in an out-of-the-way place to com-post; a tarpaulin over the pile excludes light and discourages sprouting. Never add wiry quack grass runners to the regular compost. Instead, spread them out in the sun to dry thoroughly. Or as an old neighbor jokes, "Burn them and be careful when you spread the ashes."

Fall is an excellent time to clear ground. Winter freezing works wonders on soil tex-ture, especially heavy clay, mellowing and

This 4-foot-wide (120-cm-wide) bed is intensively planted with a double row of peas, two rows of lettuce at different stages of maturity, and a row of radishes. Leaves eventually touch to make a living mulch that keeps the soil cool and moist and crowds out weeds.

pulverizing it. As weed seeds and roots sprout in early spring, you have another chance to round up potential troublemakers. I like to start new beds with a clean slate.

MAKING BEDS

With the land cleared and level, we use stakes and string to mark out the growing beds. Because beds are tended by hand from paths on either side, their width is determined by your reach. You'll need to reach at least to the middle while standing or kneeling on one side or the other.

Most of our beds are 3 to 4 feet (90 to 120 cm) wide, and all of them are raised a few inches higher than the paths. In spring, a raised bed warms up sooner than the surrounding ground; and in all seasons, it drains water better. Both states are desirable where cool, damp clay is the medium. Larkwhistle's sandy earth drains only too well.

Why raise the beds then? Primarily, to provide the plants with a greater depth of topsoil, not imported soil but earth from the paths. As we stake out the beds and run string, we are also delineating the paths between them. We then rake and shovel up a few inches of path soil and scatter this over the bed. The uneven earth on the beds is raked smartly up to the string as the bed is leveled. At this point, the back of a rake is useful for tamping and firming the gently sloping sides of the raised bed to prevent mini-landslides later on. Lately, we have been

raking up a raised rim of earth around the perimeter of each bed as we go. This ridge keeps water from flowing out into the path when we flood the bed with a hose or watering can. A few passes with the back of the rake over the path gives a smooth walking surface and a neat line between path and bed.

Over the course of a season the edges of beds may get blurred, the growing space getting wider and the walking space shrinking as we seed, transplant or cultivate. It is wise to leave corner stakes in the ground permanently, so that beds may be brought back into line quickly by sight at the end of the season, without running a line of string again.

ON THE PATH

We have a neighbor who gardens on stony clay soil. As she shaped her raised beds, she lay down a layer of porous landscape fabric over areas designated as paths. She then tossed stones from the bed into the pathways and left them there. Later she leveled the stones as best she could and filled around and over them with gravelly sand. This left fairly stone-free beds and dry serviceable paths that would otherwise be clogged with sticky clay after every rain. The landscape fabric was vital though; without it, the paths would sprout masses of weeds very difficult to extract.

Our kitchen garden paths are nothing fancier than the naturally sandy earth. Years of foot traffic have made them hard and smooth. The few weeds that do sprout are easily sliced off at ground level without churning up the soil. Sandy paths drain quickly and are never muddy.

We often spread newspapers over pathways and top the paper with old hay or straw. Nothing sprouts through that. The simplest way to handle newspapers for mulch is to open up a whole section and lay it lengthwise for a narrower path, crosswise for a wider one, overlapping the sections. Since almost all newpapers are printed with a carbon-based ink, they present no toxic danger—just ask the earthworms that chew their way through the soggy pulp.

The width of a path, like a road, depends on the amount and type of traffic. Two main streets bisect our kitchen garden. These 4-foot-wide (120-cm-wide) paths make it easy to wheel a barrow full of jostling corn stalks on their way to the compost. From the big paths run 2-foot (60-cm) side streets—for pedestrians only—between beds. A path narrower than one foot is sure to disappear as foliage closes in from either side. A two-wheel garden cart probably needs a 5-foot-wide (150-cm-wide) highway.

ENCLOSING BEDS

For greater tidiness and permanence, raised beds can by surrounded with bricks, cement blocks, railroad ties or boards. Perhaps the best material is rough-cut (unplaned), untreated cedar boards, measuring 1 to 2 inches (2.5 to 5 cm) thick and 6 to 12 inches (15 to 30 cm) wide. On average, one-by-eights do nicely. There is no trick to setting up the enclosure. You may have to dig a little trench around the bed, the better to jiggle the boards into a level position. Shim with stones if necessary. Use a spirit-level, set on a straight board spanning the bed, to bring both sides to the same height. At all corners, sledge a chunk of two-by-four securely into the soil, on the inside of the boards, and nail boards to it. If boards bow, align them with additional pieces of wood pounded into the ground along their length.

Enclosed raised beds may be the only way to get around the problem of shallow soil, impenetrable hardpan (subsoil you can barely pierce with a pick) or bedrock close to the surface. I know several gardeners who have built such board enclosures, dug out all the topsoil within them, broken up the sub-soil as best they could and then returned the topsoil mixed with compost, manure and peat. Add a measured dose of natural fertilizer to the mix and vegetables are bound to thrive.

PLANTING IN BEDS

In the 1800s, market gardeners on the out-skirts of Paris took to growing their crops in beds for the maximum yield in the minimum space. The technique they devised is still called "the French Intensive Method." If let-tuces ordinarily stand a foot apart in a row, they reasoned, why not plant several rows side by side, the same distance apart. As the plants in such a bed approach maturity, their leaves touch and the space becomes a sheet of green, with very little if any earth visible. This is a good thing. The canopy of foliage shading the ground creates a cool, moist microclimate beneath. At the same time, weeds have a hard time sprouting.

The principle of spacing plants in an intensive raised bed can be summed up like this: the distance normally left between plants in a row is roughly the same as the distance between rows in a bed. Thus, if we normally set our broccoli transplants 18 inches (45 cm) apart in a row, we can line up a second row 18 inches from the first. Or instead of broccoli for the adjacent row, we might choose cabbages or Brussels sprouts—plants of equal bulk and similar culture—for the same bed. Often plants are staggered from row to row to use the space even more efficiently. And sometimes a little more "breathing space" is left between the rows to improve air circulation and prevent fungal diseases. As a rule, I leave a minimum of 8 inches (20 cm)—a conveniently measured hand-span—between rows in a bed so that I can run a narrow hoe between them.

The chart on page 28 gives typical spac-ing and some workable companion vegetables for an intensive bed.

ORNAMENTAL EDIBLES

Enclosed vegetable beds intersected by mulched or stone-paved paths are refine-ments that get a kitchen garden off to a beautiful start, but boards and stones are only the bare bones. Whatever the design, plants add a livelier beauty of color, form and texture.

Virtually all food plants have some charm of leaf, flower or fruit. Who can deny the beauty of a pepper bush burning with thin, scarlet chilies; or the eggplant's starry mauve flowers and polished purple fruit. Red let-tuces and ferny carrot tops are pretty enough

SPACING PLANTS IN AN INTENSIVE BED

	Distance between plants within a row	Distance between rows
Asparagus	18 inches (45 cm)	18–24 inches (45–60 cm)
Beans, bush	4–6 inches (10–15 cm)	8 inches (20 cm)
Beans, pole	8 inches (20 cm) along trellis	poles 2 feet (60 cm) apart, 3–5 plants per pole
Beets	3–5 inches (8–12 cm)	8 inches (20 cm)
Broccoli	18 inches (45 cm)	18 inches (45 cm)
Brussels sprouts	18–24 inches (45–60 cm)	18–24 inches (45–60 cm)
Cabbage	18 inches (45 inches)	18 inches (45 cm)
Carrots	2–3 inches (5–8 cm)	8 inches (20 cm) or in 8-inch/20-cm-wide bands
Cauliflower	18 inches (45 cm)	18 inches (45 cm)
Celery	8 inches (20 cm)	8 inches (20 cm)
Chard	12 inches (30 cm)	12 inches (30 cm)
Chicory	8 inches (20 cm)	8 inches (20 cm)
Chinese Cabbage	8–24 inches (20–60 cm)	18–24 inches (45–60 cm)
Corn	12–18 inches (30–45 cm)	18 inches (45 cm)
Cucumbers	12–18 inches (30–45 cm)	24 inches (60 cm) trained up trellis
Eggplant	18 inches (45 cm)	18 inches (45 cm)
Kale	12 inches (30 cm)	12 inches (30 cm)
Kohlrabi	6 inches (15 cm)	8 inches (20 cm)
Leeks	6 inches (15 cm)	12 inches (30 cm)
Lettuce, head	12 inches (30 cm)	12 inches (30 cm)
Lettuce, leaf	8–10 inches (20–25 cm)	8–10 inches (20–25 cm)
Melons	24 inches (60 cm)	one row per bed
Onions/Garlic	4 inches (10 cm)	8 inches (20 cm)
Parsnips	3 inches (8 cm)	8 inches (20 cm)
Peas	1–3 inches (2.5–8 cm)	8 inches (20 cm)
Peppers	15 inches (38 cm)	15 inches (38 cm)
Potatoes	10–15 inches (25–38 cm)	18 inches (45 cm), mulched 30 inches (75 cm) if hilled
Radishes	2 inches (5 cm)	4 inches (10 cm)
Rutabaga	6 inches (15 cm)	8 inches (20 cm)
Spinach	6 inches (15 cm)	8 inches (20 cm)
Squash, winter	24 inches (60 cm)	one row per wide bed
Tomatoes	24 inches (60 cm)	36 inches (90 cm)
Zucchini	18 inches (45 cm)	24 inches (60 cm)

to edge flowerbeds. Other vegetables, too, stand out for their special decorative value. Here are some vegetables you might plant even if they weren't edible.

Swiss chard gets top marks for its glossy, crumpled dark-green leaves and broad contrasting stems. Red-stemmed chard is lovely enough for a prominent spot in any flowerbed and there are color mixtures that include red, white, yellow and pale orange chard.

Kale, whether blue-green or reddish-purple, displays wonderfully textured, crinkled leaves, like a great frilly flower, from early summer until December—it also happens to be the most nutritious thing you can eat.

Scarlet runner beans wind their way decoratively up poles, trellises or porch pillars in the sun. By midsummer the spot is alight with stems of brilliant blossoms that are very enticing to hummingbirds. The clusters of green beans are a welcome bonus. Closer to the ground, purple-podded "green" beans grow among heart-shaped leaves tinted with some of the bean's dark ink.

Radicchio folds into heads of lovely wine-red heads, like leafy roses; if some go to seed, you'll enjoy the flowers on the way.

Artichoke are very decorative—cut silvery foliage below plump scaly buds—and will fruit the first season if started from seeds under lights as early as January. In the north they seldom survive the winter.

The alpine strawberry is a jaunty small perennial for edging; its fruit, either red or white, is the size of the nail on your baby finger. Grow this ornamental edible from seed or start with plants for quicker pickings.

When my friend and I started our first garden in the city, two things never occurred to us. The first was to spray the vegetables with chemicals—that would defeat the purpose. The other was to lay out the garden in rows with unproductive paths between—we didn't have room to waste. By July you could

barely find an island of bare ground to stand on in the sea of green. When we came to the country, we had all the space we could want. But still we laid out the garden in a series of beds right from the start. The vegetable beds suit us. They are easy to tend, as productive as we could hope for and as lovely as we could wish. In the kitchen garden, use and beauty meet.

The heart-shaped leaves of bush beans and the ferny fronds of asparagus are every bit as decorative as the ornamental grass (foreground) that shares this corner of Larkwhistle's kitchen garden.

Spring Steps
Indoor Seeding, Outdoor Cold Frames

Sometime after New Year's, a gardener's fancy turns to thoughts of seeds and soil. By April, some of us are once again under the spell of a "springtime passion for the earth." Between those first green thoughts and the appearance of green seedlings, a new season bows in. What a pleasure, after a long stuffy winter, to be out in the garden, spade and seeds in hand. Drinking in the cool spring air, we feel freed from winter's huddle and heavy clothes—expanded, relaxed, eager. The rhythmic work of raking a bed becomes a kind of active meditation. The dark earth is full of lively potential.

For gardeners, April is far from being "the cruelest month," but the tentative weeks between winter and spring—April here, March or even May in other areas—are surely the most tantalizing. A glorious morning entices us out with warm promises; the next drives us indoors with cold winds, scowling skies and the sting of freezing rain. Who can sit by warming their heels while the new season dances two steps forward, one step back? Besides, if you do, you lose precious weeks of growth. While the weather dithers, gardeners can get the garden under way inside. Seedlings started indoors will be garden-ready by the time spring decides to stay.

An Indoor Start
Starting seeds of certain vegetables indoors takes a bit of organization—the gathering of equipment and seeds, some forethought and timing—but it always makes a positive difference in the outcome of the garden. Lettuce and broccoli grow better in cooler weather; an indoor start leads to improved growth before summer begins to swelter. Slow-growing leeks and Brussels sprouts take months to mature; for them, a few extra weeks indoors result in a more abundant fall

harvest. Peppers, tomatoes, melons and egg-plant are long-season, heat-loving tropicals that don't get moving until the weather warms up, and then come to an abrupt end on the first frosty fall night. A month on the windowsill in spring may make the difference between a fruitful summer and slim pickings.

In many cases, a protected period indoors helps plants through their infancy away from drought and deluge, frost or frying heat, hungry slugs and earwigs. Swiss chard, for example, is normally sown directly outdoors, but in our garden its first leaves are often decimated by earwigs. Since 8 or 10 Swiss chard plants are all we need, we seed a few 4-inch (10-cm) pots in April for May transplanting. Earwigs are a lot less interested in the slightly older specimens.

Seeding Schedule
The indoor seed-sowing season may extend over a number of weeks, from late February to mid-May in most regions. It's a mistake to think that the sooner you start, the quicker you'll pick. Unless conditions in the house are close to perfect—lots of sunlight and cool night temperatures—there is nothing to be gained by rushing things. Low light and high heat make for weak, wobbly seedlings. As an example, we used to sow broccoli the third week in March, when days are often cloudy and the house is kept fairly warm. Leaning toward the pale light, seedlings were forced into growth by the heat. We now wait until the sunnier days of mid-April before seeding indoors. The strong and stocky month-old seedlings that go out in mid-May settle into the garden without much ado. Better results come from setting out stocky younger seedlings rather than older ones that have grown weak and lanky.

In May seedlings of squash, cucumbers and melons take windowsill space as cool weather seedlings—broccoli, lettuce, onions, cabbage and leeks— are transplanted to the garden.

The snow may still be flying outside when we start seeds indoors in a sunny window.

HOME GROWN

Gardeners who tend to be seed-shy, take heart. Vegetable seeds are among the easiest to sprout, most making an appearance within a week or ten days. Lettuce may show through in three days. But why bother to start your own vegetable seedlings when you can buy them ready-grown at any nursery in May? The main reason is this: starting your own seeds allows you access to a far greater variety. A garden center may stock once or two varieties of lettuce, but seeds open the door to red Bostons, mini-romaines, European exotics, oakleaf lettuces and many more. You will always find 'Beefsteak' tomato plants at a nursery, but it happens to be a type that ripens much later than varieties you can easily raise yourself from seed. Also, with the heightened awareness of the need to preserve heritage seeds from the past, home gardens can avail themselves of interesting old-time seeds that carry a valuable genetic resource into the future.

Many commercial seedlings are cramped, tangled and root-bound by the time you get them. You're forced to wrench roots apart, a traumatic start for a plant that also has to face the rigors of sun and wind for the first time. At home you can schedule seeding and use fair-sized containers. The result is superior plants that suffer very little at transplanting time.

Setting Up: Pots, Flats and Soil for Seedlings

Seedlings are started in all manner of quirky containers, from half-eggshells and egg cartons (too small for the purpose) to toilet-paper rolls snugged together in a watertight tray (quite good).

There may be little need to buy seedling containers. All kinds of things—yogurt and cottage-cheese containers with drainage holes poked through, the bottom half of waxed cardboard milk cartons, paper or plastic drinking cups—can be reused. The plastic cell packs that held your petunias from the nursery last spring can grow your lettuce seedlings this time around. Pots left over from nursery perennials serve admirably as containers for larger seedling vegetables such as tomatoes, peppers, lettuce and cabbage. One company sells a wooden cylinder for rolling your own seedling pots from newspaper and, for those who like to muck around, there is a gizmo that presses wet earth into soil blocks. At Larkwhistle, most vegetable seedlings are started in 2- to 4-inch (5- to 10-cm) reused plastic pots.

Containers at hand, we turn our attention to the growing medium. We always stir together our own seed-starting mix, using three or four parts sandy topsoil from the garden and one part each damp peat moss and sifted compost. To each wheelbarrow full of the blended ingredients we add half a spadeful of bone meal, or a handful to each bucket of mix. Even though we do not sterilize the mix, as is often recommended—baking soil in the oven at 300°F (150°C) for ninety minutes is a messy, smelly business, and an impossible task in any volume—disease or fungus problems have been negligible.

You may lack the inclination to blend and bake a batch of soil; you may not have access to the sandy earth that makes such a good base—clay ground quickly puts a stranglehold on tender sprouts. If so, commercial seeding mixes are an easy alternative, as is a homemade blend of equal parts potting soil and perlite. Store-bought ingredients have several advantages over garden soil. They are available at a time when the garden may be muddy or crusty with frost. They are weed-free, so you are not left scratching your head, wondering which bits of green are pepper seedlings and which are weeds. Commercial mixes are formulated to be lightweight and porous to both air and water, while holding moisture that seedlings need. Most significantly, the blends you buy are sterile, free of the fungus spores that may menace seedlings in unsterilized ground. You avoid the discouraging prospect of watching your nice young tomatoes suddenly keel over from "damping off."

Damping-off spores breed and attack at soil level, causing stems to wither. As a preventive step, we sometime top pots or flats with a half-inch layer of vermiculite ("puffed" mica), or milled sphagnum moss (not peat moss). Seeds are planted right in the vermiculite, and the resulting seedlings will have a sterile "collar" around their vulnerable necks. You can also foil fungus growth by cultivating around seedlings with an ordinary kitchen fork, leaving a layer of fine dry soil on top. A spray of cool chamomile tea seems to stop the fungus, as does a dusting of crushed chamomile flowers (those sold for tea). Growing seedlings a little on the dry side with good ventilation also reduces the chance of damping off.

Seeding Steps

1. Fill pots or other containers almost to the top with moistened soil mix and tamp down gently to level soil and press out air pockets. Top up with more of the growing medium.
2. Make a little indentation in the soil surface of each pot, or each compartment in a cell-tray.
3. Drop three or four seeds into each indentation. Cover seeds lightly with a quarter-inch of soil—less for very fine seeds—and pat to firm.
4. As seedlings grow, thin to the sturdiest one in each pot or cell. Scissors are handy to snip away the surplus without disturbing roots of seedlings you wish to keep.

Seeded containers are watered from below by sitting them in a tray of lukewarm water; or "rained" from above with a hand sprayer tuned to a fine mist, or the gentlest of watering cans. Soil must be kept moist but never soggy until seeds sprout. Tepid water is better than a shocking cold shower.

Bottom Heat

Once pots and flats are seeded, they need a warm spot for germination. Gentle bottom heat rouses dormant seeds. We balance flats on a base of inverted clay pots set directly on top of the wood stove until soil in the flats feels warm to the touch. Often, one warming is enough. An electric heating pad or radiator also warms pots and flats. Useful for large batches of seedlings are special heating cables to run under your flats; or a "grow-mat," a rubber square embedded with heating cables. Or you could simply put seeded trays on a nearby kitchen counter when the oven is in use. Seeded containers can also be set in the sun in front of a window and loosely draped with clear plastic—a simple greenhouse. Be sure to remove the plastic as soon as seeds sprout lest they fry under there.

Let There Be Light

As soon as little green sprouts show through, seedlings need sunlight and lots of it—at least six hours for lettuce and parsley; more for broccoli and onions; and a minimum of eight hours for the tomatoes, peppers and eggplant. An unshaded bay window facing southeast to southwest is perfect. East and west windows are fine, too, if you are home to shift your seedlings. Supplementing the sun with fluorescent lights helps. A cool room temperature is better than too much

At Larkwhistle, where the last spring frost occurs in late May (circled), this is the spring schedule of seeding indoors and transplanting outdoors. To make a customized calendar for your garden, determine your spring frost-free date and circle the appropriate period. Using check marks, shift the schedule backward or forward the corresponding number of boxes. For example, where frost is finished in early May, leeks and onions are seeded indoors in Mid-February, hardened off in early April, and transplanted outdoors in mid-April.

	Mid-Feb. 10–20	Late Feb. 20–28	Early March 1–10	Mid-March 10–20	Late March 20–31	Early April 1–10	Mid-April 10–20	Late April 20–30	Early May 1–10	Mid-May 10–20	Late May 20–31 (FROST-FREE)	Early June 1–10	Mid-June 10–20
Leeks Onions			seed indoors					harden	trans-plant				
Parsley				seed indoors				harden	trans-plant				
Peppers Eggplant					seed indoors					harden	trans-plant*		
Tomatoes					seed indoors				harden	trans-plant*			
Lettuce						seed (1) indoors		seed (2) indoors	harden	trans-plant (1)	trans-plant (2)		
Cabbage Broccoli (early) Kale Swiss chard							seed indoors		harden	trans-plant			
Melons Winter squash Zucchini Cucumber Basil									seed indoors		harden		trans-plant
Cabbage Broccoli (late)											seed indoors		trans-plant

* Protect from frost if necessary

SPRING SCHEDULE OF OUTDOOR SEED SOWING

Sowing seeds in the garden need not be a frantic, one-day task. Better to relax and do a little seeding now and again from early spring until mid-summer. Hardy vegetables withstand frost and grow better in the cooler weeks of spring. Others, such as tropical tomatoes and melons, thrive in warm weather. The charts below show you when to seed (and, in some cases, transplant) into the garden, using spring's last frost and fall's first frost as benchmarks.

Approximate Date Of Last Spring Frost: _____

Very Hardy	Hardy	Semi-hardy	Tender	Heat-loving
Sow 5-7 weeks before last frost	Sow 2-3 weeks before last frost	Sow 1-2 weeks before last frost	Sow on or just after last frost	Sow 1-2 weeks after last frost
leeks	lettuce	beets	beans	cucumber
onions (seeds/sets)	mustard	carrots	corn	lima beans
peas	turnip greens	parsnips	pumpkin	eggplants*
spinach	chervil	radish	summer squash	tomatoes*
dill	coriander	broccoli*	winter squash	peppers*
garlic	parsley	Brussels sprouts*	zucchini	cantaloupe*
shallots		cabbage*		watermelon
		cauliflower*		peanuts
		kale		sweet potatoes
		kohlrabi		
		Swiss chard		
		potatoes		

* Best as transplants

SUMMER SCHEDULE OF OUTDOOR SEED SOWING

Approximate Date Of First Fall Frost: _____

Sow 10-12 weeks before fall frost	Sow 8 weeks before fall frost
beets	bok choy
carrots	lettuce
Chinese cabbage	kohlrabi
endive	Oriental radish
radicchio	snow peas
rutabaga	spinach
	turnips

heat, which forces weak stretchy growth.

In the absence of sunlight, seedlings will grow along under fluorescent lights, either the standard cool-white ones or special (and costlier) grow-lights that include more of the infrared spectrum. Because fluorescents radiate very little heat, plants can sit a mere 3 inches (7.5 cm) away from them. It is handy to be able to raise the lights or lower the plants as necessary. Small plants need about the same amount of rest as you do, so it's lights out for eight or nine hours every night. We rarely feed seedlings—the compost and bone meal are nourishment enough—but if they show hunger signs, such as pale or purpling leaves or lackadaisical growth, a reviving drink of liquid organic fertilizer such as fish emulsion, mixed half-strength, makes a visible difference.

Cold Frames

If seedlings are moved directly from the windless, protected indoors into the open garden, they are sure to suffer a traumatic set-back. A period of gradual adjustment to the outdoors—a process called hardening-off—acclimatizes seedlings to unfiltered sun and drying winds. Nothing is more useful for the days between indoor safety and unpredictable outdoor conditions than a simple cold frame, a bottomless sloping wooden box topped with a transparent cover. There are several choices for glazing. Clear plastic is cheap; a sheet of clear corru-

gated acrylic is much more lasting. Both are lighter and easier to work with than the old storm windows that we have always used to cover our cold frames.

Starting with second-hand storm windows (usually available free for the hauling) in good repair, we build the cold frames to fit, using leftover lumber and odd pieces of plywood. Not surprisingly no two frames are alike. The important design feature, though, is that the back of a frame is approximately twice as high as the front, and the front is at least 5 inches (12 cm) high but no taller than 8 inches (20 cm) or you'll shade the interior. A neat and sturdy cold frame may be fashioned with one length of 2 by 8 cedar lumber as the front piece, and two lengths of the same stock forming the back. Sides are made with the same lumber, or pieces of plywood, cut diagonally from corner to corner, with corner "posts" in place for nailing everything together.

For "high-tech" and well-heeled gardeners there are aluminum and acrylic cold frames fitted with an electronic device that automatically raises and lowers the top to keep the interior temperature steady.

A cold frame should be situated in a sheltered spot, facing the sun and handy to the house if possible. Our frames, oriented vaguely south, sit on the ground in the garden. The first seedlings, barely two weeks old, go into the frames in late April when frosty nights are still commonplace. These

Planning is the key to making the fullest use of garden space. The diagrams below and opposite illustrate two examples of how beds can change over the course of the season. Planted in spring, the first crop of vegetables gives way to a second, as new plants are either seeded or transplanted in midsummer for fresh eating in fall. Careful spacing puts plants quite close together without overcrowding them. The distances between rows add up to a total width of four feet (1.2 m), a handy size for tending from paths on either side. The length of the bed depends on the space you have available.

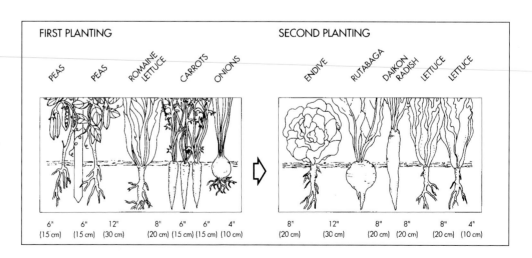

FIRST PLANTING

PEAS   PEAS   ROMAINE LETTUCE   CARROTS   ONIONS

6" (15 cm)   6" (15 cm)   12" (30 cm)   8" (20 cm)   6" (15 cm)   6" (15 cm)   4" (10 cm)

SECOND PLANTING

ENDIVE   RUTABAGA   DAIKON RADISH   LETTUCE   LETTUCE

8" (20 cm)   12" (30 cm)   8" (20 cm)   8" (20 cm)   8" (20 cm)   4" (10 cm)

are the cool-weather crops: lettuce, cabbage, broccoli, Swiss chard, leeks and parsley and with them such hardy annual flowers as asters, sweet peas, stocks, mignonette and snapdragons.

Nights may be chilly in April, but a calm sunny day sends temperatures in the frame soaring to a degree that might well kill tiny plants inside. By mid-morning we check to see if windows need to be propped open for ventilation, an airing that accustoms seedlings to the winds they will soon be facing. If you leave home for a day forecast to be sunny and mild, take the sash off completely and soak flats and pots thoroughly. A few hours before sunset, windows go back on to retain warmth for the night. If an unseasonably cold night threatens, we cover frames with an assortment of old woolen blankets and feather-spewing sleeping bags—thrift shops are a good source.

By mid-May, as we transplant hardy vegetables, vacant frame space is filled with pots of heat-loving tomatoes, peppers, eggplant, cucumbers and melons. If night temperatures are predicted to dip much below 45°F (7°C), we haul these sensitive sorts back indoors until morning.

If you want to grow some starter plants, but lack suitable window space and don't care for the fuss and expense of fluorescent lights, a cold frame makes a fine nursery right from the start. It is not lack of light in early spring that inhibits growth—the sun is on the rise and days are long enough—but the absence of heat. Buffer the breezes, warm the ground with a frame, and you can sow seeds in a frame weeks before you could plant them outside.

To start seedlings directly in a frame, position it in a sunny corner of the garden, or by the south wall of the house or outbuilding. Set up flats and pots as described above, and follow the steps. Better yet, germinate seeds indoors where it is warm and move containers into the frame as soon as seeds have sprouted.

TRANSPLANTING

There comes a time in May when a gardener is looking at a frame or windowsill full of seedlings and the forecasts are calling for a mild week, a few overcast days, a chance of showers—perfect transplanting weather. After tending seedlings for a month or more, I always get a bit nervous about setting them out. What if frost strikes in the night, a fat cutworm slices stems, earwigs chew them up, the sun fries the small fries? It's not exactly a jungle out there, but threats lurk.

It is strange but true that insects are more apt to bother plants that are enduring some stress—too much fertilizer, lack of water, or faltering growth. Transplanting is potentially very stressful, but there are ways to reduce the trauma. Care taken at this juncture will be repaid abundantly later on.

First, if at all possible, choose a calm

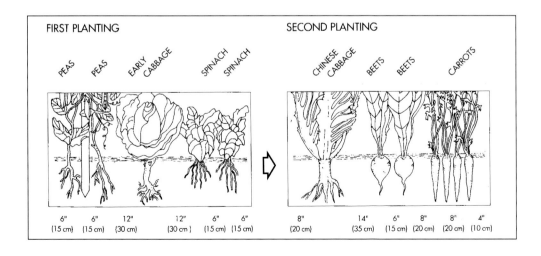

FIRST PLANTING							SECOND PLANTING					
PEAS	PEAS	EARLY CABBAGE		SPINACH	SPINACH		CHINESE CABBAGE		BEETS	BEETS		CARROTS
6" (15 cm)	6" (15 cm)	12" (30 cm)		12" (30 cm)	6" (15 cm)	6" (15 cm)	8" (20 cm)		14" (35 cm)	6" (15 cm)	8" (20 cm)	8" (20 cm)	4" (10 cm)

About a week before transplanting, slice through the soil between flat-grown seedlings. Later, each lettuce or cabbage can be lifted with a block of soil intact and minimal root disturbance.

overcast day for transplanting; if a drizzly day follows, so much the better. In sunny weather, transplant in the late afternoon or early evening. Before setting out small plants, it is wise to stir something nourishing into the soil for each one. Sifted compost or very old, fine-textured manure is excellent, especially when boosted with bone meal, kelp meal or a balanced granular organic fertilizer.

A pint-sized spade or a large, strong trowel is the tool for transplanting. After measuring and marking the distance between plants, dig an oversized hole for each seedling. Then dump a couple of handfuls of compost and a sprinkling of fertilizer

into the holes, and stir the organic stuff into the bottom and surrounding soil. Firm the earth with a gloved fist.

Pots and trays should be watered thoroughly before transplanting so the damp soil clings to roots. Most seedlings can go into the ground a little deeper than they were growing in containers; deeper planting helps to anchor and stabilize lanky plants, leaving them less prone to a wind whipping. Set in up to its bottom leaves, a tomato plant quickly sprouts new roots from its buried stem; the same applies to broccoli and cabbage. Lettuce and onions, however, resent a depth change.

Nestle transplants into the soil, making sure there are no air pockets under them. Fill in around roots with fine earth or the transplanting mix, then poke around with fingers or the trowel handle to ensure good earth-root contact. Firm the soil by pressing down gently around the transplant. At this point, we sculpt the earth by hand around each plant to form a shallow "soupbowl"; water poured on now and throughout the season will be funneled right to the plant's roots. Transplants are often given a dose of fish emulsion or liquid seaweed mixed to half the usual strength.

Cutoffs

Is there anything more frustrating than going through all these steps only to find gaps in the row next morning? Closer inspection

Where cutworms are active, protect new transplants with: A) sticks or nails pushed into the ground next to stems, B) bottomless paper cups or tin cons snugged over seedlings or C) a collar of corrugated cardboard held in place with a paper clip.

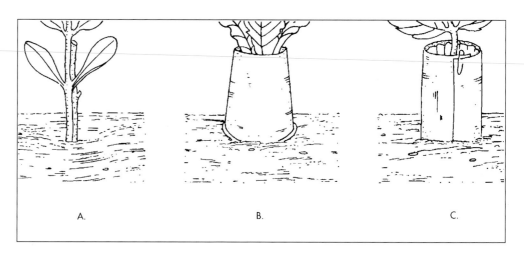

A.   B.   C.

reveals cutoff seedlings wilted on the ground. Dig around the stub with your finger and chances are you'll unearth a fat gray cutworm that spews a stream of green—your digested seedling—when stepped on. All God's creatures have a role, but this smacks of vandalism. What kind of a meal is a millimeter of stem? There are ways to outwit a cutworm, a common pest that does its dirty work at night, curling around stems near ground level and chewing through. Most effective is a physical barrier: we sometimes stick two nails an inch into the ground, one on either side of vulnerable stems. Some gardeners wrap stems loosely with a collar of tarpaper, tinfoil or cardboard, pushed into the ground. Paper cups (bottoms removed) or tin cans (minus tops and bottoms) also keep cutworms away; and a circle of ashes or crushed eggshells is said to deter ol' cutty, too. As you cultivate around recent transplants or along a row of just-sprouted seedlings, you'll likely turn up a number of the curled culprits for quick dispatch underfoot.

Earwigs love to snack on seedlings—they are as fond of basil as you are. Their trademark damage is a lacy network of holes. A spray of insecticidal soap is a sure control, but you must hit the insects directly, not just coat the leaves. And that entails a flashlit garden tour some time after 10 p.m. when earwigs begin to come out for dinner.

At transplanting time, dig oversized holes and stir in sifted compost to concentrate nutrients around each plant. Set most seedlings slightly deeper than they were growing, firm soil well and water.

BELOW: In spring, cold frames are invaluable, whether for acclimatizing indoor seedlings to outdoor conditions, growing early greens or sheltering pepper plants from chilly winds.

Trouble
Insects, Weeds, Frost and Water

FROST PROOFING

All the seedlings are in the ground. Gentle rains fall on schedule; the late spring sun is warm and encouraging. The garden is coming along beautifully. Suddenly winds shift into the north; by evening, under a clear sky, they die down, leaving chill air in their wake. Over the horizon a full moon rises. You can see your breath. All signs point to a frosty night. It's time to take steps to protect the plants.

Our garden lies in a slight hollow on the north side of the woods where cold air settles on a calm night—a classic frost pocket. Although the "official" frost-free date here is June 1, every couple of years the garden feels the silver sting as late as June 10. Passersby must wonder at a garden spread with blankets and rows of inverted flower pots lined up on the beds.

Even a light covering will deflect frost. In the garden shed we keep a stack of large flower pots that we pop over the heads of susceptible seedlings. Since frost usually strikes on a calm night, we don't weight pots down but simply "screw" them a little into the ground. Bigger pots—the kind shrubs and potted mums are sold in—slip nicely over tender zucchini or tomato plants, keeping them safe if not particularly warm.

Threadbare blankets, propped up on short sticks, are useful for covering beds of small bean plants or blooming strawberries. As a last resort we carry a few armloads of bedsheets and bath towels into the garden and drape them gingerly over susceptible seedlings. We may wake up the next morning to a south wind returning and no frost, but why risk it? Who wants to see two months of work ruined in a night?

As a season stretcher and frost deflector, plastic sheeting has its advantages. Clear plastic tunnels held up by wire hoops protect plants beneath. To protect an entire bed of larger tomato plants from frost, we drape a sheet of plastic over lengths of flexible, black, 1-inch-diameter PVC water pipe, bent into a hoops, the ends snugged over dowelling hammered into the ground at intervals along either side of the bed, so that 5 inches (12 cm) of dowel extends above ground. This can be left in place, with ends open, during a spell of cool days to keep the tomato plants moving along.

Designed especially for garden use, slitted plastic row covers exhale the buildup of hot air. Then there are water-filled plastic teepees (Wall-O'-Water) that sit over individual plants; the water absorbs heat during the day, releases it at night, warding off frost in the process. One catalog shows a plastic "cloche" meant to give seedlings a head start and shed frost, but the translucent cylinders strike me as too small and too expensive. In any event, you can reuse any big clear plastic jug for the purpose: slice off the bottom and unscrew the cap to vent hot air.

Recently we have made good use of the new lightweight fabric covers—floating row covers—sold under several trade names. Made of "spun and bonded" polyester fibers, the cloth lets in about 85 percent of available light and all the rain. It also buffers the winds to create a cozy microclimate underneath. Because they weigh next to nothing, cloth covers "float" ever so lightly, right on top of plants; as your cauliflowers grow, the fabric billows up like rising bread dough. We secure the sides with stones, long sticks or lengths of lumber. On the down side, the stuff tears easily; if you get three seasons out of it you're doing well. We reuse torn row cover by folding a rip over on itself and keeping it together with stones. Even fairly small remnants are useful to cover small

OPPOSITE: An array of herbs and flowers weave through the beds of edibles. Silver Artemisia absinthium and feathery green yarrow lend their pungent, bug-repelling scents to a mix that includes Rugosa roses, dianthus or pinks, and big blue Italian bugloss, a giant forget-me-not relative with edible blue flowers that draw bees and butterflies.

sections of garden. Garden fabric offers some frost protection as well.

INSECTS

There may never be complete peace between gardeners and insects, but it is a mistake to cast all bugs in a bad light because of a handful of troublemakers.

Natural Balance

A healthy garden is literally—and quite naturally—swarming with flying insects and crawling with earthbound creatures. Bug counters estimate that every square yard in an average garden is home to more than 1,000 insects of many kinds. Obviously, only a fraction pose any threat to plants; otherwise the garden would be eaten to shreds in no time. The rest do the beneficial work of returning organic matter to the soil, opening up underground air channels, pollinating your cucumbers and keeping the birds well fed. Some bugs—bless 'em—eat other bugs: spiders, ladybugs, praying mantises, assassin bugs, rove beetles and parasitic wasps are among a gardener's best allies.

All this is easy to forget when earwigs are mowing down carrot sprouts or turning basil into lace; when cutworms are toppling tomato seedlings and flea beetles are riddling the radish leaves. The temptation may be to reach for the "big guns"—a sprayer full of chemicals—and show the bugs who's boss. The problem is that many chemicals kill friend and foe alike. You may win the battle, but you'll never win the war. When the next generation of aphids appears, where are the ladybugs that devour them? If insect-eating birds haven't been harmed outright by the spray, they may leave when their food supply suddenly dwindles. The lull in plant damage by insects is sure to prove a short-lived illusion.

It is no coincidence that talk of pesticides often takes on a military tone. Much of the arsenal of garden chemicals was originally developed and stockpiled as weaponry— nerve gases, defoliants, and the like—during the wars of the twentieth century. In peacetime, the chemical companies targeted farmers and gardeners as a ready market for the toxic leftover inventory.

A garden is a place of peaceful cooperation, not a battlefield. Insects are part of the natural balance. Our approach to bugs can be summed up as: innocent until proven guilty. When we need to protect our plants, we do. But if we're not sure about the eating habits of a mysterious iridescent beetle that comes to light as we dig, we let it be. (Sometimes, as a precaution we'll throw the creature over the garden fence, a tactic that works only if you have no neighbors within bug-tossing distance.) After a while, you come to recognize the garden's principal pests; you learn the difference between leaf-eating Mexican bean beetles and their near look-alikes, the aphid-eating ladybugs. You can spot the calling cards of creatures that dine by night: a silver slug trail, the telltale toothmarks of earwigs. You can take specific steps to correct the balance only when you know what you're up against.

Prevention

When it comes to trouble (with a capital T and that rhymes with P and that stands for pests) prevention is better than cure. Tests have shown that insects are drawn to plants that are weak, ailing, pumped up with chemical fertilizers or otherwise stressed. A healthy garden, built on a foundation of lively organic soil, is less apt to be bothered by bugs. If insects are giving you a rough time, look to the soil first.

Diversity is another key to a balanced environment. Snakes and toads should always be welcome in a natural garden. A big old clay pot, inverted and propped up on one side with a stone, may persuade a toad to set up house in a shady corner. Enticing birdhouses and shrubbery offer shelter to swallows, flycatchers and finches. Last season a pair of perky redstarts took up residence in our garden. From dawn till dusk they flashed from fence to branch, to cabbage patch, to rosebush in a tireless search for insects—regular little bug-catching vacuum cleaners. Robins, cliff swallows, phoebes and catbirds joined the hunt.

Companion planting has its adherents. Some books provide detailed lists of good and bad companions: plant beans next to potatoes to repel the Mexican bean beetle; chives near tomatoes, strawberries and broccoli will ward off aphids. Although I'm intrigued by the possibilities, our approach to companion planting is rather more chaotic—but companionable nonetheless. Woven throughout our kitchen garden are an array of aromatic herbs that add randomly to the bug-baffling mix. At the ends of kitchen-garden beds, clumps of sage, winter savory, chives, tarragon and Greek oregano are within easy reach as we gather ingredients for cooking. Seldom picked for use, rue and wormwood lend their pungent presence to the jumble. Catnip, chamomile and horehound pop up as volunteers.

One of the simplest things you can do to prevent a pests population explosion is to clean up the garden thoroughly in fall, a time when insects are searching for a place to lay eggs or hibernate. There is no point working against yourself by leaving a litter of spent vines and stalks, old fruit and foliage lying around the garden. If you can bury all debris in a hot compost heap, so much the better. Turning the soil in fall also exposes various eggs and grubs to the birds or freezing temperatures.

Getting the Bugs Out

As sure as plants grow, some insects eventually show up to feed on them. The first step is to identify the culprits. A comprehensive illustrated insect guide is a valuable tool. *The Healthy Garden Handbook* from the editors of *Mother Earth News* gives clear mugshots of the garden's "most wanted" and suggests a choice of controls.

Plants can cope with a certain amount of grazing and may even rebound with increased vigor after the pest's cycle is over. Let's face it: often a gardener's pride suffers more damage than do the plants themselves. If the problem escalates, handpicking is a benign and effective way to control many insects. If potato beetles are getting the best of the patch, knock them off into a pail of

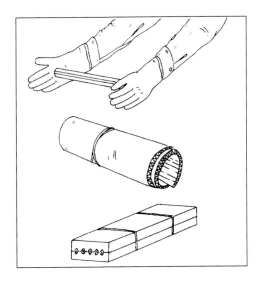

Earwigs like to crawl into dark, close quarters. Trap these nocturnal pests in pieces of old garden hose, a loosely rolled cardboard cylinder or two pieces of grooved wood, held together with elastic bands. Such simple traps often lure a number of earwigs.

water with a dash of dish soap in it. Better yet, search the undersides of leaves early in the season and crush the egg clusters by hand. Provided that the garden is not vast, handpicking is an excellent way to control larger, slow-moving pests that eat by day. Many a slug, earwig and caterpillar has felt the full force of the sole of a wooden clog in our garden. Sometimes, as I grind, I'll say something like "May your dead body enrich the earth" to ease my conscience and remind me that nothing is wasted in nature.

Slugs and Earwigs

I've tried handpicking slugs by night, but the slimy things slip through my fingers. A few shakes of salt reduce a slug to bubbling gel in no time, but too much salt can injure foliage. A neighbor stalks slugs with a flashlight in one hand and scissors in the other. I'll spare you the gory details except to say that I've heard her referred to as the "slug slasher."

Here is an improvement on beer-baited slug traps: sink yogurt or cottage-cheese containers into the ground up to their rim; fill them almost to the top with a 50/50 mix of molasses and water into which is stirred a few teaspoons of brewer's yeast and bran. Empty the drowned slugs into the compost every few days.

Earwigs have become notorious pests recently in this area. I hate to pinch them because they pinch back. Insecticidal soap kills earwigs on contact but that entails a midnight garden tour with a spray bottle at the ready. You may prefer to set some traps and get some sleep. Earwigs love to hide in tight dark places. One gardener reports wonderful success trapping earwigs in foot-long lengths of old garden hose laid on the ground in places where the nocturnal eaters have been busy—in the carrot patch, for instance, or near Chinese cabbages. A few drops of cod-liver oil or fish emulsion in the hose sweetens the trap. In the morning she picks up the hose gingerly with gloved hands, being careful to first block the exits at both ends, and shakes the earwigs into a pail of water with a slick of soap on top. Lacking old hose, roll up tight tubes of corrugated cardboard. Earwigs crawl into crevices in wood as well. Chisel or cut some grooves into two small pieces of board; clamp the boards together with rubber bands and lay the trap in the garden. Balls of crumpled newspapers or cloth, baited with fish oil, draw the pincered nightcrawlers for morning collection.

Barriers and Live Traps

Sometimes a physical barrier is the best way to ward off pests. Crushed eggshells or sharp sand spread in a band around susceptible plants may keep soft-bellied slugs and snails at bay. A dusting of wood ash is said to discourage a range of insects. The new "floating row covers," made of very lightweight translucent fabric, exclude flying pests such as cabbage moths, flea beetles and root maggot flies.

In many areas, deer and rabbits freeload off a gardener's efforts. Both mammals are forever sniffing the air for threatening scents. Some gardeners sprinkle blood meal around beds, or hang it in cotton bags at waist height from a fence or branches, to signal "danger zone—stay away." Live traps capture nocturnal bandits, like raccoons, that raid garden produce.

Sprays and Dusts

For an organic gardener, insect sprays are a last resort. The choice is between either homemade or commercial. From the kitchen come several recipes that are more repellant than lethal.

- **ALL-PURPOSE SPRAY:** Blend together a few peeled garlic bulbs, a small onion or a handful of chives, a tablespoon of cayenne pepper in a quart of water. The addition of pungent herbs such as peppermint, cedar leaves, wormwood or coriander boosts the brew. Let it steep for an hour or more. Strain through cloth and add a tablespoon of pure liquid soap or cooking oil to help the spray stick to leaves. Store in a cool place. Spray full strength to repel aphids, flea beetles, thrips and others. To make a "solar tea," chop the same ingredients and steep in water in a clear glass jar set in the sun for a few days.

- **GARLIC SPRAY:** Garlic's antibiotic properties make it a natural for controlling downy mildew on cucumbers and melons; rust, anthracnose and bacterial blight on beans: and the early blight that hits tomatoes. Remember, though, that it is wiser to plant disease-resistant varieties whenever possible.

  To make a pungent bug chaser, press 4 or 5 big garlic cloves into as many tablespoons (60 to 75 mL) of mineral oil. Let steep for a day. Add 2 cups (500 mL) of water and a teaspoon (5 mL) of liquid soap and whisk together. Strain through a square of cotton and store the concentrate in a glass (not metal) container. Use 2 teaspoons (10 mL) in a quart (liter) spray bottle aimed at your worst pests.

- **CEDAR LEAF SPRAY OR CEDAR MULCH:** Remember the lovely resinous scent of that big old cedar chest used to store blankets and woolens? In the garden, the repellant properties of cedarwood deters cucumber, bean and potato beetles, as well as red spiders and squash bugs from susceptible plants. Simmer a couple of double handfuls of cedar chips, bark or sawdust (from a local lumber mill) in a big pot of water. Strain and store for future use as a foliar spray. A cedar mulch should keep the potato patch beetle-free; cedar chips in the pathways may also help repel various pests. Smells nice, anyway.

NATURAL PEST CONTROLS
A Buyer's Guide

One shelf in our garden shed holds a few safe but effective natural pesticides that help protect the kitchen garden from hungry predators. As a last resort, when insects threaten to do more than cosmetic damage, we spray or dust only the infested area, trying if possible to hit the culprits directly. All of the following are available from garden centers or mail-order sources.

- **INSECTICIDAL SOAP:** High in fats and mineral salts, this specially made soap coats and smothers insects. Effective against aphids, whiteflies, earwigs, flea beetles, leafhoppers and others, soap spray does not harm beneficial insects and quickly biodegrades. The ready-mixed pump-spray bottle—a little soap, a lot of water and plastic—is an over-packaged waste of money compared to the concentrate that you can mix easily yourself. I like to have a spray bottle full and ready to grab—"Quick, get the soap!"—whenever a nest of earwigs is uncovered.

- **BACILLUS THURINGIENSIS (BT):** This biological control for a variety of caterpillars, loopers and cutworms should be on the shelf of any gardener wanting to grow cabbages and kin. Trade names include Thuricide, Dipel or simply Liquid Organic (Biological) Insecticide. Used as needed, BT all but guarantees worm-free broccoli. Because it degrades quickly, we respray with BT after rains or whenever we see new caterpillar damage. Mix only what you need and use it up in a day because the active ingredient soon loses its punch.

- **DIATOMACEOUS EARTH:** Made from the pulverized shells of tiny fossilized ocean plants called diatoms, this natural dust feels like coarse flour to thick-skinned gardeners but more like broken glass to soft-bellied slugs and insects. Kills on contact by piercing ectoskeleton or innards, causing pests to dry up. Controls aphids, thrips, mites, earwigs, slugs, snails, tomato hornworm and others. For full effect, dust onto dry foliage or soil and reapply after a rain. This can get expensive.

- **PYRETHRUM:** A heavyweight botanical insecticide derived from the flowers of an innocent-looking white daisy, *Chrysanthemum cinerariafolium*, pyrethrum knocks out a range of bugs, including various beetles, caterpillars, aphids and thrips. It is also toxic to fish, frogs, snakes and beneficial insects, including bees. Spray at dusk to spare the bees, and do not use where spray can drift into garden pools or streams. Although it breaks down into harmless compound fairly quickly, you're advised to hold the spray during the week before harvest and to avoid pyrethrum products that also contain piperonyl butoxide, a suspected mutagen.

A hardy perennial, pyrethrum can be grown in the garden as a source of homemade insecticide. Sprinkle the crushed flowers, fresh or dried, around and over bugged plants. To make your own spray, steep a palmful of ground dried flowers in 2 quarts of hot water for a half-hour, strain and add a teaspoon of pure liquid soap.

- **ROTENONE:** Another widely available, plant-derived bug killer, rotenone is made from the roots of several tropical plants, including derris. Deritox is one brand name. Again look for the pure product, unadulterated with synthetics. Harmless to warm-blooded animals, rotenone controls flea beetles, cucumber and potato beetles, squash bugs, leafhoppers and various caterpillars. Dust or spray carefully on a calm evening to avoid breathing it in or spreading it beyond the infested area. Potent but not long-lasting, rotenone should be purchased fresh at the start of a new season and applied, like pyrethrum, as a last resort. This dust, too, is toxic to fish, as I learned the hard way: Once on a windy day I dusted some beans growing beside a lily pool stocked with goldfish; over the next week, sadly, a number of fish went belly up, poisoned by the rotenone.

WEEDS

"One year's seeding makes seven years weeding," runs an old saw. You can save yourself a lot of work by never allowing weeds to go to seed in and around the garden. Nip them in the bud; better yet, catch them long before. Weeds are either annual or perennial. Once you root out an annual, or sever its top, the deed is done. I prefer to rake up annuals and haul them to the compost, rather than leaving a mess of weeds strewn around the garden where they may shelter insects or take root again.

Perennials are another story. Although our kitchen garden grows on land that was once woven through with quack grass and bindweed, two of the most tenacious and "spreadaceous" perennials going, I can honestly say that weeds pose very little problem. As we broke new ground, we were careful to unearth all the roots we could find. In subsequent years, we extracted the stubborn remnants. Never add perennial weeds to a compost heap.

Bindweed is a pretty perennial morning glory intent on strangulation as it twines up its neighbors in a bid to see the sun. Its roots, like rubbery spaghetti, go down too deep to dig out entirely. Like most perennials, bindweed feeds its roots through its leaves. Whenever we turn over a bed, we yank out as much root as possible. Later, during cultivation, we slice off the top growth. Over the years, bindweed has scaled down its ambitious takeover plans, and has even given up altogether in some places.

Smothering weeds with mulch is a good plan, especially in pathways where a thick layer of overlapped newspaper or cardboard under hay, leaves or straw will keep even the most determined interloper in the dark. A closely planted vegetable bed leaves little room for weeds.

Weeding conscientiously at least once a week in the early part of the season will make your work easier later when it's hot. And it's best to turf out small weeds before they have a chance to steal food, water and light from garden plants. A small sharp hoe is useful for close work in intensive beds; a pronged weeder snaps off taprooted weeds, such as dandelion and burdock, underground. And then there are fingers, handiest and most precise of weeding tools. A lot of gardeners grumble about weeding, but with a shift in attitude—think how nice a weed-free garden looks and how much better your plants will do—weeding can become almost fun.

WATER
Doing More with Less

Larkwhistle Garden is watered entirely by hand. Throughout the garden there are a number of strategically placed concrete pools—two in the kitchen garden—all linked by underground pipes to a holding tank under the farm's original old hand-pump. Water from the slightly elevated wellhead flows by gravity into all the pools where it sits, warming in the sun. To water, we dip cans and buckets into the pools and go from there. I get a great kick out of paddling around barefoot, plunging the pails into the water, splashing around, getting soaked with the garden. When children visit, watering is their favorite activity.

Because we water by hand, we've found ways to do more with less. Whether you use cans, hose or sprinkler, the following conservation techniques are appropriate to any garden.

- Start with the soil: add an abundance of spongy organic matter every season; humus (paradoxically) soaks up and holds moisture while opening the soil for improved drainage.
- Plant garden beds so that the leaves of maturing plants touch to create a cooling and water-conserving "living mulch."
- Sculpt the earth to hold water where you want it. With your hand, make a shallow "soup bowl" around individual tomato, lettuce and broccoli plants. Form a water-holding trough between double rows of peas, carrots, onions and spinach. Rake a raised rim of soil around the perimeter of a bed to prevent runoff. Such earth sculpting helps funnel water to roots.
- Localize water on beds and around individual plants and apply it to the soil rather than to foliage, if possible.
- Water deeply about once a week—think soak, drench, saturate. The soil should be moist down about one foot (30 cm). If in

doubt, check with a long trowel or small spade. Water seedlings and small plants more often if you can.

- Water early in the morning to send plants into the heat of the day with a reviving drink. Alternatively, water in the late afternoon until dusk; cold water will be moderated somewhat as it filters through sun-warmed soil. Remember to water early enough in the evening so that foliage dries by nightfall; damp leaves are a breeding ground for mildew and fungus. Working in a wet garden may also spread diseases.
- Once the soil has warmed up somewhat in June, wait for a real soaking rain, then lay an organic mulch around the thirstiest plants to conserve moisture.
- Pay attention to signs of wilting leaves in the morning or evening—time to water. A certain amount of wilting is natural under a hot mid-day sun. Avoid watering at mid-day because it tricks plants into opening their "pores" then when you turn off the tap, they may actually lose more water through their leaves than they take up through their roots. Also, much of the water applied at mid-day evaporates.
- Sink large, perforated, topless tin cans or plastic jugs into the ground next to tomatoes, peppers and such; filled with water, the container will gradually leak moisture to roots.
- Pay particular attention to watering when fruits such as cucumbers and tomatoes are swelling, when broccoli heads are expanding, when ears of corn are growing plump—that is when the parts you want for food are moving toward maturity.
- Use a round of hand watering as a good excuse to feed plants a drink of liquid fertilizer in the form of fish or seaweed emulsion or a garden tea made from manure or compost.
- Cultivate often.

At any season, garden fabric protects susceptible plants from flying insects. Permeable to sunlight and rain, the cloth floats lightly over vegetables as they grow.

The Cultivated Garden

Cultivation is the practice of scratching and stirring a shallow surface layer of soil—and it is one of the best things you can do for the garden. The tool for the job is a pronged cultivator—a "scratcher" we call it—with either a long or a short handle. On clay ground, a loose top layer prevents baking, cracking and crusting over. In a sandy garden, surface cultivation creates a "dust mulch," a crumbly dryish layer that blocks the upward evaporation of moisture from below by breaking the continuous soil "wick." After every rainfall, we cultivate all the unmulched kitchen-garden beds. After watering, we fluff up the soil around plants. Stirring the soil conserves water and lets the earth breathe—and a freshly cultivated bed looks so lovely. Weeding and cultivating go hand in hand. I have a combination hoe/cultivator, a gift from an older gardener. The blade slices weeds; flipped over, the four-pronged flip side loosens the soil. Think of cultivation as giving the earth a good back-scratch.

Sow Cool
Peas, Spinach, Onions and Leeks

"They're hoeing the snow up there," was the story that circulated among our neighbors (and finally returned to us) our first spring in the country. Eager to dig in, we did indeed chase the last remnants of snow with hoe and rake—and we've done the same thing many an April since. Larkwhistle's light sandy soil is by nature "early" soil; that is, it warms and dries sooner than heavier ground, which is just as well since we are by nature impatient gardeners, especially in April. Sand also drains better than clay soil, so that melting snow leaves it moist but not sodden. Most years, the very day after snow recedes, we are able to open shallow furrows in the cool earth for onion sets, peas and spinach seed. In April we're grateful for early soil that brings snow peas and scallions for the wok by mid-June, lettuce and radishes for the salad bowl by the end of May, a time when many gardeners are just getting around to sowing their first seeds outdoors.

NEW TRADITIONS

"Sow as soon as the ground is workable," say the instructions on the back of a packet of spinach seeds. "Better safe than sorry: The 24th of May is the time to put in the garden," says traditional wisdom. Trust the seed packet.

A May harvest depends on an April planting. "But it's still so cold," I hear you protest. And yet, look around: all kinds of wild plants and weeds are putting on a burst of growth in April. Certain vegetables, too, some of them related to the dandelions and lamb's quarters sprouting in lawn and garden, are built to survive frost, thaw out and keep growing. Not only do the hardy ones endure cool weather, most actually need it for best growth.

PEAS
Snap, Shelling and Sugar

Cool weather crops include one of the best-tasting vegetables—fresh green peas. My first mouthful of peas right from the pod came as a sweet surprise. The peas I knew as a child, straight from the tin, were more gray then green, more starch than sugar—a miserable fate for such a good vegetable.

Many vegetables can be grown from nursery transplants, but not peas: the first step is to look for seeds. There are three kinds of peas—shelling peas, snow peas and snap peas. Each come in a range of heights. Shelling peas—the kind you remove from the pods—take up the most space for what you get, but are probably the most delicious. Flat, edible-podded snow peas—the French *mangetout*—are very productive of flat pods for stir-frys and crudités, but lack sweetness and tend to toughen as the peas fill out.

A few years ago snap peas—the now famous 'Sugar Snap' started it all—made a splash in seed catalogs. Here, after years of work, was a brand-new vegetable combining the fiberless pods of snow peas with plump sweet seeds inside. A great treat right off the vine, 'Sugar Snaps' are as close to candy as you can grow. Those vines, however, stretch to an unwieldy 6 feet (1.8 m) or more, a drawback for many gardeners. In our experience shorter versions of snap peas such as 'Sugar Ann' have lost not only stature but also a measure of sweetness—we stay with the original green giant and trellis them up.

Peas Ease

Virtually free of pests and diseases, peas are one of the easiest of vegetables to grow, provided their few needs are met. These are: early planting, cool moist soil and support for the taller types.

OPPOSITE: Trained to climb up chicken-wire fencing, pea vines occupy much less space and are easier to pick than unsupported plants. Across the hay-mulched path, lettuces and leeks share a bed bordered by self-sown calendulas and sweet alyssum.

All three kinds of peas are among the earliest seed we plant, with the first batch usually going in at the beginning of April, soon after the snow has faded. Early planting brings the vines to fruitful maturity by July, so that most of their growth takes place in the cooler days of May and June. Hot dry weather is a pea plant's idea of stress, and stressed plants, like stressed people, are more susceptible to sickness. To extend the harvest of shelling peas, we sow a second time, three weeks to a month later.

Peas do well in a range of soils, with a preference for rich sandy loam. Fertilizers high in phosphorus and potash—phosphate rock and kelp meal are two choices along with compost or well aged manure—help produce sturdy vines full of fruit. But too much nitrogen pushes foliage at the expense of pods.

Think Ahead

To get a jump on spring, it's wise—but not absolutely necessary—to prepare the earth in the pea patch the fall before, spreading the required fertilizers and digging them in. If your soil stays cold and damp for weeks in April, rake the space into a raised flat-topped bed in October; a rise of even a few inches means better drainage and faster warming. Where the soil tends to be hot and dry, sculpt a shallow, rain-catching trough for pea seeds instead.

A band about 18 inches (45 cm) wide will accommodate a double row of peas with space for cultivating or mulching on either side. A wider raised area, however, makes room for other vegetables and cuts down on unproductive paths. In our garden, peas typically grow along the north side of a 4-foot-wide (120-cm-wide) intensive bed; for company they may have lettuce, onions, carrots and spinach in front, an arrangement that gives way to a second planting of endive, Chinese cabbage and late lettuce in midsummer. I can't say that the peas are the easiest to pick in this wide-bed setup—it would be much handier with a path on both sides—but the inconvenience is balanced by the full use of space. And it makes a lovely planting, too, with red and green lettuces snugged up to the pea vines and a feathery edge of carrot tops. For greater convenience and an extended harvest, plant two double rows of peas three to four weeks apart, on either side of a wide bed, with a narrow path between.

Peas are gregarious; there is no point planting a skimpy single row when you can get double the pods in a little extra space. To plant, hoe open two side-by-side furrows, about 3 inches (8 cm) deep and a hand-span apart. Drop seeds in one by one, leaving an inch or so between them. Use a rake to knock in the sides of the furrows, covering seeds with about 1½ inches (4 cm) of earth; thump the back of the rake gently along the row to firm. Sculpt the earth to leave a ridge of soil on each side of the band of peas; then, when vines are laden with pods in a hot, dry July, you can flood the little trench, and water will be funneled to thirsty roots.

I have to confess that the first pea seeds we plant are usually pink, coated with fungicide that sterilizes soil around each seed so they will not rot in the cool ground. I know that this is heresy coming from an organic gardener, but pink peas are our one concession to chemical help.

Pea Props

All but the shortest pea vines need some support; left to topple they take up more than their share of space, and pods are hard to find in the leafy tangle. Ideally the time to put in props is just before the rows are seeded. We seldom do, but always wish we had when, wincing at possible root damage later on, we are hammering in posts between young plants already entwined.

Pea tendrils will curl around anything fine. For hip-high varieties such as "Green Arrow" shelling peas or "Oregon Giant" snow peas, we use lengths of wide-mesh chicken wire nailed to slim posts, or 2 by 4's, spaced 5 feet (1.5 m) apart. Usable year after year, the fence is unrolled, stretched tight, and sledged into place each spring—this is a job for four hands.

If available, twiggy branches pushed into

the ground between a double row provide a network of support and make for easy picking. Once, when a neighbor thinned out a stand of birch trees, we hauled home bundles of tall tree tops for a double row of 'Sugar Snaps'; laced together with binder twine, the branches looked first like a leafless hedge and then like trees full of peas. Typically, though, we erect a 6-foot-high fence of posts and chicken wire for 'Sugar Snaps.' Other options are various arrangements of lumber and twine (which I find both awkward and flimsy) or special nylon pea netting.

Usually spring rains keep peas watered, but if a dry spell hits as vines are flowering and fruiting, be sure to soak the patch deeply twice a week, if possible flooding the soil—here's where that trough comes in—rather than wetting the leaves. A ground-covering mulch of grass clippings, straw or last fall's leaves, snugged up to the base of the vines, goes a long way toward keeping the earth moist and cool, conditions very much to their liking.

Harvest Time

Quick to pick, snow peas are ready when they are still flat and tender, before they grow puffy, curled, and fibrous; once flowers appear, pods are close at hand. Pick 'Sugar Snaps' (or equivalent) when they are plump, bright green, and tender; if you pierce the pod with a thumbnail, just under the little green cap, you can pull out and down to pick the pod while removing both the cap and string all in one step—a real kitchen time-saver.

It can be tricky to know when shelling peas are ready; pods may look full but be only inflated, the peas mere pebbles inside. If squeezing doesn't tell you, unzip a few pods to see. If you are tempted to leave pods on the vine a few extra days, remember that all peas change quickly from sweet and tender to bland and grainy. For best flavor, pick peas just before you intend to cook them—if you cook them, that is.

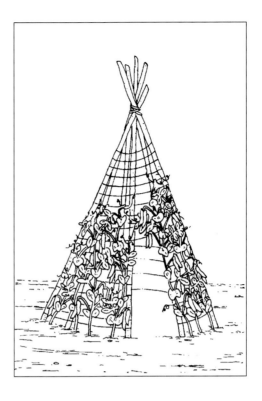

'Sugar Snap' peas climbing up strings or netting quickly transform a teepee of poles into an edible hideaway for children.

In the Kitchen

Shelling and snap peas are the favorite grazing food in the garden; a certain percentage never make it to the kitchen. Of those that do, some never reach the kettle; handfuls are munched raw while shelling, and even the cat pounces on rolling peas and eats them eagerly. Snow peas get the classic stir-fry treatment with garlic, ginger, and soy sauce. 'Sugar Snaps' are sweet as can be raw, and delicious steamed and dressed with a bit of butter and salt. Brief cooking makes shelling peas even more succulent.

Risi e Bisi is a perfectly simple Italian dish of rice and peas. Cook them separately, then gently stir together; season with a little sweet butter and salt, lots of grated Parmesan or Romano cheese and freshly ground pepper. A few sautéed mushrooms are a nice touch, but simpler may be better.

SPINACH

On that first spring planting day, a packet of spinach seeds always rattles around with the peas and onion sets in the garden basket. Here is a cold-hardy crop that must go into the ground early for decent results. The reason? Spinach thrives in cool weather during spring's shorter days, but responds directly to higher temperature and June's lengthening days by sending up a seed stalk—end of harvest. The sooner it sprouts, the more time spinach has to grow leaves before the bolt. Certain varieties are listed as "longstanding" and "slow bolting," but nothing will postpone the inevitable except an early start.

Gardeners like to say that there is no comparing the taste of store-bought with fresh-picked. Well, yes and no: I doubt that you could tell the difference between acorn squash from the market and from the garden; you may not know store-bought zucchini, peppers or eggplant from those you grow, except that you know what's on them. But other vegetables, spinach among them, lose a fair bit of sparkle sitting in a truck and on the produce shelf for even a few days.

Seeding and Thinning

The lively crunch of a spinach salad just minutes from the earth is within easy reach of anyone with a bit of space in the sun—even a little shade will do. As a leafy crop, spinach responds with lush, dark green growth to an extra helping of nitrogen in the soil. To that end, we turn in a few inches of decayed cow manure or compost along the row; a dusting of blood meal also boosts the N rating, while a blended organic fertilizer covers the spectrum of nutrients. Lime is needed to bring the pH up to around 6.5, a level that spinach demands. Even in our alkaline soil, a dusting of powdered lime stirred in at planting time improves growth.

A maxim of intensive gardening says that the distance between plants in a row can also be roughly the distance between rows, as long as you leave room to cultivate. Since full-grown spinach plants should stand 5 or 6 inches (12 or 15 cm) apart along a row, we plant spinach seed in either double or triple rows, with a hand-span between each row. Drop the largish seed one by one, about 1 inch apart, into a shallow furrow, then cover with ½ to ¼ inch of fine-textured earth,

before tamping gently with the back of a rake or by hand. If your soil tends to crust over, consider topping the seeds with sifted compost instead.

When seedlings grow to touch each other, it's time to thin. I know several otherwise sensible gardeners who balk at this step; and I can understand why: I'm still surprised that seeds sprout at all and, when they do, I feel like an ingrate, somehow, tearing half of them out. But there's nothing gained by crowding plants.

The first thinning leaves small plants about 3 inches (8 cm) apart. Later, when they touch again, you can go over the rows once more, removing every other plant, a thinning that counts as a harvest and may last a few days. After that, harvesting means picking larger outside leaves, allowing the rest to fill out for the next time.

A tip: If spinach growth has stalled or slowed, a drink of dilute fish emulsion usually shows dramatic results in a spurt of growth and darker leaves. Spinach is a thirsty vegetable in any case and, if spring rains fail, plan to soak the patch every three or four days; avoid sprinkling in the evening for fear of encouraging fungus. To further ward off blights and blue mold, look for hybrids such as 'Melody,' 'Indian Summer' and 'Tyee' with built-in tolerance. We habitually plant the old-fashioned 'Longstanding Bloomsdale,' but have been astonished lately by the exhuberant growth and long season of a variety called 'Unipak.'

Pests

Although disease is rare in our spinach rows, several bugs routinely show up. Most destructive are some species of cutworm—worldwide there are a frightening 20,000 variations on this grayish-brown caterpillar (the larvae of night-flying moths). The cutworm helps itself to a spinach salad during a night out of the ground. By day the coward hides, but the damage is done. Spraying spinach with *Bacillus thuringiensis* ensures that the cutworms eat their last meal, otherwise you will probably unearth the curled-up creatures as you cultivate alongside the rows. They pop horribly when stepped on.

Flea beetles can riddle young spinach, but the tiny dark hopping insects are easily foiled by a covering of horticultural cloth, floating row cover such as Reemay, draped over the rows. Even in the absence of beetles, spinach seems to thrive under such cloth, especially during the first month of growth.

Once it grows seed stalks in late June, spinach is only fit for the compost heap. Pulling up seedy spinach opens up space for a midsummer planting for fall picking. You can reserve the row for another spinach seeding in August that should yield new greens as the maples turn. Other follow-up vegetables include endive, Chinese cabbage, daikon radish, late lettuce, fall turnips—see Second Season (see page 115) for details.

Pick of the Crop

Cooked (or, rather, overcooked) is how many people learned to hate spinach. Raw is how many learned to love it. Much of our pickings go directly into the salad bowl, by way of a grit-removing deluge and a quick turn in the salad spinner. But lightly cooked, fresh-picked spinach, drained, chopped and simply dressed with butter or olive oil is simply delicious. Spinach Parmesan, an elaboration, is another way to enjoy this vegetable.

ONIONS

If leeks are the gentry among alliums, onions are the peasant cousins, hard-working, handy, and sometimes taken for granted. But so many dishes start with a skillet full of sautéed onions that I can't imagine cooking without them. To "know your onions" is said to be a mark of wisdom, and it is a wise gardener, indeed, who can sort them out: red, white and yellow; sets; Spanish and Egyptian.

The simplest way to grow onions is from sets. Plant an onion set in spring, harvest a full-grown bulb in September. A set is a miniature bulb grown from crowded seeds the year before. You could grow sets your-

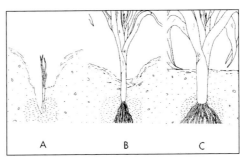

self, but nobody does—wicker baskets at hardware stores filled with crackling sets are another sign of spring. A tip: If you are picking out sets by hand, go for the smallest of them; bigger ones may already have a flower stalk in embryonic form at their centers and you don't want your row of onions going to seed at the expense of bulbs. Sets are available for yellow, white, red and Spanish onions.

Some garden centers sell onion seedlings in early spring, often quite interesting varieties and usually growing on top of each other in a too-small containers. We buy seedlings as soon as available, preferably in April, and shift them into a flat, spaced 2 inches (5 cm) apart. Grown until transplanting in mid-May or about a week before the last spring frost, the seedlings have a grand head-start. This method has done very well for us, sometimes better than sets.

Lately, we have had excellent results starting both onions and leeks in cell packs, those flimsy plastic containers divided into four or six compartments that every gardener has left over from nursery annuals. Larger trays, divided into a hundred or more individual planting cells, work equally well. Fill cell packs or trays with growing medium, plant several seeds in each compartment and thin eventually to a single seedling in each. Start both onions and leeks indoors six to eight weeks before the spring frost-free date. At transplanting time, a week or two before the frost-free date, simply pop the seedlings out of the cells and set them in the garden. Roots are not disturbed, and seedlings grow on without pause or setback. For fun, try growing big mild Spanish onions this way; there is nothing better for

A) In spring, transplant leek seedlings into the bottom of a 3- or 4-inch (7.5- or 10-cm) deep trench. B) As leeks grow, gradually fill the trenches with soil. C) At harvest time, you'll dig long, beautifully blanched leeks with lots of the tender, mild white portion.

Orange tulips in the background show just how early in spring spinach can be ready to eat.

summer salads and burgers from the barbeque.

Being quite cold-hardy, sets go into the ground first thing in spring with the peas and spinach. Before planting, turn an inch or two of fine-textured compost and/or a measured amount of a blended organic fertilizer into the soil; manure used at this stage should be old, dark and crumbly. Lacking a complete fertilizer, bone meal or phosphate rock and a very light dusting of wood ashes and blood meal will help. See that the ingredients are well mixed through the top 8 inches (20 cm) of soil before raking the space smooth.

We always plan to harvest both green onions (or scallions) and mature cooking bulbs from the same row. To do this, push onion sets, pointed side up, into the loose soil to the depth of your knuckle, spacing the individual sets about 2 inches (5 cm) apart. This distance is much too close for full-sized bulbs, but later, if you pull every other one as salad onions in early summer, the remaining bulbs will be properly spaced to fill out to maturity. In a bed devoted solely to onions, space rows 8 inches (20 cm) apart across a bed.

A second tip: The best part of a green onion is the white below the leaves. For extra long green onions, use a separate bed or small area of ground, and plant onion sets deep down—3 inches (8 cm) of soil over their heads—and they will stretch to see the light, blanching all of the underground portion tender and mild.

"What are you going to do with all those onions?" a visitor once asked, looking around at five 25-foot (7.5-m) rows. Lots: once they get going, we harvest onions almost every day, not only as spring scallions and mature bulbs for fall/winter use, but at any size all summer long. Onions start off stir-frys, tomato sauce and ratatouilles; season coleslaw and tabouli; are sautéed with ginger, lemon thyme, lemon juice and tamari for a sauce to pour over poached fish.

Of Mulch, Maggots and Mold

Although they will put up with a dry spell, onions need a fair bit of moisture to plump up. Plan on a soaking every seven to ten days, if rains fail. For a quick boost of nutrients, we water the rows once or twice a summer with fish emulsion or an equivalent. A mulch of grass clippings, last fall's leaves, or what-have-you, pulled right up to their little necks, keeps onions moist and discourages weedy competitors.

Some gardens are bothered by onion root maggots, the larvae of a fly that lays its eggs on the soil next to onions; mulch applied early is an effective barrier to the maggot's destructive tunneling. Infested roots should be pulled and destroyed to stop the cycle. In wet areas or in damp clay ground, mulch may encourage moldy onions; in this case, it is better to cultivate shallowly around bulbs to suppress weeds and leave a fine dryish surface. Use wood ashes or diatomaceous earth around unmulched onions if maggots are a threat.

Home Stretch

Some gardeners say you must bend onion foliage to the ground in late summer or bulbs will not mature. Others disagree. Foliage begins to ripen naturally, like any daffodil or lily, when the time is right. When most of the tops are half-toppled, we ease them all over in one direction for the sake of a tidy row.

Once leaves have withered to yellow, pull the onions and, with the remnants of foliage covering the bulbs, let them cure in the garden for a day or two, with a further drying under cover in an airy shaded place for a few weeks. When the curing is complete, twist or cut off the shriveled tops and you have onions to store for months to come.

LEEKS

The *Allium* genus brings lots of flavor to the kitchen garden in the form of onions and leeks. Onions of any color come from either seeds or sets, but leeks are grown only from seeds. Start your own or look for seedling leeks at a garden center—a local nursery may be persuaded to grow you a batch of leek seedlings, since they have the ideal space and are starting thousands of seeds anyway.

It's a mystery to me why leeks are so expensive, commonly a dollar apiece, when they are only marginally trickier to grow than ordinary cooking onions. Lack of demand may account for the price; but who is willing to pay that much? Perhaps it's the leek's association with stylish French cuisine; and yet this mildest of alliums is a staple of day-to-day home cooking in much of Europe. It is much cheaper to grow your own leeks: a patch of ground 10 feet (3 m) long by 1 foot (30 cm) wide will yield about 50 leeks from an 89-cent packet of seeds.

Leeks must be started from seed very early indoors. We sow leeks in late March, or eight weeks before the average date of the last spring frost in cell packs or cell trays as described for onions. The sooner you start them (within reason), the bigger the leeks you'll harvest. Bigger is not always better in the vegetable garden, but in the case of leeks, a big leek is every bit as good as a little one, only more so.

In the Trenches

The process for seed-grown leeks is the same as that for onions, but at transplanting time they need special treatment. Like scallions, the prized part of a leek is the white section below the leaves. Planting in trenches ensures that a good portion of the leek will be blanched white and tender underground.

We transplant leeks into the open garden when the tulips start to flower (about mid-May here), keeping an ear to the long-range forecast to avoid exposing seedlings to the trauma of a cold snap—they'll survive frost, but it's an unnecessary shock.

A hefty round-bladed hoe, the kind used for hilling up potatoes, is ideal for opening a trench about 5 inches (12 cm) deep and wide; otherwise a small shovel or border spade (half normal size) will do. Stir a 1-inch (2.5-cm) dressing of compost and/or some organic fertilizer into the trench bottom, and you are ready to plant. Ease the young leeks out of the containers. Trowel out a small hole in the bottom of the trench. Holding the seedlings by their leaves, plant each leek so that at least half of it is buried when you fill in with soil. Space seedlings 4 inches (10 cm) apart. The row complete, water gently; you don't want a mud-slide in the trench.

As the leeks grow, gradually fill the trench with soil from the sides. If times are dry, we soak the row thoroughly before adding each level of soil, fertilizing with fish emulsion twice over the summer. Once trenches are topped up, a mulch helps suppress weeds and maintain moisture. Leeks are wonderfully free of pests and diseases; indeed, like onions, they may help keep bugs at bay.

A leek is ready to eat when it is as fat as your thumb, usually sometime in August, but with the summer garden full of food, we let them grow on into October. When you dig or pull a leek, half of its roots come up with a clinging ball of dirt. I like to clean leeks next to the compost heap; pull back two or three of the tough outer leaves right to the roots, and then slice off roots and leaves with a knife. Trim away most of the foliage. To clean grit from their tops, cut a slit down into the white portion, and rinse the leeks under running water as you flip the loose flaps to dislodge grit in the crowns.

Leeks are one of the best ingredients for fall and winter soups. A simple flavorful

Plant early, harvest sooner. Sown in April, peas may be ready for picking when the roses are blooming in early July.

potage is easily made by simmering leeks, potatoes, carrots and celery in salted water until the vegetables are soft; blend the soup into a coarse puree and add your choice of milk, butter, cream or soy milk. Heat through and serve.

I like to simmer leeks and carrots in chicken stock, with bits of cooked chicken stripped from the bones used to make the broth; cooked rice goes into the soup and it's done—a warming dish in December.

RED ONION AND BLUE CHEESE PIZZA

2 or 3	red onions	2 or 3
¼ cup	olive oil	50 mL
1 tbsp	balsamic vinegar	15 mL
1 tsp	honey or brown sugar	5 mL
pinch	salt and pepper	pinch
1 tbsp	fresh oregano, finely chopped	15 mL
2 leaves	fresh sage, finely chopped	2 leaves
1	prepared pizza crust	1
	Crumbled blue cheese	

Thinly slice onions. In a heavy skillet, sauté over medium-low heat in olive oil until very soft, about 15 minutes. Add the vinegar, sweetener, salt, pepper and herbs, and cook for another 3 to 5 minutes. Spread the onion mixture over a prepared pizza crust and top with crumbled blue cheese. Bake the pizza at 375°F (190°C) for 15 to 20 minutes. Serves four.

LEEKS AND WHITE BEANS VINAIGRETTE

Make the dressing by whisking together:

½ cup	olive oil	125 mL
3 tbsp	lemon juice or vinegar of choice	50 mL
1 tbsp	prepared mustard	15 mL
handful	fresh herbs: basil, chives, lovage, Greek oregano, tarragon, finely minced	handful
	Salt and pepper to taste	

Prepare leeks and beans salad:

4	medium-size leeks	4
4 cups	water with 1 tsp (5 mL) salt	1 L
1	can (14 fl oz/398 mL) Italian white beans, drained	1
few leaves	frilly red lettuce or radicchio	few leaves
	Grated carrots for garnish	

Remove roots and green tops and wash leeks thoroughly. Cut leeks crosswise into 1-inch (2.5-cm) rounds. Bring salted water to a boil. Add the leeks and simmer 5 to 8 minutes over medium heat until just tender. Drain leeks well, reserving the liquid for soup stock. Plunge cooked leeks in cold water and drain thoroughly. Toss the leeks gently with the vinaigrette. Gently fold in the beans and let the salad stand for an hour or more to meld flavors. Serve on frilly red lettuce or radicchio leaves with a garnish of grated carrots. Serves four to six.

SPINACH PARMESAN

2 or 3 handfuls	spinach leaves	2 or 3 handfuls
2 tbsp	olive oil	25 mL
2	garlic cloves, minced	2
½ cup	grated Parmesan cheese	125 mL
½ cup	dry bread crumbs	125 mL
pinch	nutmeg	pinch
2 tsp	fresh tarragon, minced	10 mL
½ cup	milk or cream	125 mL

Carefully wash spinach and shake dry. Steam spinach gently until wilted and cooked through. Drain it in a colander, pressing out excess water. Coarsly chop the cooked spinach and return it to the pot. In a small skillet, sauté the garlic in olive oil for a few minutes over moderate heat. Do not brown garlic. Add the cheese, bread crumbs, nutmeg and tarragon to the garlic before adding the mixture to the spinach and tossing gently. Pour the milk or cream into the seasoned spinach and reheat briefly over low heat. Serve immediately. Serves two.

Spinach Parmesan can be used as the filling for a crustless quiche:

2	eggs	2
dash	milk	dash
pinch	pepper	pinch

Lightly oil an 8-inch (20-cm) pie pan. Spread the spinach mixture evenly in the pan. Beat eggs with the milk and pepper. Pour the egg mixture over the spinach and bake at 350°F (180°C) until the egg has puffed and browned a little and a knife inserted into the center comes out clean. Cut the pie into wedges and serve warm or at room temperature. Serves four.

Lettuce Alone
From Seed to Salad Bowl

Trendy salad greens come and go, but while radicchio and arugula have their moments, lettuce remains. After tomatoes, lettuce is the most popular home-garden vegetable; and of all the leafy things growing in our garden, it is the one we most often gather. Indeed, despite shifting fads, one corn-fed neighbor of ours steadfastly maintains a preference for what he calls (at every opportunity) "a honeymoon salad—lettuce alone."

Once, our garden grew a standard romaine, a green Boston and an ordinary leaf lettuce. But gardeners—"insatiable seekers after outlandish things," as one old book calls us—are ever on the lookout for something different. Recently, seed catalogs have sprouted a raft of red lettuces, fancy French imports, one-serving miniatures, rediscovered heirlooms and more. One catalog lists more than fifty cultivars, some described in such living color—"pale pink on cream in the blanched hearts and burgundy on exposed leaf surfaces"—you'd think they were flowers. All have sterling features to recommend them: heat or frost tolerance, exceptional taste or texture, sheer beauty.

Our solution to the dilemma of choice is to grow three or four tried-and-true types each year, and experiment with as many more unfamiliar lettuces. Since a fine new (to us) variety can move to the must-grow list in a season, the band of old faithfuls is a revolving lot—a summer in the garden, a hiatus, around again. To sort out the confusion of cultivars, it is helpful to group lettuces according to shape and habit of growth. Variety names listed below are meant as a rough guide, a starting point, only. New cultivars appear, older ones re-surface; experimentation is encouraged.

• **LOOSELEAF:** Plants are V-shaped with loosely opened centers. Shades of green or red, leaves may be smooth or curly. For early salads nothing is quicker than lime-green 'Black-Seeded Simpson' or the darker 'Salad Bowl,' the kinds so often grown in crowded rows. 'Oakleaf' is an older variety that has found a new audience for its light green, lobed foliage that fans out in flattish bunches. Last year we grew 'Lollo Rossa,' a frilly red lettuce better suited as a garnish or a leafy bowl for potato salad. 'Red Sails' is a big, easy, dramatically curled and colored lettuce with flaccid, slightly bitter leaves, more impressive in the garden than in the salad bowl.

Although these are all described as leaf lettuces, given space—10 to 12 inches (25 to 30 cm) apart—they will surprise you by developing full hearts much tastier than the coarse outer leaves. For an extended harvest we pick outside leaves before they grow too big, leaving the centers to develop.

• **BUTTERHEAD:** Also known as bibb or Boston, soft-textured leaves fold over into squashy, flat-topped heads. We always include 'Buttercrunch,' a sweet, easy lettuce that deserves its popularity. For a marbled row we interplant with either 'Red Boston' or the marvelous red butterhead called 'Merveille de Quatre Saisons,' or 'Four Seasons.' Lovely to look at, with reddish-bronze outer leaves wrapped around pink and butter-yellow hearts, 'Four Seasons' is a treat to munch. If we have salad-loving company, I like to serve each person a whole butterhead, the separated leaves arranged on the plate as they grew; a drizzle of vinaigrette laced with fresh herbs makes a simple, tasty salad. Other notable butterheads are 'Esmeralda' and 'Kagran Summer.'

OPPOSITE: It is amazing how much can be grown in a fairly small space. Peas, romaine lettuce, onions and carrots share a 4-foot (120-cm) bed.

Seeding lettuce with some precision makes the inevitable thinning much simpler later on. A) Make a shallow thumbprint indentation every 6 inches (15 cm) along a row or across a bed. Into each drop three or four seeds. As seedlings develop, thin to the sturdiest one in each place. B) When lettuces are about half grown, begin to cut every other one for early salads. C) Leave the rest to fill out a foot (30 cm) apart.

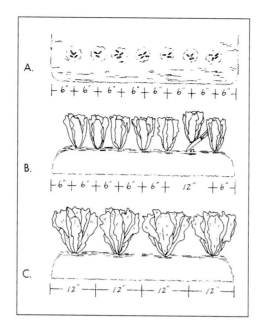

- **CRISPHEAD OR HEAD LETTUCE:** Mainstay of supermarkets, iceberg or head lettuce gets a lot of bad press from garden writers—'bland,' 'watery,' 'hard to grow—needs muckland.' I happen to like it, but for years we were dissuaded from trying it, until we read about 'Ithaca M.I.,' a head lettuce said to be 'excellent for transplanting on sandy land.' And so it proved. 'Crispino' is another head lettuce that has done well. These two have a place in our garden every summer. Some of the fun of harvesting head lettuce comes from proving the naysayers wrong.
- **ROMAINE OR COS:** Familiar in Caesar salad, crisp sturdy romaine grows into upright cylindrical heads. In the past we grew the standard 'Valmaine Cos,' a big, dark green lettuce that is quite good if cut early, before heat prompts the start of a seedy core. 'Medallion,' a large green romaine, has grown well for us seeded directly in the ground in May. 'Diamond Gem,' a small lettuce also called 'Sugar Cos,' is ideal for intensive beds. The diminutive heads can stand 8 inches (20 cm) apart in all directions. Here is a crop that almost lives up to the catalog's pitch: "the best tasting and most troublefree lettuce you can grow." There are many other fine romaines as well.

- **INTERMEDIATES:** Sometimes called French Crisp, Summer Crisp or Batavia, these lettuces (many of them European imports) combine the qualities of head and leaf lettuce. Seldom seen in markets, they are much easier to grow than head lettuce and sweetly crisp in salads. 'Canasta' jumped quickly from experimental to old-favorite status; its waved and glossy outer leaves shade from apple green to purple-red at the edges, while the hearts are filled with creamy leaves. For color contrast we plant a mixed row of 'Canasta' and 'Victoria,' a green counterpart. The all-green 'Anuenue' is sweet and dense, while 'Sierra' is red-tinged. Many other cultivars are well-worth growing.

A good seed catalog—*Johnny's Selected Seeds* and *The Cook's Garden* are both packed with interesting lettuces—tells you which varieties must have cool weather, and which thrive or flag under the summer sun. By making an informed selection, and sowing at intervals throughout the season, it is possible to keep a supply of lettuce coming from May to October.

HEAD START

Lettuces of all kinds mature best under cooler conditions of air and soil. With that in mind, we get a jump on summer by seeding lettuce indoors in April. After that we aim for additional sowings, either in pots or directly in the ground, at three-week intervals.

Start with 2-inch (5-cm) pots filled with dampened seedling mix, then sow 3 or 4 seeds, ¼ inch (5 mm) deep, in each pot. Given warmth and moisture, seeds sprout practically overnight. After a week or two in a sunny window, seedlings are thinned to the strongest pair per pot, before being shifted into a cold frame. The frame cover is adequate to deflect frost, but there is always the possibility of stressing the small fry in an overheated box. Pay particular attention to watering and ventilating on hot days. A shading cover of lathing or snow-fencing (in place of glass) keeps seedlings comfortably cool.

The first seedlings are ready for the open garden by mid-May, several weeks before the

The home gardener enjoys an array of seed-grown lettuces seldom seen in the market.

last expected frost. A few days before transplanting dig a helping of sifted compost or very old manure into the lettuce patch, if that hasn't been done the fall before. If such organics are in short supply, concentrate them where needed: a trowelful stirred into the soil for each seedling will create an adequate zone of fertility. Seedlings are planted at the same level they were growing, or slightly deeper to steady spindly stems.

If you want fat, full lettuces, give them room to stretch—set the small transplants a foot (30 cm) apart. Given a generous organic diet and steady moisture, they soon fill the gaps.

A tip: If you have a lot of extra seedlings, transplant them a measured 6 inches (15 cm) apart at first. Then, as they grow, harvest every other one for early salads, leaving the rest to fill out at the right spacing.

With transplants in, sculpt a saucer shape around each plant before pouring in fish emulsion mixed to half the usual strength; this settles the soil and provides a fast flush of plant food. The saucers remain to funnel rain water to the roots; failing rain, aim the watering can or hose into the lettuces at least once a week. Since lettuces thrive on readily available nitrogen, a full-strength dose of fish emulsion mid-way through their stay in the garden helps them along.

Not all vegetables benefit equally from mulch, but lettuce appreciates it. A thin layer of straw, old hay or grass clippings keeps the earth cool and moist. Lacking these, cultivate the soil surface shallowly to form a "dust mulch," a layer of dryish pulverized earth that keeps moisture from wicking up and away from beneath. This is especially important on clay soils that tend to harden and crack.

While the earliest salads grow from transplants, lettuce seed sown directly in the ground provides a follow-up harvest. Again, don't wait until the traditional "putting-in-the-garden" date. Sow the seeds as soon as the ground is workable. Hardy lettuce seed will sit in the ground, waiting for a warm nudge. Some catalogs offer pelleted seeds, each one encased in a small ball of clay; this makes for easier handling and better spacing. Dribble seeds thinly along a row and cover with a mere dusting of soil. Thin seedling progressively as the crowd so that they stand first 6 inches (15 cm) apart, then a full foot (30 cm).

Sometimes I get precise about spacing lettuce seeds initially; a bit of measuring saves a lot of finicky thinning later on. Once the ground is fertilized and smoothly raked, lay a measuring tape along the row. Then with fingers or trowel handle make small shallow imprints at 6-inch (15-cm) intervals. Into each little dip drop 3 to 5 seeds, close together but not on top of each other. Cover seeds lightly, pat to firm, water and wait. Sprouts soon appear in nicely spaced clusters that are thinned to the strongest seedling in each spot. As the young lettuces stretch and touch, harvest every other one for salads, leaving the rest to fill out a foot apart. This method need not be limited to single row planting; double rows or wider beds can be seeded on a 6-inch grid as well.

The opposite approach is to broadcast, in a band or bed, either your favorite lettuce, or a special mix of lettuces blended for the purpose. Lettuce seed is also teamed with salad greens such as arugula, mustard and endive in *mesclun* mixes either spicy or mild. Seeds are sown so that they land close together—as you might sow grass seed for a new lawn. The result is a fairly dense mat of leaves—green, red, what-have-you—that is harvested at the "baby" stage by shearing with scissors, a patch at a time, a bit above ground level. Plants re-sprout quickly for second and third cutting, but eventually grow seedy and useless. If you have a spare cold-frame sitting empty, sow such mixtures in the frame very early in spring for fresh salad greens about the time most gardeners are getting around to planting.

COLORFUL HARVEST

Waved, puckered or frilly; lime-green, emerald, bronze or burgundy; lettuce is as decorative as any garden vegetable. If the plants remained low and leafy all summer, they would be perfect for landscaping—an edible border for flowerbeds. Eventually, though, all lettuce bolts to seed, leaving you with a patch of shabby stalks. Enjoy their leafy aesthetics for a month and keep a new patch coming along. Every spring we plant a row of alternating reds and greens, 'Simpson' and 'Red Sails' or red and green Bostons or 'French Crisp'—a feast for the eyes, a colorful feature in the garden and the best you can get for the salad bowl. Pick lettuce in its prime, in the cool of the morning. A quick wash and spin dry, then cold storage in a closed container keeps it garden-fresh until mealtime.

CREAMY HERB SALAD DRESSING

Home-grown lettuce deserves a special dressing and fresh herbs from the garden are the ideal seasoning.

2 tbsp	mayonnaise	25 mL
5 tbsp	plain yogurt	75 mL
1 tbsp	cider (or other) vinegar	15 mL
2 tbsp	olive (or vegetable) oil	25 mL
1 tbsp	minced onion (Spanish, red, fresh green, chives or other)	15 mL
1 tsp	lime juice	5 mL
½ tsp	mustard	2 mL
4 tbsp	dill or chervil leaves, minced	60 mL
1–2 tbsp	basil and tarragon, minced	15–25 mL
	Salt to taste	

If dressing is too tart, sweeten to taste with honey (melted in a little hot water first) or sugar.

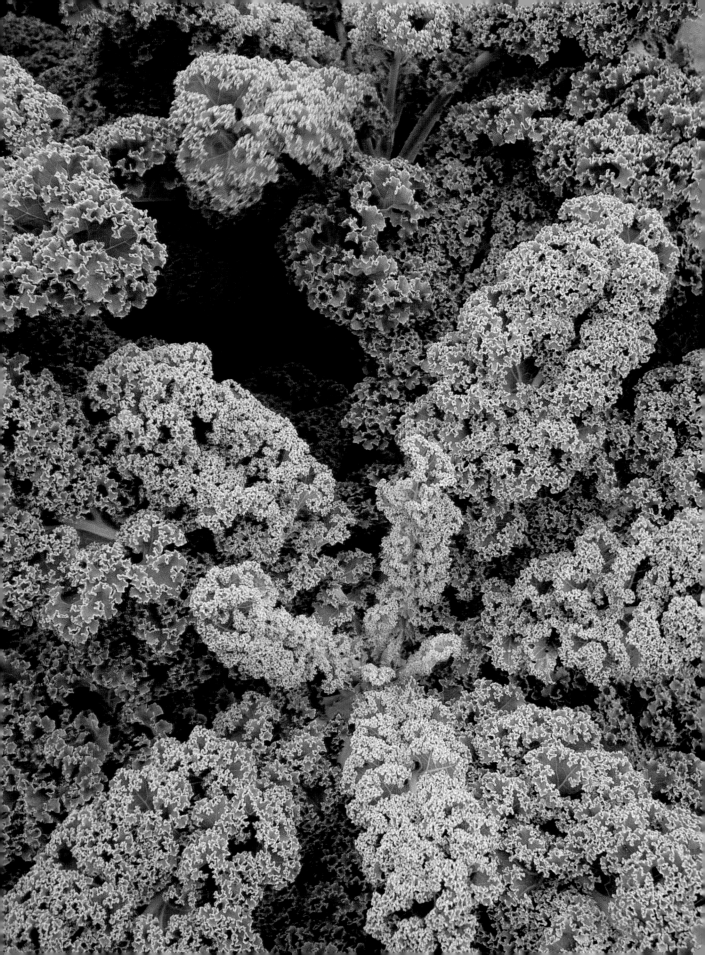

Cultivated Coles
Growing Cabbages and Kin

"I give up," a neighbor said, waving a dismissive hand toward her vegetable garden. "If it isn't one thing, it's another with those wretched plants—just look at them." The plants in question were a shabby assortment of young cabbages, broccoli and Brussels sprouts. Anemic, stunted and bug-ridden, her band of brassicas did, indeed, look wretched. They also looked familiar, facsimiles of those that once grew at Larkwhistle. We could sympathize with her frustration: there is no doubt that the cole family can tax any gardener's skill and patience. But, as we learned, a few timely steps and interventions make all the difference.

What do we mean by "brassicas" and "coles"? Botanically speaking, a number of food plants belong to the genus Brassica. Chinese cabbage is *Brassica chinensis*. Kale, kohlrabi, Brussels sprouts, cauliflower, broccoli and cabbage have all been bred from one Brassica species, the wild sea kale native to Britain. When Brassicas go underground, they become turnips and rutabagas.

"Coleworts" is an old English monicker for the whole group. The word survives today in *cole*-iflower, broc-*cole*-i, *cole*-rabi, kale (also known as bore*cole*) and, of course, that ubiquitous fast-food sidekick, *cole*slaw.

What makes cole crops so tricky to grow? In a word, and at every stage: bugs. First, cutworms prey on seedlings, either mowing them down or eating the tender centers. Next come root maggots, larvae of a fly that lays eggs at soil level around Brassicas; once hatched, larvae tunnel into roots with withering results. If coles survive these pests, they face an onslaught of hungry green caterpillars that hatch from the eggs of white cabbage butterflies. Slugs and earwigs also enter the picture. Given the potential onslaught, it is easy to grow an uninspired

Brassica patch. But it is also possible to do much better, turning out fine heads of cabbages, gorgeous broccoli, crisp kohlrabi and even fine specimens of tricky-to-grow cauliflowers.

Why cultivate cabbages and kin at all, when they are so cheap and abundant at the market? Taste and see. Every gardener knows how good vine-ripened tomatoes and fresh peas and corn can be, but one of the vegetables we wait for most eagerly is home-grown cabbage, tender, sweet and perfect for coleslaw—very different from anything one can buy. Some cabbages are long on fiber but short on flavor, so perusing seed catalogs we look for varieties noted for tenderness and taste. 'Stonehead,' a "high-quality shipper" matures hard as a rock and just about as flavorful. In contrast, 'Early Jersy Wakefield,' an heirloom variety rightly described as "one of the best tasting cabbages ever," is a treat fresh from the garden. For exceptional flavor look for 'Tendersweet,' 'Charmant' and 'Derby Day,' as well as old favorites such as 'Golden Acre' and 'Copenhagen Market.' Run your own trials with a new variety or two each year and see what you like.

Broccoli is the other stand-out in the Brassica bed, and for good reasons: first, the plants are capable of yielding a nutritious green vegetable for several months, often from July into September if adequately fed and watered. 'Emperor' is a popular broccoli that grows a succession of side shoots after the big central head is cut; the same is true for the early 'Green Comet' and later 'Cruiser.' 'Paragon' is notable not only for fine heads, but also for sweet and tender stems all the way down.

My first attempt to grow broccoli started with skinny nursery plants. After wrenching the tangled roots apart, I set the transplants

OPPOSITE: Curly kale is one of the most decorative edibles from June to November. Its leaves are packed with nutrition.

(with high hopes) a few inches apart in the fresh-dug ground of a shady city yard. They soon broke into sprays of yellow flowers, while I wondered when and where the heads would appear. Little did I know that the broccolis had come and gone, flowers following barely visible buds, all the feeble plants could muster in an effort to survive.

Live and learn. All cole crops respond to the same basic conditions. The steps here apply equally to cabbages, cauliflower, kale and Brussels sprouts. Timing of seeding and transplanting depends on whether you want a summer or fall harvest (or both) of cabbages, cauliflower and broccoli. Hardy and slow-growing, kale and Brussels sprouts are seeded once, in late spring, for a harvest that extends into early winter.

COLE CROP CALENDAR

- **EARLY CABBAGES AND BROCCOLI**: For a summer harvest, seed indoors five weeks before your average last expected spring frost; set month-old transplants in the garden about a week before that date. Once accustomed to the outdoors, seedlings can withstand several degrees of frost, and it is not difficult to protect small plants with inverted flowerpots or floating row cover.
- **LATE CABBAGES AND BROCCOLI**: For fall picking, seed indoors (or in a cold frame) a week or two after your frost-free date and transplant a month later. We use the same varieties for both early and late, often adding red or savoy cabbage for fall use. For storage cabbage, choose suitable "winterkeeper" types.
- **CAULIFLOWER**: Seed into 4-inch (10-cm) pots a week or so before the frost-free date, and transplant a month later; older plants do not establish as well. Sensitive to sudden temperature changes, cauliflower does remarkably well for us under a floating row cover—we leave the cover on from the seedling stage until the heads have formed. A June seeding and July transplanting brings cauliflower to maturity during September's cooler days.

- **BRUSSELS SPROUTS**: Seed and transplant this slow-poke cole as for early cabbage; harvest in fall. Keep fed, watered and mulched for steady growth.
- **KALE**: Extremely frost-hardy, kale is seeded like early cabbage for a summer/fall harvest; flavor is better after frost. We've had good success with 'Winterbor,' 'Redbor,' 'Blue Surf' and 'Westlandse.' Kale, the vegetable, is just as decorative (if less colorful) as the so-called flowering kale—and the most nutritious thing you can grow.
- **KOHLRABI**: Start indoors two or three weeks before the last spring frost; transplant a month later, spacing seedlings 4 inches (10 cm) apart. Like beets, kohlrabi may also be seeded directly in the ground from spring to midsummer for a continuous supply.

STEP-BY-STEP COLE CULTURE
For Starters
'Tis a brave gardener who tries to seed most coles directly in the open garden, where the young plants fall easy prey to flea beetles, drought, deluge and neglect. Brassicas do much better when started indoors or in the shelter of a cold frame, and then transplanted to the garden at the month-old stage. If you are buying nursery plants, look for those growing in "cell-paks" so you will not have to pull their roots apart.

Cabbages and kin may be started in flats, but for easier transplanting, seed into 3 or 4 inch (8 or 10 cm) pots filled with a good soil mix. As they develop, thin seedlings to the strongest single one. If grown on a windowsill or under lights, seedlings need gradual exposure to outdoor conditions. Since cool growing conditions produce stocky seedlings, coles might live in a cold frame from the second-leaf stage until they are ready for the garden. In the meantime, prepare a bed for them.

Soil Food
Cabbage, broccoli, kale and cauliflower are the garden's gourmands; the earth can hardly be too rich for them. Even if we've turned a generous dressing of manure or compost

into the bed the fall before, we often prepare an enriched zone for each plant prior to transplanting. Once the bed is raked smooth and level, measure and mark off transplanting locations 18 inches (45 cm) apart. Dig out a shovelful of earth from each spot. Put a shovel of crumbly old manure or sifted compost into each hole, along with a sprinkling of a balanced natural fertilizer (or half-and-half blood and bone meal). Stir the amendments thoroughly into the surrounding soil. Step into the hole gently to firm the ground and you are ready to transplant.

Another approach is to spread compost and manure over the bed, broadcast some natural fertilizer and dig everything under. The "zone of fertility" method just described is especially recommended if organic matter is in short supply, or if you are transplanting in a new garden where the soil is not up to par.

Transplanting

Tip seedling carefully out of their pots to avoid root damage. Young Brassicas are set in the ground a little deeper than they were growing, up to their two lowest leaves. Firm the soil carefully around roots to ensure good contact with the earth. Around each plant sculpt a shallow water-catching depression, dinner-plate diameter, to funnel water to the roots. New transplants are watered thoroughly to settle the soil and wash out air pockets.

Move Them Around

The surest prevention for diseases is rotation, more easily accomplished if Brassicas share a bed. In a 3-foot-wide (90-cm-wide) intensive bed, taller broccolis (or Brussels sprouts) stand 18 inches (45 cm) behind cabbages, both spaced the same distance apart in their rows. If possible, avoid planting cole crops in the same location for three years.

A straw mulch helps maintain the cool, moist conditions that cabbages need, and may also prevent an infestation of destructive root maggots.

A covering of sheer floating row cover protects young Brassicas from flying insects and root maggots, and creates an ideal microclimate underneath.

Pest Control

Now what about those bugs? Prevention is always better than cure. Lively organic soil gives plants the vigor to withstand some insect damage, but there are other measures that can make a difference between bug-ridden Brassicas and a clean crop.

Cutworms can be foiled at planting time by surrounding each plant with tar-paper or cardboard stapled to form a cylindrical collar that extends an inch into the ground and several inches above; tinfoil is simpler to work with and can be folded around and scrunched in place. Lately we've been using small fiber pots, or paper drinking cups, with the bottoms cut out as an effective cutworm barrier, "screwed" down into the soil, one over each Brassica.

The next step, mulching, is critical. If your coles are thriving one day and wilting the next, their roots are probably riddled with small white maggots (larvae of a fly that lays its eggs on the soil around the stems of cabbages and such). Once you see such signs above ground, the damage is almost irreversible, and plants might as well be pulled up and tossed. A thick mulch of hay, straw, grass or leaves laid around transplants and snugged up to their necks, has proven to be an effective barrier, preventing the fly from getting through to the base of the Brassicas to lay eggs.

A floating spun-fiber row cover, laid on directly after transplanting, also improves chances for bug-free broccoli and cabbage. Spread loosely over the bed and weighted at the edges with rocks or chunks of wood, the gauzy fabric excludes root maggot flies, cabbage butterflies and flea beetles. Providing some degree of frost protection, the cloth also creates a nurturing environment that young Brassicas thrive in.

Cabbage Worms and the Rest

Most gardeners have brought a dish of broccoli to the table with the extra garnish of hidden green worms. Summer brings a wave of white butterflies to the garden in search of the only food—our beleaguered Brassicas—that sustains their caterpillar stage, small worms as green as the leaves they eat. This camouflage makes them hard to spot, even though their droppings litter the chewed leaves. If worms are few, you can do a search-and-squash tour. But at the first sign of damage, we bring out a sprayer full of

Snap off lower leaves where they join the stalks to give Brussels sprouts room to expand.

Bacillus thuringiensis (BT), a biodegradable bacterium that kills cabbage worms. Remarkably effective, BT may need to be re-sprayed after a heavy rain if the butterflies persist. It is available in garden centers as BTK or Bioligical Insecticide. No cole grower should be without it.

BT keeps coles worm-free, but slugs and earwigs may crawl out from under the mulch to feed after dark. Insecticidal soap is the only organic control I know for earwigs, but the pincered pest must be hit directly with the spray ("At least they die clean," quipped a visitor.) Several times a week in early summer we inspect the garden around 11 p.m., flashlight and soap spray in hand. If small earwigs are cleaned up early in the season, they don't spawn another batch. On the same rounds, slugs are sprinkled with salt for a quick end.

Cole crops are watered deeply into that earth "soup bowl" once a week if rainfall is not enough. They are also treated to a drink of fish emulsion in mid-growth; you can practically see a spurt after such a feed. For full broccoli heads, pour on the nitrogen-rich fish-emulsion when you see small broccoli "buds" nestled in the broad, blue-green leaves.

Side-dressing is a further inducement to growth. Dust a palmful of blood meal around each Brassica after they have been in the garden for a month or so. On top of that spread a ring of very old manure or compost from stem to leaf edges. Don't be stingy; lay it on thick. Your Brassicas will show their approval by extending new roots into the organic stuff. Pull back the mulch to side-dress.

HARVEST
Cabbages

Cabbages are ready when they feel firm, but we start the harvest a week or two earlier before heads have filled out completely. Those first few are especially tender and mild. Even after cabbages have attained full size, they keep on packing leaves into their centers until finally, after a heavy rain, some may burst open from the outward pressure. Twisting the whole plant around once or twice or slicing into the ground beside it with a spade, breaks enough roots to slow growth and prevent splitting.

The broad outer leaves of cauliflower must be tied over the developing head to exclude light and blanch the curds.

Broccoli

Broccoli comes to the table when heads have expanded and the individual buds are still tightly closed. With its central stalk cut, all of the plant's juices go into smaller side spears. When the bite-sized shoots taper off, it's time to haul plants to the compost heap. Early broccoli can be conveniently followed by fall endive or lettuce; late broccoli is usually followed by snow.

Brussels Sprouts

As much as we enjoy Brussels sprouts in the fall, we do not grow this long-season cole every year since the bulky plants take up a lot of space for the yield. As the stalks lengthen, snap off leaves, starting at the bottom, to give sprouts room to develop. Soon after the first fall frost, pinch out plant tops to direct energies into the mini-cabbages. The best sprouts come from plants that are heavily fed and consistently watered all summer long; top-dressing and mulch help.

Cauliflower

To form proper pale curds, cauliflower must be "blanched" by tying the leaves together over developing heads. "Self-blanching" types grow broad upright leaves, shielding heads from sunlight. Last summer we had an excellent crop from plants growing under a floating fabric row cover from transplanting time to harvest day. On occasion we lifted the cover to check on their progress, as well as to mulch, water and feed. No insects invaded the gradually rising tent of fabric.

Kale

Curled, leafy and non-heading, kale is the most primitive cole grown today, likely a form that ancient Greek and Roman gardeners grew. It makes sense that a plant so close to its wild roots would be a rich mine of vitamins and minerals, containing ten times the vitamin A of an equal weight of lettuce, up to three times the vitamin C as the same amount of orange juice, more B vitamins than whole wheat bread, and more calcium than milk. For best flavor, pick kale after the leaves have been touched by frost, or frozen solid—this hardy green is usable into early winter, and may survive to re-sprout in spring.

Apparently insects couldn't care less about nutrition. Kale is usually untouched by the bugs that bother other Brassicas. We often feature kale's decorative foliage by planting it in a prominent corner of the garden near a group of red and green Swiss chard. Such an arrangement would work nicely in a flowerbed, sunny shrub border or a large container. Too coarse for salads, kale goes into robust fall soups, or is steamed on its own until tender. Snapping off the tough bottom leaves seems to encourage tender new growth.

Kohlrabi

Also rich in calcium and vitamin C, kohlrabi looks like a green or purple turnip growing above ground. Here is a vegetable that must be harvested small and tender, about tennis-ball size. Large bulbs are tough and tasteless. Raw young kohlrabi is as crisp and full of juice as an apple, a refreshing change on a plate of vegetables and dip.

Cole crops provide an abundance of flavor and nutrition over many months; we wouldn't know what to grow in their place. More difficult than lettuce or zucchini, they reward a gardener willing to prepare a fertile place and take timely steps to keep the bugs at bay. After a season or two, you catch on, and frustration in the Brassica bed becomes a thing of the past.

Sweet and Sour Red Cabbage

2 tbsp	vegetable oil	25 mL
1	onion, thinly sliced	1
¼ tsp	caraway seed (optional)	1 mL
1	apple, peeled, cored and sliced	1
½ head	red cabbage, shredded or thinly sliced	½ head
¼ tsp	sea salt	1 mL
3 tbsp	apple cider vinegar	50 mL
1 tbsp	honey	15 mL
¼ cup	tomato juice	50 mL
	Water	

In a deep skillet, sauté sliced onion in oil over medium heat until translucent. Add caraway seeds, sliced apple, shredded cabbage and salt and stir for a few minutes to release juices from the cabbage. Add vinegar, honey and tomato juice and enough water to just cover the bottom of the skillet. Reduce heat to low, cover the skillet and allow the cabbage to simmer and steam, stirring occasionally, for 30 to 45 minutes, or until the cabbage is soft and most of the liquid evaporated. Taste part way through cooking and add salt, vinegar and/or honey to balance the sweet and sour flavors to your liking. Serve with poultry or meat, and baked potatoes.

Gratin of Kale

Make this dish anytime in the fall, and up to Christmas—hardy kale is usually in good shape until then. The robust flavor and texture of kale teams well with a creamy sauce and a crunchy topping of bread-crumbs and parmesan. If you have plenty of kale—and you will if you grow three or four plants—use the medium-sized leaves near the top of the plants rather than tough older leaves lower down.

4–6 leaves	kale	4–6 leaves
1 tsp	butter	5 mL
1 tbsp	olive oil	15 mL
1 clove	garlic, minced	1 clove
1	onion, diced	1
1 tbsp	flour	15 mL
½ cup	low-fat milk	125 mL
½ cup	bread crumbs	125 mL
½ cup	grated parmesan	125 mL
1 tbsp	minced fresh parsley	15 mL

Strip kale leaves from central stalk and tear into pieces. Simmer kale in a little salted water until wilted and fairly tender, about 10 minutes. Drain and set aside. Sauté garlic and onion in butter and olive oil until translucent, about three minutes. Sprinkle flour over garlic and onion and stir for 30 seconds. Pour in milk and stir until thickened—if too thick add a little of the kale water or more milk. Return kale to the sauce and fold to coat leaves. Remove from heat.

Butter a casserole dish. Put the kale in the casserole dish, pressing it in evenly. Mix together breadcrumbs, parmesan and parsley and spread evenly over the kale. Bake, covered, in a 400°F (200°C) oven, for 10 minutes and uncovered for 5 minutes more, until the topping has browned slightly.

The Root of the Matter

Carrots, Parsnips, Beets, Radishes and Potatoes

At potato-digging time, children love to play prospector, rooting and sifting through the loose earth in search of stray spuds. Kids love to yank at carrot tops and come up with a fistful of greens dangling orange roots. Picking root vegetables is something of a treasure hunt, wondering what is hidden underground, the surprise as you bring to light a golden beet, monster carrot, prize parsnip or cache of potatoes. You can watch your tomatoes grow and color and see peas pass from flowers to pods, but roots remain a mystery until harvested.

Considering that the word "mundane" means "of this earth," root crops can be called the most mundane of vegetables. Everybody eats them; nobody gets too thrilled about them. But once you grow roots, you know that there is nothing dull about a popsicle-crisp carrot—pulled, rinsed and eaten Bugs Bunny style; nothing boring about new potatoes, boiled, buttered, herbed and served with the last of the green peas. Roasted parsnips or a subtle parsnip soup made from roots sweetened by winter are very different from the same vegetable simply boiled and dished.

CARROTS AND PARSNIPS

Both carrots and parsnips are umbrella-makers, or members of the botanical family *Umbelliferae*, all of which send up umbels of tiny flowers arrayed at the ends of spoke-like stems. Dill's yellow-green parasols show its connection, and when parsley goes to seed you see the resemblance; caraway, lovage, fennel, anise and sweet cicely are herbs that also belong. Wild umbelliferous plants include hemlock, cow parsnip, fool's parsley—you'd be a fool to eat this poisonous parsley—and the ubiquitous Queen Anne's lace, wild parent of garden carrots.

Root Rationale

Considering that carrots are abundant and cost so little, a new gardener might assume (as I once did) that they practically grow themselves. You soon learn that they don't, at least not during their fragile early stages. Why bother, then, growing such a cheap, abundant vegetable? First, for the space they occupy, carrots return a lot of food. Shelling peas may yield for three weeks or so; the same garden space supplies carrots for many months, from the first picking in July until the last root, perhaps stored right in the ground, is pulled next April.

Then there is the carrot's versatility in everything from soup to cake. But what keeps us growing carrots is the aromatic sweetness and juicy crispness of home-grown roots—supermarket carrots seldom compare. As often happens, the home gardener has access to varieties that may never make it to market. Over the seasons we have experimented with many carrot cultivars. Trials continue, but so far the standouts for flavor include 'Ingot' and 'A-Plus,' both with "supersweet genes" and a boosted vitamin-A content; 'Touchon Deluxe,' 'Rumba,' 'Bolero,' and 'Rondino' are a quartet of Nantes carrots, a type identified by blunt rather than tapered roots. Consensus has it that the best-tasting carrots are found under the Nantes heading, but according to one expert, "Nantes are rarely found in supermarkets because their blunt shape is less than 'classic carrot.' And their crisp texture makes them too brittle for mechanical harvesting."

Given proper care and feeding, long, straight carrots thrive in Larkwhistle's loose, sandy loam. Shorter varieties such as 'Minicor' and 'Short-and-Sweet,' or the small round 'Parmex' and 'Planet,' may be the ones for shallow or heavy clay soils, at

OPPOSITE: A dense living mulch of leafy carrot and parsnip tops shades the bed, leaving no room for weeds. A deep weekly drink may be all the care this intensive patch needs once it is established.

Even a fairly small bed will grow a surprising amount of food. Carrots, beets and parsnips are natural bedfellows that are planted at the same time and thrive in loose, humusy soil.

least until you build up raised beds of fluffy organic soil.

No such variety choice exists among parsnips, a vegetable pretty much summed up by 'Harris Model' and 'Hollow Crown Improved.' Only a parsnip connoisseur, if such a one exists, could tell the difference anyway.

Whatever varieties you choose, it is important that seeds of both carrots and parsnip be absolutely fresh. In common with other umbelliferous plants, seeds lose their spark quickly, especially if badly stored. There is no point preparing the earth carefully and then planting last year's seeds.

Root-friendly Soil

Root crops thrive in a stone-free, sandy loam, free from the competition of weeds. At Larkwhistle we are fine in the sand and no-stones department, not bad for weeds, but often short of moisture and plagued by earwigs. Here are the steps to prepare a bed for carrots and parsnips. Loosen earth down 9 inches (23 cm) or more by digging or tilling. In some gardens this may mean shoveling out topsoil, breaking up the hard subsoil and returning topsoil—a classic double-dig. If

you can plunge a spading fork into the ground to its full length, that's deep enough. A raised bed, built as described in the chapter By Design (pages 23–29), provides a greater depth. As you dig or till, remove stones; if a burrowing taproot hits a rock, you get a twisted carrot. Incorporate a layer of fine-textured, sifted compost into the topsoil—manure is neither needed nor recommended as it promotes forked and hairy roots. In a clay garden, a dressing of sharp sand or thoroughly decayed sawdust opens the soil for better root growth. To avoid recompacting the soil, keep from walking over the prepared bed.

Better Late

Books and seed packets urge you to plant carrot and parsnip seeds "as soon as the ground can be worked in spring," but don't. Both seeds and seedlings are sensitive to cold and temperature swings. In our experience, earwigs mow down sprouts that get off to a slow start. Nothing is gained by sowing too early.

When the daffodils are in bloom—early May here, or three weeks before the average frost-free date—it is time to sow parsnips and the first round of carrots. A second batch of carrots, seeded four to six weeks later, around the summer solstice, should fatten up nicely for fall meals and storage. If you want to get cosmic about it, hold off seeding until the moon is on the wane; the darkening lunar phase is said to favor root vegetables.

Weak Seed, Delicate Seedlings

Compared to the seeds of cucumbers, corn or beans, carrot and parsnip seeds are frail and slow, hardly able to break through dry, crusty ground. Ideally, sowing will be followed by two weeks of warmth and showers, but why take a chance on weather when you can lend nature a helping hand? Once the soil is prepared, we draw out a series of shallow furrows, 8 to 10 inches (20 to 25 cm) apart, across or along a bed; then sprinkle seeds fairly thickly by hand. Here's the dilemma: sown thickly, both carrots and parsnips always need thinning, a job that is either painstaking or meditative, depending on outlook. Sown thinly, seeds may sprout unevenly, and earwigs may thin them further; you're faced with resowing, which is frustrating and time-consuming. We opt for thick sowing and meditative thinning. An old saw on the subject runs: "Sow thick, thin quick." With seed sown, we cover the furrows with a scant ½ inch (1 cm) of sandy soil, less if the earth is heavy. In clay ground, a covering of sifted compost or pure sand presents less of an obstacle to wispy seed leaves than a crust of clay.

Steps must be taken to keep a newly seeded bed moist until germination. If rain is sparse, shower the rows every day or two. Some gardeners cover the patch with burlap sacks and watering through them; the bags hold moisture and prevent seeds from washing out. Others lay boards over seeded rows but earwigs flock to such shelter. We have had good results starting carrots a week or two earlier under a sheet of floating row cover, a feather weight fabric that lets in light and rain and warms the ground. The row cover stays on for several weeks—but, where earwigs are a problem, you'd better lift it and check.

Earwigs

In our garden, the earwigs head directly for tiny carrots, parsnips and beets. One day there is an unbroken green thread along the rows; the next morning there are gaps and bare patches, but no sign of bugs. Earwigs, like vampires, hide from the sun and come out to feed at night. Ignore the damage and the green line may vanish completely in a week.

Our environmentally friendly solution is a spray of insecticidal soap, or 1 teaspoon (5 mL) of pure dishwashing soap mixed in a quart (1 L) of water. This dispatches earwigs cleanly if they are hit. Simply spraying foliage may leave the insects foaming at the mouth, but alive and chewing. A late-night flashlit tour brings earwigs to light and a quick end. Running a hand over the feathertops dislodges earwigs that are hard to see; as they scatter, you spray. A tip: Earwigs

seem to prefer wilted carrot and beet leaves to fresh and growing ones. Little piles of thinnings left here and there will often be crawling with the beasties that night. A few squirts of soap spray gets the lot.

Thinning

"Never thinned a carr't in my life," a neighbor informed us—in these parts, "carrot" rhymes with "part"—as he watched us squinting into a tangled forest of seedlings, carefully plucking first one, then another. To thin or not to thin: in his rocky, clay garden, never-thin Ed grew fine carrots, odd sizes and some twined around each other, but bags enough to store in his cold cellar all winter and plenty to give away. So much for fussy soil preparation and careful thinning. But Ed had space for long rows; what his parsnips and carrots lacked in uniform quality, they made up in quantity. However, at Larkwhistle, as in many home gardens, every root counts.

When carrot and parsnip tops reach 2 or 3 inches (5 or 8 cm) high, we get down on hands and knees and thin. Carrots are thinned first to 1 inch (2.5 cm) apart. The strongest seedlings stay, others between them are gingerly plucked. About three weeks later we start to pick small roots for the table, and over the summer thin to a final 1-inch (2.5-cm) spacing. Parsnips are thinned once to about 2 inches (5 cm) apart. It's advisable to water a dry root bed before and after thinning.

Pelleted Seeds

Seeds for some carrot varieties, notably 'Bolero,' are available in pelleted form. Each carrot seed is encased in a ball or pellet of fine white clay that dissolves on contact with moist soil. The clay coating enlarges tiny carrot seeds to the size of radish seeds, making them much easier to sow. Lately, we have been using pelleted seeds with excellent results: quicker sowing, an even stand of seedlings and a much easier job of thinning. Sow pelleted carrot seeds ¼ to ½ inch (0.6 to 1.2 cm) apart. Do a first thinning when carrots are pencil thin but big enough to eat—a sweet treat. Thin again, over the course of weeks, when carrots are half grown, leaving those in the ground standing 1 to 2 inches (2.5 to 5 cm) apart. Given enough water, thinned carrots will grow impressively large, filling the space you give them. Having used pelleted carrot seeds for several seasons now, I would be reluctant to go back to tiny seeds thickly sown and laboriously thinned.

Home Stretch

Thinning accomplished, we have only to see that our roots are kept weeded and nicely moist; a deep watering twice a week is preferable to a daily light shower, especially once taproots have stretched deep in search of food and moisture. After every rain or watering, I run a pronged cultivator between the rows to loosen the top layer of soil; this crumbly "dust-mulch" impedes moisture from wicking up from below and evaporating. If carrots and parsnips are planted in close rows, their tops eventually form a dense canopy, a living mulch that shades the ground, inhibits weeds and holds moisture.

There is no urgency about picking carrots. Peas and corn may rush past their prime, but carrots can stay in the ground for weeks—even months—beyond their official sixty or seventy "days to maturity." A deep orange color is the clearest sign of readiness and full flavor. Says one expert, "As long as the carrot is pale, its flavour will be pale and its nutritional value low—color is a strong indicator of vitamin A content. The deeper the orange the more beta carotene the root contains."

A May seeding gives you carrots to shred into summer salads and coleslaw. Seeds sown in early summer yield roots for hearty fall minestrones, carrot soups, energizing juice or simple steamed carrots. If you are not keen on carrots, or the kids push them away, grow a row and be prepared for a taste surprise.

Parsnips tend to be bland in the fall. By spring, after cold weather has changed their starch to sugar, they are a whole new vegetable. Parsnips can be stored in the ground all winter. Once the snow goes, the harvest lasts for a few weeks before new leaf growth saps the roots and spoils their texture. We also leave a few rows of carrots in the ground over winter. Protected from freezing by armloads of leaves or hay and, later, snow, the roots stay sweet and fresh until April. Digging carrots and parsnips from the cool, dark earth in spring, we pause to remember that the Earth is generous with her gifts—all we need for life—at every season.

BEETS

In winter, market shelves are laden with broccoli, cucumbers, tomatoes and fancy lettuces—summer food trucked in from afar—while locally grown roots often sit shriveled and overlooked in out-of-the-way corners. Among the ranks of unappreciated roots are rutabaga (big yellow 'Swede' turnips), parsnips, 'Purple-Top White Globe' turnips and beets. I know several people who will eat any vegetable but beets. "Too earthy," says one. A fourteen-year-old friend is more blunt, "Beets, ugh—taste like dirt." A long-time beet grower tells me that some varieties tend to "take on the taste of soil, but not 'Early Flat Egyptian.'" I can't say I've ever noticed a "dirt" taste in garden-grown beets.

'Burbee's Golden Beets' yield pleasantly mild, tawny orange roots. Marble-sized thinnings can be steamed, with their yellow-stemmed tops, for a vegetable dish that tastes more like spinach or chard. Small golden beets are lovely cooked whole, sliced and marinated; slivered for stir-frys, they taste almost like corn. 'Chiogga' is an Italian "heirloom" beet showing red-and-white rings when cut; the sweet roots are less prone to bleeding than all-red beets. 'Formanova' means "new form," but engravings from the last century show that long cylindrical beets have been around for a while. Perfect for slicing, the fat carrot-shaped roots cook faster than the round ones. Growing best in the deep, loose soil that favors carrots, 'Formanova' beets can stand closer together than round beets. 'Albina Veredun' is as round and white as a summer turnip, but the resemblance ends there. Wonderfully sweet, with none of the earthiness of some red roots, this beet does not bleed when cut or cooked—highly recommended. 'Winter Keeper' or 'Long Season' is a storage beet that keeps getting larger, without losing a trace of sweetness, until late fall; plant these big boys in late May or early June. Because they take a long time to boil, we put 'Winter Keeper' beets in the oven while other things are baking; over the next few days, slices are used in salads or warmed in butter with a few drops of cider vinegar as a side dish.

In Europe beets—fresh, not canned—are sold already cooked, a treat for travelers who picnic. Beets are anything but a convenience food. "I never cook them," says a friend, "too messy, and they take so long." But the same woman told me that, when she was pregnant, she often ate a salad of grated raw beets and apples dressed with lemon juice and herbed salt, "for the iron." Beet root is a mine not only of iron but of calcium and phosphorus as well. Wonderful fall and winter food, such a salad could be elaborated with grated carrot and Chinese radish (or daikon), endive and Chinese cabbage—all discussed in the chapter Second Season (page 115). Add a handful of minced fresh parsley, tarragon, lovage, and chives for both flavor and nutrition. However you dress it—oil and lemon, seasoned yogurt or mayonnaise—the salad turns pink as you toss.

Best Beets

The same rich, deep, stone-free earth that suits carrots also grows the best beets. Adequate amounts of potash (from kelp meal or wood ashes applied with a light hand) and phosphorus (from bone meal or phosphate rock) go toward smooth, properly sized roots, while a high dose of nitrogen from blood meal or fresh manure rushes to beet tops and may leave roots stunted and oddly shaped.

Same soil, same schedule: we seed our first beets with the early carrots at daffodil time, then sow again a month later. In all but the hottest regions beets can also be seeded in July, following early lettuce or peas, for a batch of young roots in fall.

The "sow thick, thin quick" rule applies

Big but still tender and sweet, 'Winterkeeper' beets will store for several months in a cold, slightly damp place.

to beets as to carrots, only more so. What you sow as beet "seed" is actually a fruit husk holding two or more true seeds. No matter how precisely you space the seeds, sprouts come up in clusters that must be thinned. In an intensive bed, sow beets in rows 8 to 12 inches (20 to 30 cm) apart, farther depending on how you will cultivate. Drop seed into shallow furrows, spacing them about an inch (2.5 cm) apart; cover and pat soil lightly. In heavy soil cover seeds with fluffy compost or lighter ground.

When seedlings start to crowd each other, we thin carefully to give each plant a few inches of space, room enough to develop small globes. Subsequent thinning, which may last for weeks, counts as a harvest as you gradually pull golfball beets, leaving the rest about 5 inches (12 cm) apart. Bulky "Winter Keepers" need 8 inches (20 cm) between them. Fast growth makes for tender sweet beets. All else being equal, nothing slows a root crop like dry soil. In dry weather, a morning soaking twice a week is preferable to an evening shower, which may encourage fungus to infect damp foliage overnight.

With beets, and throughout our kitchen garden generally, the story of pests and diseases is soon told. As Stokes's seed catalog says, "Since pests and diseases are not major concerns, beets are relatively easy to grow." Just as seedlings emerge we keep a sharp eye out for earwig damage and pounce with the soap spray after dark. Various skin scabs, interior white zoning and brown patches all point to a soil out of balance, a problem best remedied by consistent applications of compost, old manure and organic fertilizers.

Cool Roots

Beets for storage are left in the ground until quite late in fall—early light frosts leave them unharmed. Cut or twist tops off before squirreling away roots in a very cold but not freezing place.

RADISHES

Gardeners may assume that if they can grow anything, they can grow radishes. Seed catalogs proclaimed them "very easy," and articles recommended them for a child's first garden. But after many years of growing vegetables, we are still surprised if we bring in a decent crop. Planted in April—"as early as the soil can be worked" is the usual advice—radishes poke along and mostly feed flea beetles, tiny black jumpers that leave foliage riddled with holes. Planted a month later, radishes may be host to root maggots—end of harvest. During dry, hot weather, summertime radishes turn pungent and pithy.

What's a gardener to do? "Quick in, quick out" is the rule for radishes, which often serve as a spring "catch crop" in a space reserved for tomatoes or peppers later on. Since our peppers grow in a tall cold-frame that sits empty until mid-May, we wondered if it might serve for radishes in the meantime. Why waste that warm sheltered space for six weeks in spring?

One April we sowed the ground in the frame with 'French Breakfast' radishes. Before sowing, we turned in some fine compost; radishes need relatively small amounts of plant food accessible in the top layer of soil. In the loose earth, it was easy to draw shallow furrows, spaced 4 inches (10 cm) apart, with a finger. Seeds were dropped in an inch (2.5 cm) apart, covered and watered. With its glass top in place, the frame captured and held the spring warmth, prompting sprouts in two days—a good start. The frame was watered by hand every other day, since adequate moisture means quick-growing, mild roots. After sprouts had grown a few leaves, we thinned to 2 inches (5 cm) apart—crowded radishes may be all leaves and no roots. Untouched by flea beetles or frost, the pampered radishes were ready by mid-May, a colorful addition to the first salads of spinach, green onions, lettuce and wild greens. Even the slightly bristly radish tops went into the salad bowl. The framed radishes had been our best crop yet. A floating row cover acts like a covered frame to keep root maggot flies and flea bottles away—just remember to water the radishes under there often.

An Array of Radishes

Although some types are naturally hotter than others, variety in radishes has more to do with shape and color than taste. Any variety, well grown, will be a treat. 'White Icicle' grows salad-quality greens and mild, tapered white roots. Round and colorful, 'Easter Egg' radishes pop up red, white, rose, and purple. Maturing in three weeks under ideal conditions, round, red 'Cherry Belle' and 'Champion' are the quickest of a quick crop. 'Sparkler' is red and white and round. 'French Breakfast' is red and white, long and tapered—I wondered at the name until I started eating it and other radishes with toast for breakfast.

Pests

If grown in the open air, radishes may need some protection from flea beetles—tiny shiny-black hoppers—and maggots. Stirring a thin layer of wood ashes into the soil should ward off maggots; more ashes can be dusted around young radishes as a further deterrent. Also avoid planting radishes where broccoli and/or cabbages grew the previous season. Both are radish relatives

bothered by the same bugs. A garlic spray may scare away flea beetles; rotenone and diatomaceous earth should kill them. But no cure (as mentioned) is as effective as physically blocking the pest with glass or fabric.

If a row of radishes is thriving, you can soon get too many—feast or famine. Roots left for even a few days past their prime grow hot and corky. Better to sow another short row of radishes every ten days and eat them young, tender and mild. If they are getting ahead of you, radishes keep better in the refrigerator than in the ground.

POTATOES

I think of potatoes as two vegetables: big, mature tubers for fall and winter eating, and new potatoes, mouthwatering morsels for summer. Potatoes new and old can be gathered from the same plants at different times. A few weeks after bushes have flowered, feel around in the loose soil or under the hay mulch, and steal a few meals of small spuds, leaving the rest to size up. In August, well before green tops have withered, we pull up several whole plants to get at the cache of odd-sized new potatoes underneath. Even if garden space were limited, we would still grow a few plants for the wonderful taste and texture of young tubers.

Family Ties

Considering that potatoes have been cultivated in their native South America since at least 2000 B.C., and that they are the one vegetable that everyone eats today, I find it surprising that they were not grown to any extent in England until the 1800s. In an 1833 gardening book, Englishman William Cobbett wrote of the potato that it "shouldn't be used as a substitute for bread—I never eat of it myself, finding so many things far preferable."

The potato's family ties may explain the longstanding reluctance to "eat of it." Tubers of *Solanum tuberosum*, wild mother of all potatoes, are both bitter and toxic, characteristics shared by the green leafy parts of tomatoes, eggplant and peppers, all related to potatoes under the family

Soon after potato plants flower, dig around their roots by hand to unearth small new potatoes for summer meals; tubers that are left will grow to full size.

name Solanaceae, the ominous-sounding Nightshade. I shy away from green peppers and green tomatoes, and never eat a green potato, whether from the store or the garden, unless it is peeled deeply. Left to green up from exposure to light, potatoes become harsh-tasting, indigestible and mildly toxic.

Colorful Cultivars

Before we pick a growing method, we need to choose our tubers. Until I began to garden, I had no notion that potatoes were anything but tan outside, white inside—no-name spuds. Variety in potatoes had more to do with how you fixed them and what you put on them, than with the tubers themselves. A trip to the local feed-store to pick up potato "seeds" for our first patch taught us that potatoes do have names—at least four were available—and they can be red-skinned as well as tan. And that was just the start.

The adventure really began when a visitor brought a sack of potatoes shaped like pudgy toes: "German Fingerlings," he called them, "the favorite in the old country for potato salad." Since then we have saved a handful of tubers every fall to replant in spring; and a few "Fingerlings" usually pop up on their own as "volunteers" from tubers missed during last year's harvest. Rarely growing bigger than thumb-sized, the waxy, yellow-fleshed potatoes hold together when tossed warm with a herbed yogurt or a mayonnaise dressing. Justly popular, 'Yukon Gold' potatoes are even more flavorful from that garden; 'Ruby Gold' is a red-skinned counterpart with the same waxy texture. When baked, russet-skinned potatoes such as 'Netted Gem' or 'Gem Russet' are sweet, dry and nutty, unlike any potato you have tasted.

In their native Peru, potatoes crop up in surprising shades: red, tan, purple, rose, russet, yellow and blue. A blue potato? Every year we try an exotic potato or two, but unusual color is not all we look for as we go through the list of cultivars. First priority is scab resistance, since in our sweet (alkaline) soil potatoes are very scab-prone—a quantity of pH-reducing maple leaves turned into the potato bed the fall before helps a lot. Early maturity is desirable in a short-season area, and any potato described as "drought tolerant" and "an excellent storer" is worth a trial.

What, When and How to Plant

To grow potatoes, you plant a potato. You could plant sprouting store-bought spuds—assuming that they do sprout, since most have been sprayed with a growth-inhibiting chemical—but it's not a good idea. Specially grown seed potatoes look exactly like eating potatoes, but there is a healthy difference: potatoes for planting have been inspected and certified to be free of virus and disease, a boon to all gardeners. Under ideal conditions a pound of planting stock may yield 14 pounds (6 kg) of potatoes—usually 4–8 tubers per plant.

Traditionally, preparation for planting begins the day before, when whole seed potatoes are cut into chunky egg-sized pieces, each with at least one, but not more than three, sprouting "eyes." Cut pieces are left exposed to the air overnight to form a callus over the cut surfaces and are often dusted with a fungicide, rendering them less likely to rot in cool spring ground. Alternately, plant whole potatoes, the size of an egg—again, look for stock certified free of fungi and diseases. With no cut surfaces, the chances of whole potatoes rotting are virtually nil (unless the soil is cold and wet). Pick or rub off any eyes clustered together at the ends of a whole potato, leaving all the juice to flow to the remaining two or three sprouts. The consensus is that whole potatoes give rise to vigorous plants less prone to various potato ailments.

Recently we have experimented with potato "sets," melon-ball pieces scooped from whole potatoes. Available from suppliers specializing in potatoes (see Sources), the sets have been carefully dried and callused. In early May, we hoe open trenches, 6 inches (15 cm) deep and 24 inches (60 cm) apart, across a wide intensive bed; or a long single row in our "little field," an area devoted to bulkier vegetables. Two sets or one small whole potatoes or a cut chunk are spaced

10 inches (25 cm) apart, snugged into the loose soil, eyes up, in the bottom of the trench. Back-fill with earth, leaving tubers 3 inches (8 cm) under. As tops grow, hoe earth up along each side of the rows. Soon after a soaking June rain, lay down a layer of hay, leaves or grass clippings over the entire potato patch. If enough rain falls thereafter, the work may be done for the season. If not, try to soak the bed at least once every couple of weeks, especially as the plants are coming into flower and after. Mulch is not strictly necessary, but it does save continual hoeing and hilling.

While potato tubers themselves are fairly cold-tolerant, tops are withered by the lightest frost. Plant potatoes two or three weeks before the last expected spring frost. By the time leaves emerge, the danger is usually past. If an unseasonable frost is predicted, cover foliage with old blankets, or simply heap earth over each plant, burying leaves completely; new growth shows through in a few days.

We have an old friend who loves to figure out how to grow things in a garden that is mostly limestone outcroppings, deep fissures and boulders of all sizes. One summer, he picked and shoveled a deep and wide rectangular pit where, over a couple of seasons, he dumped in masses of maple, birch and poplar leaves. Digging into the pit one spring, he came up with handfuls of dark, crumbly leaf mold, and he decided to bury some leftover seed potatoes in the stuff as an experiment. If they grew, fine; if not, no loss. Planting them was all he did. Come fall, to his surprise, he retrieved a heavy crop of well-formed, thin-skinned tubers, so clean they needed only a quick rinse. Growing in leaves alone, the impromptu potato patch had been an unqualified success. No doubt the slight acidity of the leaf pile had kept his spuds scab-free, since a pH hovering around 5.5 inhibits potato-scab organisms.

Newfoundland gardeners tell of laying their seed potatoes directly on flat rock and heaping seaweed over them. Other growers set chunks of potato on the soil surface and lay on a foot of hay or straw; green tops push through the mulch and tubers form underneath. Another approach involves piling leaves, sappy green stuff, unseedy weeds, manure and the like to a depth of a foot or two (30 to 60 cm) over a garden bed in fall, in essence building a long, low compost heap that will rot and settle somewhat by spring. At potato planting time you nestle seed pieces into the deep mulch and, again, cover with 6 to 10 inches (15 to 25 cm) of straw, hay or loose leaves. If any tubers show through, you cover them with more mulch. Reports say that potatoes so grown are less prone to bug damage and diseases—worth a try.

Bugged Spuds

Other than earwigs, which can turn young potato leaves into lace, our spuds have not been bothered much. Many gardens, however, attract the black-and-yellow striped Colorado potato beetle (alias potato bug). Handpicking the orange eggs, larvae and adult beetles is the safest control, but time-consuming in a big, badly infested patch. Marigolds and garlic are said to repel, and a deep mulch impedes movement. Horseradish is another repellant, but we've had more than enough trouble trying to get rid of this invasive herb. Potato bugs, apparently, will eat bran sprinkled on damp leaves, swell up and explode. Toads eat potato bugs. Old-time gardeners used to boil up cedar boughs until the water turned to weak tea for a foliar spray. Finally, from the garden center come two organic dusts, rotenone and pyrethrum, which should prove effective, as a last resort.

Treasure Trove

Potatoes are ready to dig when their green tops have yellowed and withered. A spading fork is the tool of choice for the job. What fun to turn up a hill, uncovering a batch of colorful tubers. Some spuds come up attached to the roots. Others hide in the soil and have to be ferreted out by hand; you could use the fork, but it's more fun to find potatoes with your fingers and you avoid shish-kebabing them on the tines.

To prepare them for storage, spread potatoes out in a single layer in a dry, airy, shaded place for a day to set their skins; clods of soil are brushed off beforehand and tubers turned several times to cure evenly. Any small or damaged tubers are set aside for immediate use. Potatoes store well in a cool, airy place in closed cardboard boxes. It is important that the storage locale be dark; otherwise all that careful hilling and mulching is quickly undone as the tubers turn green and bitter. Warmth and damp prompts potatoes to sprout in due course.

Usually considered a field crop, potatoes are often left out of smaller gardens. True, the plants are bulky, but they occupy less space than the home gardener's top crop, tomatoes. Like vine-ripened tomatoes, home-grown potatoes are one of the kitchen garden's most delicious gifts. When so much of the garden's output is green and succulent like lettuce and cucumbers, there is something comforting about being able to provide what a Caribbean friend refers to as "food"— a starchy staple that you could almost live on if need be.

MARINATED BEETS

The quantities for this recipe are flexible according to servings required.

Medium-size beets
Olive oil
Vinegar (cider or other)
Fresh tarragon, basil,
and parsley, minced
Spanish onion, sliced
Salt and pepper to taste

Boil whole beets until tender, leaving the taproots and tops intact to prevent bleeding and flavor loss. Let beets cool, then peel and slice or cube. For the dressing, mix together 3 parts olive oil, 1 part vinegar, the herbs and Spanish onion, adding salt and pepper to taste. Toss beets in dressing. Chill dressed beets for several hours or overnight.

LEEK AND POTATO SOUP

This is a hearty, warming fall soup that makes a meal with an endive-and-carrot salad and crusty bread.

4	leeks (white part)	4
1 tsp	curry powder	5 mL
2	bay leaves	2
pinch	cayenne pepper	pinch
pinch	fresh nutmeg	pinch
3	medium potatoes, peeled and cubed	3
4 cups	water or stock	1 L
1½ tsp	salt	7 mL
handful	celery or lovage leaves	handful
1 cup	milk or soy milk	250 mL

Wash leeks well and thinly slice them crosswise. Sauté leeks in butter or oil until soft, about 5 minutes. Add the curry powder, bay leaves, cayenne pepper and nutmeg to the leeks and stir. Add the cubed potatoes and stir to coat with seasonings. Add the water, salt and celery or lovage leaves. Bring soup to boil, then immediately reduce heat and simmer gently until potatoes are quite soft. Using a potato masher, purée the potatoes right in the soup pot, or blend the soup into a coarse purée. Stir in the milk and reheat. Serves four.

NEW POTATO SALAD WITH HERBED DRESSING

This salad works especially well with firm, waxy potatoes. Quantities have not been given because they are flexible, so the salad can be prepared for a picnic for two or a family get-together of twenty.

Potatoes
Red onions or scallions, chopped
Celery, chopped
Red peppers, chopped

Boil potatoes in salted water until cooked through but not mushy. Drain well and set aside to cool. When cool, combine potatoes in a big mixing bowl with chopped red onions (or scallions), celery and red peppers.

For the dressing:

Plain yogurt
Mayonnaise
A combination of fresh herbs
(in quantity): parsley, chervil,
tarragon and/or basil; in lesser
amounts: lovage, chives and/or
spearmint
Garlic cloves, pressed
Salt
Pepper
Dry mustard to taste
Vinegar to taste
Sugar to taste
Frilly red lettuce or radicchio leaves

Whisk together equal parts of plain yogurt and mayonnaise. Finely chop the herbs. Add the herbs and pressed garlic to the dressing. Season with salt, pepper and perhaps a little mustard, vinegar and sugar to taste. Pour the dressing over the potatoes and mix gently but well. Let the salad stand for an hour or so. Serve on a bed of frilly red lettuce or radicchio leaves.

Tropical Fruits
Tomatoes, Peppers and Eggplant

"After you taste them ripe from the garden," commented a visitor, "you're just not interested in out-of-season tomatoes from the store—there's no comparison." Anyone who has ever harvested his or her own tomatoes probably seconds the sentiment. Tomatoes are the most popular home-grown food.

When tomatoes are ripening, we eat them every day in many ways. There is no better start to a summer meal than sliced tomatoes dressed with olive oil, balsamic vinegar, rings of Spanish onion and minced fresh basil. Simple and refreshing, such a salad reminds us of why we do the work of seeding, planting, weeding and watering. And who doesn't like tomatoes on toast?

It is no coincidence that tomatoes, peppers and eggplant mature together in the mid-summer garden. Botanically related, the three belong to the Solanaceae, or Nightshade, family. Included in the group are such familiar annual flowers as petunias, nicotiana and datura, as well as noxious weeds like nightshade, jimson and tobacco; potatoes are an underground Solanaceae.

Wild tomatoes survive year round on lush mountain slopes in equatorial Peru, where temperatures seldom dip below 50°F (10°C). In Mexico, peppers stretch into perennial shrubs the size of lilacs, and the eggplant's ancestors still grow wild in torrid India. The three need similar growing conditions. Given their tropical origins, they respond to plentiful heat and sun, and all are understandably touchy on the subject of frost.

You can't expect to sow a row of pepper, tomato or eggplant seeds and hope for a harvest. These tropical fruits call for (and are certainly worth) some extra effort. Like many gardeners, we have devised ways of making the southerners at home in a north. The reward is plump, ripe fruit that graces the table with tropical colors—red, yellow, orange, purple—wonderful flavor and more nutrition than any pill can pack.

All of these how-to-grow details apply equally to tomatoes, peppers and eggplant. Here are the steps:

- Choose early varieties if your season is short and/or cool, and look for built-in resistance to disease.
- Six to nine weeks before your average last spring frost date, start seeds indoors in 4- or 6-inch (10- or 15-cm) pots, sowing four or five seeds in each.
- Germinate in a warm environment and set container in the sunniest window as soon as seeds sprout.
- Thin small plants as they grow to the strongest single one per pot.
- Water as necessary to keep soil moist but not soggy, allowing soil to dry somewhat between waterings to foster strong roots.
- If starting extra early, shift seedlings to 8-inch (20-cm) containers about halfway through their windowsill life.
- Accustom plants gradually to unfiltered sun and drying winds by exposing them to outdoor conditions for a longer time each day over a week before transplanting.
- When frosts are past, set transplants in full sun, in earth enriched with compost, old manure and organic fertilizers high in phosphorus such as bone meal and rock phosphate.
- If transplants are on the small side, foil cutworms with protective collars around stems.
- Water deeply once a week, soaking the soil not the plant.
- Avoid working around plants when foliage is wet to prevent the spread of fungus.

OPPOSITE: From two mini greenhouses made of cast-off storm windows come plump purple eggplants ripe for grilling, baking or ratatouille and sweet red peppers ready for roasting.

Whether yellow or red, vine-ripened tomatoes are among the favorites fresh from the garden. Trimmed, staked and tied, the vines take up little space and are quite decorative.

- Mulch after the soil is thoroughly warm to retain moisture and suppress weeds.

TOMATOES

One spring my partner and I were away from the garden in early April, the time we normally start tomato plants indoors. During the winter we had sent tomato seeds to a friend, with a request that she start them for us, which she did—a month before our usual schedule. Expecting to pick up nice little seedlings in late April, we were presented with hefty 10-inchers, six weeks old, almost on the verge of flowering. "What'll we do with them," John lamented on the way home, "we can't put them in the garden for a month or more—they'll be huge!"

Since the seedlings were outgrowing their smallish pots, we repotted them in deep 8-inch (20-cm) containers filled with sandy garden soil, sifted compost and bone meal. Plants were shifted daily with the sun from a southeast to a southwest window and watered as necessary. We were careful to let the surface soil dry between drinks. The plants were fed once with half-strength

fish emulsion, as if they needed the extra push.

During the third week of May we set two long cold frames over garden beds, after turning a layer of compost into the soil. Every 2 feet (60 cm) within the frame we dug a hole deep enough to take the flowering tomato plants up to their bottom leaves. Two reasons for the deep planting: first, tomatoes will root out from the buried stem; and second, we had to get our big babies down low enough so that their tops would not be crushed by the frames' storm-window covering. Before planting we stirred a cupful of bone meal into each hole; afterwards we watered thoroughly to settle soil and wash out air pockets.

By early June, when frost danger was over, leaves were pushing at the glass for headroom. Off came the windows and away went the plants. June visitors wondered at the thigh-high bushes already sporting sizable fruit—and so did we. Thanks to our friend's mistiming, we had learned a lesson about starting tomatoes extra early indoors and giving them plenty of root room. Now we seed indoors in mid-March, about eight or nine weeks before we expect to transplant, and shift seedlings into 8-inch pots before they are too far along.

When to transplant tomatoes is a gardener's perennial dilemma, as spring moves two steps forward and one potentially fatal step back. Like all seedlings, tomatoes need to be hardened to the elements for a week before transplanting. Even so, they will not tolerate a breath of frost, and it's a shame to lose plants overnight when a slight covering would see them through. There are many ways to deflect frost: old blankets, bedsheets or other cloths propped on sticks or simply draped over seedlings; flower pots ample enough to cover without crushing; or paper grocery bags anchored with soil or stones. A sheet of clear plastic, laid over hoops of flexible plastic water pipe, does an admirable job of frost-protection and may be left in place, slightly ventilated, during chilly late spring days.

Choose and Pick

A fruitful summer starts in winter when we select tomato varieties. Everyone hankers after the first ripe tomatoes, and earliness is a further virtue where frost often wraps things up in September. Remember, too, that bigger is not always tastier—some of the bite-sized cherry tomatoes are packed with flavor—and taste is sometimes sacrificed for earliness.

Our list of standbys includes:

- 'EARLY CASCADE VFN': These tennis-ball tomatoes in heavy clusters are usually the first to color. The flavorful tomatoes are firm when picked but mellow after a few days in the house. This year we'll leave fruit on the vine past what growers call the 'firm ripe stage.'
- 'EARLY GIRL': Ripening first and continuing into fall, this older hybrid lacks the built-in disease resistance that is crucial in some areas. Here it remains healthy.
- 'ULTRA GIRL VFN': This plant is resistant to several tomato afflictions later in the season. Round, firm fruit weigh in at 7 to 9 ounces (250 g).
- 'SWEET MILLION' AND 'SWEET 100': These sugary cherry tomatoes grow in profuse clusters, like grapes, on vines that, according to one gardener, can reach the roof of a two-story house—we've managed 6 feet (1.8 m), which is tall enough, thank you. 'Sweet Million' trades a touch of sweetness for disease resistance.
- 'BIG BEEF': Even a northern gardener longs for big meaty tomatoes oozing juice and flavor. With an early start, this disease-resistant hybrid brings in Beefsteak-style fruit about seventy days after transplanting.
- 'LEMON BOY': These are big and bright yellow and less acidic than most reds.

Since we are growing in a short-season area, the list is limited to tomatoes that will ripen here. What works for us may fail elsewhere, and you may have wonderful luck with some of the delicious late-season tomatoes that stay green and boring here. Part of the fun of food gardening comes from trying something new. Experimentation eventually leads to tomatoes that suit a gardener's needs, space, soil and climate.

Degrees of Health

Under certain conditions tomatoes are notoriously prone to various wilts and blights. The initials after a tomato's name refer to a specific disease or pest that the plant is genetically able to resist. Give us a V for vanquished verticillium wilt; an F for forgotten fusarium; an N for no nematodes; and a T for tolerance to tobacco mosaic. Pile on the letters as thickly as compost, and the tomatoes are likely to be a picture of health and vigor. If possible, we choose cultivars with the horticultural equivalent of a degree in health.

Disease problems can be further minimized by:

- planting in lively organic soil fed with a balanced diet of compost, manure, mulch, and natural fertilizers;
- situating plants in an open sunny spot;
- pruning to open vines to breezes that dry up fungus spores;
- rooting out wild nightshade vines from around the garden;
- ensuring uninterrupted growth with adequate water and a few drinks of liquid fertilizer;
- soaking the soil, not the plants, and forgoing the hose in the evening;
- not planting tomatoes in ground used for potatoes, eggplant and/or peppers the year before;
- adopting a no-smoking policy in the tomato patch, because tobacco is a sister plant that may harbor tomato-afflicting viruses.

Sprawlers or Climbers

Whether starting from seed or buying nursery plants, pay attention to whether the variety is determinate or indeterminate. The two are grown quite differently. Determinate or bush tomatoes branch freely, but the length of each stem is fixed or "determinate." After producing a flower cluster or two, each branch ends. Determinate types are usually left to ramble at will without pruning or

Well staked and trained to two or three branches, tomatoes might be considered as pretty as the pink and crimson sweet William flanking them.

Aiming for a double triple-branched plant, we leave the main stem to grow, plus the first one or two side branches. Any shoots that sprout after that from leaf axils—the place where leaves attach to the chosen stems—are pinched out before they get too long. You'd be surprised how quickly side shoots, or suckers, appear. If plants are not "suckered" once a week, a lot of useless greenery saps juice that could be plumping up fruit.

Tomato stakes must be tall and strong enough to support the weight of a fruit-laden branch. We use sturdy branches cut from dead trees in the woods across the way. Old broom or rake handles, snapped hockey sticks, and the like are fine, as are 6-foot (1.8-m) lengths of one-by-two lumber, or stout bamboo canes. Position stakes close enough to plants so that branches can be easily tied, but avoid jamming stakes right into the root zone near the plant's stem. With stakes along the north side of the row, plants are open to the sunny south. Soft cloth or old nylon stockings are better for securing branches than choking twine.

Earthing Up

Here's a trick picked up from my tomato-growing grandfather: when plants are half-grown, heap fertile earth, fine compost, or extra-old manure thickly around their base. You'll be surprised how quickly new roots sprout to take up nutrients.

Bugs, Cracks and Cat-facing

Our tale of tomato bugs is thankfully soon told. One menace is the yellow-striped green hornworm, a creature so perfectly camouflaged you might not see it. I can't say I've ever seen one, nor the ragged foliage and droppings it leaves behind.

Hornworms can be handpicked, but unless you are plagued with caterpillars, don't step on them—they turn into lovely sphinx (or hawk) moths that you'll enjoy in the evening as they hover like hummingbirds over flowers sipping nectar.

If an infestation of Colorado potato beetles threatens to reduce tomatoes to

staking. The result is a low, sprawling octopus of a plant loaded with tomatoes that tend to ripen all at once. Inevitably some are out of sight under foliage, or lying on the ground where they may rot in wet weather. A straw (or other dry) mulch cushions fruit above the damp earth. Because they need so little attention, determinates may be the tomato of choice if you have more space than time.

Indeterminate, or vining, tomatoes, in contrast, branch out into side shoot that continue to grow until checked by frost or a gardener's pinch. More climbing vine than sprawler, an unpruned indeterminate tomato can become a tall, confused tangle. Traditionally, indeterminate tomatoes are trained to one, two, or three stems, each tied to its own stake.

Of Suckers and Stakes

At Larkwhistle we grow indeterminate tomatoes because they take up a lot less space than the sprawlers. True, they need more tending than bush types, but it is a pleasure to potter in the tomato bed, pushing in stakes, plucking suckers, tying the hairy stems with strips of old bedsheets, watching the fruit swell from week to week, then blush and finally turn red.

skeletons, a dusting or two of rotenone should halt their progress.

Tomato plants work hardest during July and August, months that are often plagued by drought. Vines may not show signs of dry-weather stress, but a prolonged dry spell followed by heavy rain can cause blossom-end rot, a dark scab that starts at the base (or blossom end) and spreads into a nasty mush that spoils the fruit. A deep weekly drink helps prevent the affliction, as does the removal of any affected fruit. Mulch laid down after the first fruits have formed maintains even moisture. The same steps may prevent fissures, or cat-facing, from appearing in the tops of tomatoes, a breeding place for fungus. Some varieties are listed as crack-resistant.

Tomato Juice

What is there to say about harvesting tomatoes: let them ripen thoroughly, let every drop of green chlorophyll transform to "a red carotenoid called lycopene"—it tastes much better than it sounds. Pick your tomatoes at their peak and let the juice run down your chin.

Protection from Frost

It's late September or October. Tomatoes are laden with red and ripening fruit. Suddenly the wind shifts into the north and the temperature drops; by evening winds are calm but a new air mass, clear and chill, has rolled in from the Arctic. Frost tonight—tomorrow all of the fair-weather crops may be reduced to limp black flags mourning summer's unofficial but very real end, unless you take steps.

Here are the options:

- Pick all red tomatoes, any that are barely blushing and everything in between; pick them all if you plan green-tomato anything. Left on counters and windowsills, half-ripe fruit will slowly turn; others can be wrapped in newspaper and stowed away in drawers or boxes, the greenest at the bottom, those approaching ripeness on top. Tomatoes have an uncanny ability to turn red and soft off the vine, which accounts for those bland pink billiard balls pawned off as tomatoes in winter. Those you ripen indoors are bound to be an improvement.

- Toss big blankets over the vines to deflect frost; some gardeners lay vines on the ground, the better to cover them. Chances are there will be some summery days or weeks after the first frost.

- Pull up your tomato vines, roots and all, and hang them upside-down in a warm shed or garage—fruit will continue to ripen.

PEPPERS AND EGGPLANT

For years we gave peppers and eggplant the same treatment as tomatoes. We'd start with early maturing peppers such as 'Gypsy,' 'Stokes Early Hybrid,' 'Early Sweet Banana,' and 'Crimson Hot'; early eggplants 'Dusky' and 'Early Bird.' Then we'd follow the steps. But these two tropical fruits need even more heat than tomatoes to amount to anything.

In many areas, June flirts with both spring and summer—a warm "growthy" spell, followed by cool days and downright chilly nights. While peas run up their chicken wire and lettuces grow plump, peppers and eggplant sit still, waiting for heat. If warmth doesn't arrive until July, they've lost a month. The result is a ho-hum harvest of green peppers and small eggplant hardly worth the work and garden space. The problem we faced was how to coax these tropical fruits to succulent maturity within the deadlines of our season.

Framed Fruit

Enter the pepper and eggplant frame, a homemade variation on a cold frame that makes quite a difference. One chilly June day it was clear that our miserable peppers and eggplant would be better off under glass of some kind. A traditional sloped frame was too low to accommodate their growth, but the idea was sound. They needed a tall frame, so that they would not hit the roof before outgrowing their need for contained warmth. "What if we stood storm windows

Easy to tend, this homemade glass enclosure creates a protective environment that brings peppers and eggplant to maturity in our cold garden.

on their sides and built a special little greenhouse to hold peppers and eggplant all season," John mused. "After all, we grow only six of each." It was worth a try.

Rooting through a stack of old storm windows, we found two matched pairs, one set longer than the other. It was a simple matter to nail the four windows together, the pairs opposite each other, to form a 2½-foot-high (75-cm-high) rectangular glass box with no top or bottom. We were careful to wield the hammer with a light hand for fear of shattering the glass. Wood screws would have been better for the job than nails, but when the hardware store is 12 miles away and enthusiasm keen, you use what you have. With a fifth window sitting on top, the prototype pepper frame was set for a trial run in the garden.

The new frame did everything we hoped it would: by August it was filled with bushy plants loaded with ripening fruit. This simple construction adds six to eight weeks to our pepper and eggplant growing season.

The pepper frame sits neatly at one end of a vegetable bed. Maintenance consists of removing the top window for winter storage. The frame itself may stay in place over win-

ter but should be relocated for the next growing season to avoid disease. When the putty fell out, we secured the window with metal glazing points. Once in a while we scrape the peeling paint onto a drop sheet—lead paint and soil don't mix. The bare wood eventually weathered to gray.

Each spring we turn some old cow manure into the earth within the frame, along with a dusting of bone meal or rock phosphate, fertilizers high in phosphorus, to spur fruiting. A neighbor fed her framed peppers only blood meal (concentrated nitrogen), and had lush leafy plants barren of fruit. With the organic stuff dug in, soil is tamped down lightly and leveled.

Pepper and eggplant seedlings are transplanted into the frames, about 16 inches (40 cm) apart, during the third week in May. There they stay for the whole season. The frame is not a temporary shelter but a little pocket of tropicana in the north.

With the top window on, the glass walls are soon misty with condensation, a sign that the enclosure is suitably steamy. Like any cold frame, these glass houses buffer chilly breezes, warm both soil and air and create a tropical microclimate. The peppers and eggplants never miss a beat; stretching roots into the fertile soil, they grow on merrily whatever the weather outside. Inside temperatures may push 90°F (32°C). On hot days we slide the lid aside; there are lots of gaps in the glass box anyway.

Peppers and eggplant flowers are self-pollinating. Every little breeze shakes pollen from stamen to pistil within each flower. Sheltered frame plants may need a gardener's helping hand. Every few days when plants are in flower we reach in and give them a jostle.

By mid-July, as plants reach the top of the box, we take off the lid, leaving the frame in place for extra protection. A pail or two of sun-warmed water is poured into the frame twice a week; a compost mulch does weed-and-feed duty.

Growing steadily without setbacks, seldom bothered by bugs, framed peppers and eggplant tend to be healthy and fruitful. Through August and September peppers gradually ripen red or golden, and eggplants grow plump and purple. When the weather turns cool, we replace the window lid; no matter that leaves are squashed a bit at this stage. Fruit keeps maturing under these conditions long after the tender plants would have been blackened by frost in the open.

Gardeners with greenhouses or sunrooms should know that peppers do very well planted in large pots—12-inch (30-cm) diameter minimum—kept inside all summer. We have had excellent results with cayenne and chili peppers, as well as long banana peppers (sweet and hot) grown all season long in oversized containers (the kind shrubs and trees are sold in), sitting on a bench in front of the south-facing windows of our garden shed—windows in the roof let in the high summer sun (and even some rain).

HERBED RATATOUILLE

1	onion, diced	1
1 clove	garlic, minced	1 clove
1	eggplant, cubed	1
1	zucchini, quartered and sliced	1
1	yellow summer squash, quartered and sliced	1
2	tomatoes, diced	2
2 tbsp each	fresh oregano and fresh basil, finely chopped	25 mL each
2 tbsp	olive oil	25 mL
	Salt and pepper to taste	
1	hot chili pepper (optional)	1

Heat the oil in a skillet. Sauté onion and garlic until soft. If using the chili pepper, add it now. Add eggplant and sauté until soft. Add zucchini and summer squash and cook for 2 minutes more. Add tomatoes, herbs, salt and pepper and simmer for 3 to 5 minutes. Ratatouille may be served as a side dish, hot, warm or cool, or spooned over grilled fish or chicken.

EGGPLANT TERRINE

1	eggplant	1
1 or more	garlic cloves, pressed	1 or more
3	eggs	3
1½ cups	milk	375 mL
handful	a combination of fresh herbs (use up to five: basil, tarragon, fennel leaves, chervil, parsley, dillweed, lemon thyme; in smaller amounts: oregano, rosemary, marjoram, lovage, thyme)	handful
1 cup	dry bread crumbs	250 mL
2 tbsp	grated Parmesan cheese	25 mL
	Salt and pepper to taste	

Slice a medium-size eggplant into rounds, then dice the slabs. Toss eggplant in oil to coat and roast in the oven at 400°F (200°C) on baking sheet until soft and slightly brown. Oven roast garlic, also tossed with oil, in a small casserole dish until soft.

Whip together the eggs, milk, and fresh herbs. Mash the roasted eggplant and garlic coarsely. Stir in the egg mixture and blend well, adding bread crumbs, grated Parmesan cheese and salt and pepper to taste.

Spoon the mixture into an oiled terrine dish, spring mold or loaf pan. Bake, uncovered, for 30 minutes at 350°F (180°C), then reduce heat to 300°F (150°C) and continue baking the terrine for another 30 to 40 minutes, or until a knife or toothpick poked in the center comes out clean. Serve slices of the terrine warm or cool, sprinkled with one of the fresh herbs, with some bread and a green or tomato salad. Serves six to eight.

To make a savory eggplant dip (instead of a terrine), roast eggplant and garlic as above, mash with a fork and season to taste with olive oil, lemon juice, fresh herbs, salt and pepper.

Note: A young fresh eggplant should not need the salting and draining that removes some of the strong flavor from tough older fruit, and you can leave a garden-grown eggplant unpeeled.

Three Sisters of Life
Corn, Squash and Beans

The original inhabitants of "this Turtle Island," later renamed North America, knew themselves to be "one strand in the web of life." Out of such an understanding grows the wisdom of Native Chief Seattle: "Whatever we do to the web, we do to ourselves." Now, more than ever, we need to remember that we are vitally connected, for better or worse, to the Earth. This is not some vague romanticism, but a truth to keep in mind and heart as if our lives depended on it. They do.

For Native people, "all our relatives" encompasses not only family, but also "the perfumed flowers…the bear, the deer, the great eagle"—all aspects of creation. A special respect is due to the plants and animals that provide food—the direct, day-to-day links between human life and the Earth. "If your philosophy doesn't grow corn," an Elder once said to me, "I don't want to hear about it," which is to say that a view that neglects the lively bonds between the land and its people is not only incomplete but dangerous to the health and well-being of both.

For indigenous people, corn, squash and beans are the Three Sisters of Life—foods you can live on. These sustaining staples grow out of the harmonious interaction between another triad—humans, humus and Manitou, the Great Spirit. As often happens, science eventually catches up with traditional knowledge. Nutritionists tell us that corn and beans complement each other to provide complete protein; the sweet yellow squash gives a wealth of vitamins A, B and C; iron; calcium; phosphorus and energizing sugars.

CORN

Once, in an outdoor market in Guatemala, I watched a Mayan woman gathering up some dried corn she had spilled. On hands and knees, she slowly picked the kernels from the cobblestoned square until she had retrieved every last one. Before coming south, I had worked in a restaurant where I routinely scraped perfectly good food into the garbage can. What a contrast between that careless waste and this demonstration of a healthy appreciation for the stuff and staff of life. I trust that the lesson in true economics—meeting the needs of a household with thrift and care—sank in. As an old neighbor of ours says, "A willful waste makes a woeful want."

To Native people, corn is more than nutrition, it is a gift to be cherished and shared. Often called Sacred Mother, corn stands for fertility, renewal and power—the "fire in the belly." When the new crop comes in, it is a time of celebration and thanksgiving.

Eating and gardening are perhaps the two activities that most clearly remind us that our physical life-line is tied to the Earth. More than food grows in a garden. Plant a corn seed, pick an armload of cobs for dinner and in the moment's quiet your awareness of the source may deepen.

Coming originally from Central and South America, corn is a member of the Gramineae or grass family. As early as the eighth century, the Aztecs cultivated dry corn for grinding into nutritious cornmeal, a year-round staple. Specialty seed catalogs continue to list heirloom dry corn for gardeners interested in following in traditional footsteps. Most of us, however, grow sweet corn-on-the-cob, a gift of the gods if ever there was one. Corn lovers have their own harvest rituals: get the water boiling; pick the corn and rush it into the kitchen; three minutes in the pot, butter and salt it. For

OPPOSITE: Snap beans, whether yellow, purple or green, are prolific and easy to grow in average soil.

me, a "feed o' corn," as everyone around here says, always feels like a special occasion—rolling the cobs in the communal butter, eating with your fingers, the delicious messiness of it all. No wonder outdoor corn roasts and boils—seething kettle on an open fire—mark summer celebrations, family picnics and community get-togethers.

Corn Varieties

When the lilacs are in bloom, usually during the last week in May, we seed corn. With a view to harvesting cobs over a number of weeks, we sow two varieties, one early-maturing and one late, both at the same time. Every spring we mull over which varieties to plant. With one catalog listing more than sixty cultivars, choosing can be confusing. The selection has become more complicated with the recent addition of "sugar enhanced" and "supersweet" types to the list of "normal" corn.

Let's sort through the distinctions. Regular "old-fashioned" sweet corn—now called "sugary normal" to distinguish it from the newer kinds—begins to convert its sugar to starch quickly after harvest, or if cobs are left unpicked for a few days past their prime. Varieties are identified by "(su)" after their names.

Working with corn genes, breeders have modified the sugar-to-starch trait, giving rise to corn that remains sweeter longer, either on or off the plant. Called "sugar enhanced" corn, such varieties are followed by "(se)" in seed catalogs. They may also be tagged "EH," denoting an extended harvest. Because such corn holds its good-eating quality for a longer time, there is no rush to pick the corn all at once, before it gets past its best, or to cook it within minutes.

Between normal and enhanced corn are "all sweets," or high sugar normal types "(su)," regular corn with a higher sugar content than normal, but with the same rapid loss of sweetness.

Then there are "supersweet" corn cultivars, bred to stay sweet for hours, even days, after harvest. The code "(sh2)" refers to the "shrunken" gene responsible for the slow change of sucrose to starch (with a fructose stage on the way), and to the shrunken appearance of the dry seed. Supersweet corn has a rather crisp texture, even when cooked, unlike the nice chewiness of both normal and enhanced corn. Because the seeds are very sensitive to soil temperature, supersweets should not be planted until the soil has warmed to at least 65°F (18°C), usually a week or two after the spring frost-free date. Another quirk: Supersweet corn must be kept well away from other types or the flavor and texture of all will suffer. Either separate supersweet corn from other types by 25 feet (7.5 m) or more, or, if space is limited, choose a supersweet type that matures at least ten days earlier or later than the rest.

All that said, I leave it to each gardener to choose corn varieties—except to say that white-and-yellow "Peaches and Cream" corns seem to be enjoyed by everybody.

Seeding and Planting

At one time, we assumed that corn took up too much room for a home garden. True, the plants are tall and bulky, but in fertile soil they can stand fairly close together, making corn as suitable for intensive beds as broccoli or tomatoes. What it takes is some precision at seeding time. At Larkwhistle, we plant corn, like most of our food crops, in a wide (intensive) bed. Once the soil is fertilized, dug and raked smooth, we use a foot-long (30-cm) stick to mark out a grid of planting spots along and across the bed. A 4-foot-wide (120-cm) bed accommodates four rows, a foot apart, with outside rows 6 inches (15 cm) from either edge. Every foot along the rows we plant three seeds, in a close cluster, about an inch (2.5 cm) apart. Seeds are covered with 1½ inches (4 cm) of earth, roughly the distance between fingertip and knuckle. If the earth is soft, we simply push the seeds in with a finger. The adjacent row is the same, except that the groups of seeds are not directly opposite but staggered. Although this one-foot (30-cm) grid-planting saves space, I'll admit that corn grows rather better and is much easier to tend if you can spare 18 inches or 2 feet (45 or 60 cm) between the rows, while retaining the one foot (30 cm) in-row spacing.

You are advised never to plant a single, long row of corn, but rather three or more rows side by side. Corn is wind-pollinated; pollen grains shaken by breezes from tassels atop the stalks rain down on the silks protruding from the immature ears. Planting in an intensive block ensures that most cobs will be well pollinated and filled to the tip with kernels.

Whatever the starting distance, the next step, thinning, cannot be skipped. Once seedlings have grown 3 or 4 inches (8 or 10 cm) tall, remove all but the strongest one from each spot. Pulling up a lusty young plant is not easy—the instinct is to leave everything that grows—but steel yourself. Three corn stalks growing on top of one another will not amount to much.

Raising Corn

Like other grasses, corn is a strong, self-sufficient plant that will make the best of a range of soils and sites. For tall stalks and fat cobs, three elements are needed: full sun, adequate water and deep, rich organic soil. Nothing creates the last two conditions—moisture and fertility—as well as a thick layer of manure or compost turned into the corn patch in fall or early spring.

Several summers ago, in the middle of a hot, dry spell, our corn stopped growing and leaves began to shrivel and curl. Like fields all around, our patch looked stunted. Watering helped, but in a few days the ground was dusty again. Our instinct was to pile a thick mulch of half-decayed, strawy manure around the base of stalks. We then poured on buckets of water, which carried a quick shot of manure "tea" as it filtered through to the corn's roots. What a dramatic difference! Almost overnight, leaves turned green and turgid again; growth resumed. Before long the corn was sinking new roots into the dark, damp mulch. Visitors, having traveled through fields of suffering corn, wondered at the tall, thriving stalks, a result of the necessary care at the right time.

Where space is at a premium, corn can be intensively planted on a grid. Mark off rows 12 inches (30 cm) apart and sow a cluster of three seeds the same distance apart along the rows. When seedlings begin to crowd each other, thin to the strongest single corn plant in each spot.

Insects, Diseases and Corn Bandits

Most corn diseases are better prevented than cured. As always, planting disease-resistant types is the first line of defense. Cleaning up the corn patch in fall, and (if possible) moving corn around the garden from one year to the next, reduces the chance of disease. If corn earworms pose a threat, a spray of *Bacillus thuringiensis* (BT) is the remedy, but it must be used before larvae have burrowed into ears. Corn borers are harder to control without chemicals. Look for varieties that have been bred with a very tight husk of leaves around the cob, a physical barrier to borers.

One of the (many) strikes against chemical pesticides is that they kill insects indiscriminately, friend and foe alike. "Insect friends?" you ask. Every garden is home to a host of helpful insects—tachina flies and trichogramma wasps are two—that prey on an array of potential pests. The wasps, for example, lay their eggs in the eggs of a corn earworm; little wasps hatch, earworms don't. The flowers of several umbelliferous plants—dill, parsley, Queen Anne's lace—provide the nectar that trichogramma wasps need if they are to stay in the garden. I've noticed that flowering lovage, a green giant among aromatic herbs, is always humming with a bevy of these nonstinging insects, welcome helpers in pest control. Nature

Spacing corn 1 foot (30 cm) apart in a bed makes it possible to grow this favorite summer vegetable in the home garden. A mulch of compost or well-rotted manure ensures lush, steady growth; each time rain falls or the bed is watered, the corn plants receive a shot of plant food.

teaches gardeners that diversity is one of the hallmarks of a healthy balance.

As the harvest approaches, gardeners are not the only ones sniffing around the corn patch for signs of ripeness. Wily raccoons pay an early visit, maul a cob or two, make a mental note, and return when the corn is prime. How many times have we anticipated a lovely feed the next day, only to find chaos in the corn patch: torn-down, ripped-up stalks and half-chewed cobs strewn around. A raccoon is one messy eater. Some gardeners swear by a chicken-wire fence, with the mesh fastened to its supports only halfway up; the raccoon climbs the wobbly wire, which then bends backward with the weight, landing the creature on its ear—end of raid. How about a radio, tuned to an all-night rock station, set under a bucket in the corn patch? I hear it works, but our garden is too close to bedroom windows for such a noisy scheme.

So far we've had reasonable luck live-trapping raccoons and taking them for a ride into the woods. Rather than waiting for signs of damage, we bait the trap with apple halves or melon rinds soon after we plant the corn. If we capture the local bandits early enough, there will be none around to steal the corn—we hope. As the cobs reach ripeness we may drop a chunk of fish skin into the trap, muttering all the while "Some nice, smelly old fish for you, Mr. Raccoon? Much tastier than corn, you know…"

The Harvest

Everyone agrees: harvest corn when it is at a peak of tender sweetness. Signs of ripeness are silks that are light brown, dry but not altogether withered; and ears that are rounded at the ends rather than pointed; firm but not hard. If this sounds too mysterious, you can pull back the husk a bit and

Started in individual 4-inch (10-cm) containers about a month before their transplanting date (a week after spring's last frost), squash, zucchini, cucumbers, and melons need all the indoor sunlight you can give them—at least seven hours a day.

puncture a kernel with a fingernail; if the sap is milky, as opposed to watery, pick the corn. Be warned, though: peeled corn may attract birds and raccoons.

SQUASH

With their boisterous growth, lush leaves and abundant fruit, squash seems to stand for the exuberance of summer. A Native name for gourds, *ascutasquash*, has come into English as *squash*, a term that, like the plants themselves, covers a lot of ground from tiny courgettes to big, knobbly blue Hubbards, from curious crooknecks to giant pumpkins that tip the scales at 400 pounds (180 kg) plus.

Summer and Winter

For a gardener the most useful distinction is between summer and winter squash, and their variations. Summer squash includes green and yellow zucchini, round pattypan or scallop squash (also green or golden), several pale-green Lebanese and Italian types, vegetable marrows, and knobbly crookneck squash. The differences between them are mostly skin-deep; shape and color aside, all summer squash tend to be rather bland-tasting, a sponge for the herbs, garlic, onions, tomatoes and chilies often cooked

with them. Of those we've sampled unadorned, the old-fashioned yellow crook-neck has the most taste and substance. All are picked while still immature, a few days to a week after pollination. If a thumbnail pierces the skin easily, a summer squash is still fit for the table.

Winter squash, in contrast, must stay on the vine as long as possible. As fruits mature, they develop their full sweet flavor. In early October, the day before frost threatens, we search for the rock-hard fruit hidden in the leafy tangle. Only those with a firm, tough shell and a rather dull finish are worth taking; shiny, soft skin is the mark of tasteless, half-grown fruit that will not keep well. We use rose pruners to cut squash from the vines with an inch (2.5 cm) or so of stem intact.

There is something comforting about this end-of-summer ritual: piling the fruit carefully in a wheelbarrow, laying them out in a single layer in a patch of sun on the living-room floor. The same instinct that prompts chipmunks to bury acorns and bears to put on weight in fall is satisfied by the sight of squash spread out to cure indoors. Colorful Indian corn and a sheaf of dried grasses complete an autumn still-life, a wistful reminder of summer's glory as the sun heads

OPPOSITE: *Planted*
atop the compost pile
in late May, squash
vines crawl over and
through the snow
fence enclosure and
climb over anything
within reach.

south and cold grips the garden. By
November, the squash have been squirreled
away, perhaps under the bed if all the storage
shelves are full. Once a mainstay in pioneer
gardens, winter squash keeps for months in
a cool (45° to 60°F/7° to 15.5°C), dry locale.
An hour in the oven melts the hard flesh,
releasing the stored, sun-ripened sweetness.

Winter Varieties

Like related cucumbers and melons,
squashes interbreed easily, a trait responsible
for their many shapes, sizes and colors.
Gourds are nothing more than weird, wonderful and inedible squashes. A varied
selection of winter squashes includes:

- **ACORN OR PEPPER SQUASH:** Usually dark
green, the acorn-shaped, hard-skinned fruit
may also be orange or white. All tend to be
moist, fibrous, nutty, and only mildly sweet
when baked.
- **SWEET POTATO SQUASH:** 'Delicata' and
'Sweet Dumpling' are two that show the
characteristic pale yellow skin striped with
dark green; the first is cylindrical, the other
is rounder. Ideal for one or two servings,
these smaller, orange-fleshed fruits bake up
sweet and moist.
- **BUTTERNUT SQUASH:** Shaped like a fat
cylinder with a bulbous base, butternuts
have beige or light tan skin and orange flesh.
Excellent for storage, they are moderately
sweet and moist when cooked. 'Waltham
Butternut,' a garden classic, yields four or
five hefty fruits on a ranging vine, while the
"semi-bush" vines of 'Early Butternut
Hybrid'—an All America Winner—need
only half the space. Because their vines are
almost solid compared to the hollow stems
of other squash, butternuts are less susceptible to the destructive squash vine borer.
- **BUTTERCUP SQUASH:** Characterized by
smooth, blocky, dark green fruits striped
with gray, buttercups are our favorite for
their wonderfully sweet taste and dry texture—if you like sweet potatoes, you'll
enjoy buttercup squash. We often grow
the Burgess strain, long-keeping, 3- or 4-
pound (1- or 2-kg) fruits with a gray-green

button or turban at their base; vines ramble
far and wide, scaling a split-rail fence, climbing into a pear tree—strange fruit hanging
from the pear boughs—or ramping into the
tall grass.
- **NAKED-SEEDED SQUASH:** This novelty is a
sterling snack food, tasty and nutritious.
Resembling a small jack o' lantern, the fruit
is filled with hull-less seeds. Kids might
enjoy the messy job of separating the seeds
from the slippery membranes. Spread the
rinsed, lightly salted seeds in a single layer
on a cookie sheet and toast in the oven on
very low heat until dry and crunchy—home-
grown pepitas.
- **HUBBARD SQUASH:** Weighing in at 10 to
20 pounds (4.5 to 9 kg), Hubbards are blue-
gray or golden, hard-shelled, knobbly
squash for long storage. The oversized fruits
are more impressive for fall fairs than practical for a small family. 'Blue Ballet' is a smaller
version, while the reddish-orange 'Red Kuri'
is described in seed catalogs as "excellent for
soups and pies" and "dry, buttery and sweet"
when baked.

Of Hills and Heaps

Given their prolific growth, squash makes
good use of all the compost and manure you
can spare. For summer squash, we concentrate the nutrients in a fertile zone or "hill"
by marking off a circle of ground 2 to 3 feet
(60 to 90 cm) across, digging out of the top
6 or 8 inches (15 or 20 cm) of soil and
dumping in two or three pails of compost or
old manure and a handful of all-purpose natural fertilizer. Stir the organics into the soil,
trying not to bring up subsoil, and top the
hill with the reserved soil. Flatten the top of
the mound with a rake or by hand, and
sculpt the earth to form a rim or lip around a
slightly concave circle. Such a space will
accommodate three summer-squash plants.
One hill may be enough and two, spaced 4
feet (1.2 m) from center to center, should
provide an overflow crop of zucchini, patty-
pans and other summer squash.

Occasionally, we seed summer squash
directly in the ground outdoors, a few days
after spring's average frost-free date, when

the soil feels warm to the touch. In that case, we poke eight or ten of the big seeds into the loose earth of the hill, covering with an inch of soil. Seeds are spaced a hand-span apart. As seedlings sprout and grow, we thin them to the sturdiest three per hill, preferably choosing plants that stand at least a foot apart. Eventually the three entwine and look like one big bush.

Most seasons, however, we start both summer and winter squash indoors on precisely the same schedule and in the same way as described for melons and cucumbers (see the chapter Fruit of the Vine, page 107); that is, seeding in early May, in 4-inch (10-cm) pots, transplanting no more than a month later or about a week after the last spring frost. An early start is especially important for winter squash in northerly areas where fruit might otherwise not mature before frost blasts the vines. If possible, with an ear to the long-range forecast, we time transplanting to coincide with the onset of a warm spell. A covering of translucent garden fabric—floating row cover—keeps the young plants cozy for a few weeks; when the first fruiting blossoms appear, the veil should be lifted to admit bees for pollination.

Like zucchini, winter squash can also be seeded outdoors in somewhat larger hills, two vines in each, the hills spaced at least 5 feet (1.5 m) apart. Remember that most squash vines range for yards in every direction. In recent years we have come up with a way to satisfy the plants' prodigious appetite while curbing their enthusiastic spread.

Noting that volunteer vines often grow with great vigor from the compost heap, we decided to locate the pile where we wanted the squash. The process begins the fall before, during garden cleanup, as we gather wheelbarrow loads of compostable material—everything from seedy lettuces to frosted tomato plants, to armloads of stems from perennials being cut back at this time. The compost heap is built directly over one of the wide vegetable beds. Because the pile will become growing space next year, we make the effort to chop bulky stalks and leaves into smaller pieces with a machete. The pile begins with a foot-high (30-cm) layer of bulky garden residues. As we stomp and chop, the rough green stuff subsides to 6 inches (15 cm) or so of finer material. This layer is topped with several inches of the freshest manure we can get—fresh, because we want the pile to heat up quickly and cook as long as possible into the fall. Lacking manure, we might use topsoil or last year's compost as the brown layer between layers of green stuff. The heap is built up to a height of about 3 feet (90 cm). It is then topped with a few inches of earth (over the last manure layer) an "icing" of topsoil removed from the bed before the whole process was started.

Come spring, the compost warms quickly; the manure layers hold moisture. In early June we transplant our winter squash seedlings, 2 feet (60 cm) apart, right into the pile. If the material looks too coarse as we trowel out transplanting holes, we "line" each hole with fine soil and fill in around roots with the same. The squash plants soon sink roots into the damp fertility and on down to the ground beneath. Before long they are off and running. At this point we surround the pile with snow-fencing, a barrier that provides some support for the climbing vines, and more or less contains them; if space is tight, stray shoots can be tucked back into the enclosure.

After the harvest, when the frosted vines have been hauled away to a new pile, the compost is ready for spreading around the garden, a year after it was put together. I like to think that the squash roots have helped to break it down, saving us the back-breaking job of turning. Needless to say, the place where the pile stood will be much more fertile than before.

The compost-as-growing-space technique can be modified to fit into any sized garden and would be suitable for cucumbers and bush (unstaked) tomatoes, too. The essentials are: build the heap in the fall, chop the ingredients, use generous layers of manure or soil throughout, top with earth.

Trouble

The same insects and afflictions that menace cucumbers and melons (see page 109 and 112) affect squash as well. The remedies are also the same. Sheer garden cloth goes a long way to keeping young plants out of the reach of various borers and beetles; older plants are generally safer. A heavy mulch prevents moths from reaching the soil where they lay eggs that hatch into squash vine borers. Lacking the cloth or mulch, dust the base of vines with rotenone, ashes or black pepper if borers have been problematic in the past. Once in, borers can be gingerly hooked out with a hairpin or wire; cover the wound in the vine with a mound of earth to induce new roots. Several sanitation steps discourage a buggy population boom: clear away and compost all squash residues in fall; keep garden borders mowed; dig or till a squash patch in spring. So far (knock on wood), our squash plants have enjoyed the best of health, whether due to the deep spring digging or the compost planting, the diversity of our kitchen garden—some people don't see the vegetables for the tangle of flowers and herbs—or simply our northerly location.

BEANS

Beans are a home gardener's crop insurance. If the melon vines wilt and raccoons get the corn, we can usually count on beans to provide something good to eat for eight weeks or more. As they are feeding us, the plants feed the soil: on their roots are little bumps or nodules, colonies of bacteria that work to change nitrogen from the air into nitrates, free fertilizer for plant use. Gardeners can stimulate this process by dusting damp bean seed, prior to planting, with "legume inoculant," a dry black powder containing the nitrogen-fixing bacteria. As one catalog notes, "It's a natural, simple process that takes just a moment, but pays benefits all season long." After beans have been rotated throughout the garden, you can stop powdering seeds because the organisms remain in the soil and attach themselves to the roots

Against a warm southwest wall, summer squash thrives under a mulch of strawy, aged manure. Every time it rains, the vines receive a shot of plant food.

of any legumes—members of the bean and pea family—you might plant.

Although I am intrigued by the possibility of growing dried beans for the winter, their cultivation and threshing take up more space and time than we can spare. Like most gardeners, we focus on snap beans for fresh summer use. Snap beans, your old string beans minus the strings, grow on either branching, knee-high bushes or tall, twining, climbing plants that need the support of poles, strings, netting or wire fencing. Pole beans may take a week or two longer to bear, but they grow more food in less space than bush beans; some say that the flavor of a pole bean is "superior to even the best bush bean." In our cool locale, pole beans do not thrive as well as their bushy counterparts, but we keep trying.

A Bevy of Beans

Seed catalogs insist that certain snap beans (i.e., the ones they list) have "exceptional taste," "rich, beany flavor," "superior eating quality." To test the claims, we try a new bean or two every year. Frankly, I find the flavor nuances so subtle that an extra minute on the stove seems to make more difference than which bean is in the pot, and yet, we have our favorites. 'Green Crop' we grow every year for its abundant flat, wide pods that are easy to sliver for cooking. Widely available, 'Provider' is a popular early green bean, resistant to several common diseases. 'Bush Blue Lake,' a short version of classic pole beans, needs more space than others.

'Beurre de Rocquefort' is a long-bearing, yellow bush bean from France that takes to cool northern summers and can be planted earlier than others. 'Rocdor' and 'Cherokee Wax' are also fine wax (yellow) beans with some disease tolerance. Next year we'll try 'Dragon Tongue,' a flat, bronze-mottled yellow bean said to be "one of the tastiest beans around," and 'Dutch Stringless' for "real bean taste"—the search goes on.

From France come skinny "filet" beans that are picked young and served whole. 'Triomphe de Farcy' and 'Marbel' are universally praised for earliness and fine flavor, but the purple-streaked green pods must be picked when very thin, almost every day at their height. Once they attain snap-bean size, filets lose their appeal, growing tough and stringy. Filets are not for freezing.

'Purple Queen' and 'Royalty Purple Pod' are ornamental and prolific. Give the bushes a foot between them and they'll fill out with lilac flowers, followed by dangling dark-purple beans. After two minutes in boiling water, the purple turns to green, telling you when the beans are blanched for freezing.

The Bean Bed

Coming originally from Central and South America, beans of all kinds respond to warm soil and air; a whisper of frost is enough to kill them. In cool soil the seeds may rot, and those that do sprout lack vigor. Although beans may be started indoors—two seeds in a 2-inch (5-cm) pot, thinning to one—a few weeks ahead of time, most gardeners sow them outdoors a week after spring's last frost. When the maple trees are in full leaf and the soil is warm to the touch, our beans go in. A second and third planting, at two- or three-week intervals, gives a steady supply until frost. Because the plants bear fairly heavily over several weeks, a succession of smaller seedings is the only way to go if you want beans for fresh eating rather than freezing.

Beans need a place in full sun and earth lightened and enriched with compost or leaf mold, but not clogged with nitrogen-rich manure; excessive nitrogen pushes foliage at the expense of fruit. Pole beans need relatively more nutrients to support their vigorous growth and heavy fruiting. Here, we turn an inch of compost, sometimes augmented with a dusting of bone and kelp meal, into the bean bed a few days before planting. The goal is to boost the potash and phosphorus levels. But since beans prefer a slightly acidic ground, wood ashes, a potent source of both potash and alkalinity, tends to raise soil pH above the comfort level.

My grandmother grew fine pole beans in a tiny city garden that has never seen manure, "real" compost, or chemical fertilizer. All she did was bury her garden leftovers—frosted plants, leaves from the peach tree, spent bean vines, the residue from tomato canning—in the ground. In many gardens, beans prosper without fussy soil preparation—just dig, rake and plant. You'll know in a season whether the earth is out of balance or deficient; if beans fail to thrive, you have some soil-building to do.

Bush beans do well an intensive bed, but should not be crowded. A tangle of plants may lead to rot in a wet season, and makes it hard to find pods amid the overflow of foliage. The recommended distance between bean plants in a row is 8 inches (20 cm); traditional methods would put the rows 18 inches (45 cm) or more apart. Intensive gardening, however, makes the usual distance between plants in a row the same as the distance between the rows themselves. With that in mind, hoe open bean furrows, 1 inch (2.5 cm) deep, 8 inches (20 cm) apart, across the width of a bed. Plant one seed every 2 inches (5 cm)—some may not sprout and earwigs may chew off a few more. In clay soil, it is advisable to cover the seeds

with sifted compost or lighter ground; beans have a hard time hoisting their hefty leaves through crusty ground. If germination is good and earwigs few, you're left with a crowded bed of beans—and a hard-to-pick forest if all are left. As the small bushes expand, pluck out the surplus so that the remainder are properly space. I can thin carrots, just fine, but always have trouble pulling up extra bean plants, even knowing that crowding creates problems later on. Old habits die hard, but, be it resolved: next year we thin the beans. Even at the proper spacing, beans will fill gaps between them and crowd out weeds. Giving beans room to breathe not only makes for easier picking, it also fosters better health as circulating breezes dry foliage, inhibiting the spread of fungal diseases. On one point all experts agree: Working among wet bean plants can spread disease.

To grow pole beans, first set up supports. Traditionally, slender 10-foot (3-m) saplings, with bark left on, are pushed firmly into the ground at 18-inch (45-cm) intervals. A crowbar is handy to loosen the earth first. At the base of each pole sow eight to ten beans, thinning later to four to six plants. Variations on the method are possible. Three or more poles, lashed together at the top, teepee style, make an interesting feature in a sunny corner of the garden. Make it bigger and the kids can hide out in its leafy shade. One teepee may be all you need; otherwise, space them on 4-foot (120-cm) centers. Beans will climb special nylon netting or tall, wide-mesh chicken wire. One grower recommends two tall, sturdy posts set in firmly, 8 feet (2.4 m) apart, with a cross piece between them, top and bottom. On this frame you weave a grid of untreated twine. At season's end, twine and vines come down together for composting. As an annual climber, pole beans, and especially the striking 'Scarlet Runners,' can decorate trellis work, porch front or chain-link fence.

Plants take in nutrients from both roots and leaves. Last summer, we gave the bean patch a foliar feed of seaweed emulsion, a dark green liquid mixed into a concentrate from powder and further diluted for use. The results were dramatic as leaves turned noticeably greener during the ensuing spurt of growth.

Bean Bugs

Beans are one of the healthiest, most insect-free crops we grow. In the cause of prevention we shift the patch around the garden so that they grow in the same place only once in three years. We also bury spent plants either in the ground or in an active compost pile in fall, and remove any ailing bushes as soon as trouble appears. The Mexican bean beetle is almost a dead-ringer for the beneficial ladybug, except that the beetle is more orange than reddish, has no spots on the segment between head and body and turns bean leaves to lace. Handpick both beetles and their tiny yellow, spiny larvae; clusters of orange eggs can be crushed in the process. Planting beans next to potatoes is a time-honored way of deterring both bean beetles and potato bugs. As always, a mix of flowers and aromatic herbs—specifically savory, garlic, nasturtium, hyssop, sage and petunias—adds to the bug-baffling diversity that helps protect the beans and the rest of the garden from predators. Our kitchen garden is laid out in permanent plots that are worked by hand, an arrangement that allows for groups of perennial herbs at the ends of beds. Hardy annual flowers such as alyssum, cornflowers, California poppies, calendulas, borage and Shirley poppies self-sow freely along pathways and among the vegetables to create a colorful jumble that (we can only hope) is more confusing to insects than a large tract of their favorite food.

Pick of the Pods

When beans are at their peak, we pick them every few days, before the pods are lumpy with developing seeds. Mature beans should be picked so that new pods will continue to form.

CORN, BEAN AND TOMATO STEW

Corn, beans and tomatoes are all native to the Americas and team well with cilantro, parsley and something oniony in a colorful stew. Fresh shelled green lima beans are lovely in this dish, but frozen baby limas may be used. Other beans, whether canned or home-cooked, also work well. But there are no substitutes for fresh sweet corn, ripe tomatoes and fresh herbs.

1	onion	1
1 tbsp	butter	15 mL
1 tbsp	vegetable oil	15 mL
2 cups	corn kernels, cut from 4 cobs of corn	500 mL
1 cup	lima beans, fresh shelled or frozen, or cooked kidney or black beans, or 1 can (19 oz/540 mL) kidney or black beans, drained and well rinsed	250 mL
2	tomatoes	2
1 handful	parsley and cilantro leaves, finely chopped	1 handful
pinch	cayenne	pinch
	Salt and pepper to taste	

Dice onion. Heat butter and oil in a large skillet. Sauté onion until soft. Add corn kernels and cook for another minute or two. Add limas or other beans and continue cooking for about 5 minutes. (Frozen limas will slow cooking momentarily, but will thaw and cook quickly.) If using canned beans, drain and rinse thoroughly before adding. Add tomatoes, chopped, along with salt and pepper (and cayenne) and cook for another 5 minutes. Stir in the finely chopped herbs, cook for an additional minute or two. Turn off heat. You can let the stew sit, covered, while you get the rest of the meal together. Serve with rice or as a (hefty) side dish with grilled meat or poultry.

SAVORY SNAP BEANS

Summer savory is the classic bean herb. Here is a simple and flavorful way to serve snap beans at a summer supper.

several handfuls	snap beans, green or yellow	several handfuls
several sprigs	fresh summer savory	several sprigs
1 tbsp	olive oil	15 mL
1 clove	garlic, pressed or minced	1 clove
	Lemon juice, salt and pepper to taste	

Cut snap beans on a sharp slant into thin strips and place in a heavy-bottomed pot with water just covering the bottom. Add a pinch of salt and whole sprigs of summer savory.

Cook over medium heat, stirring occasionally to redistribute the beans, until beans are quite tender but not mushy, to bring out their natural sweetness. If water starts to evaporate, add a little more; there should be almost no water left when the beans are done. Remove beans from skillet and drain if necessary; discard sprigs of savory. Heat olive oil in same skillet and sauté garlic very briefly. Return beans to skillet and season with lemon juice, salt and pepper to taste. Sprinkle with minced summer savory. Stir beans and seasonings together briefly to meld flavors.

Fruit of the Vine
Melons and Cucumbers

CANTALOUPES AND WATERMELONS

In August, if all goes well, melons begin to ripen, one by one. Then, the rising sun finds us crouched among the vines, searching for fragrant cantaloupes ready to "slip"; listening for watermelons that answer our rapping and tapping with a low-pitched echo of ripeness. Melons, according to Mark Twain, are "the proper food of angels." At least two earthbound gardeners agree: nothing could be finer for a summertime breakfast than a ripe melon taken from the vine in the dewy cool of the morning.

Pollen Exchange

Melon plants, botanists tell us, are "highly polymorphic," meaning the various species are free and easy about swapping pollen. This exchange, whether spontaneous in nature or planned in breeders' fields, has given rise to an array of shapes, sizes and colors. But round or oblong; smooth-skinned or roughly pebbled; orange, yellow or red inside, home-grown melons are bound to be ambrosial.

A dream of garden melons begins in winter when we send for seed. Those big Texas blimps that need 100 hot days to mature are not for us, nor are exotic honeydew, casaba or Crenshaw melons. Instead, we look for quick cantaloupes (or muskmelons) and "icebox" watermelons seldom larger than a volleyball—melons that will make it to maturity within the deadlines of our season.

Fortunately for gardeners, the folks who juggle melon genes have come up with varieties whose very names promise to extend the borders of cultivation into cooler short-season areas. So far we have had good success with 'Quick Sweet,' 'Earlisweet,' 'Alaska,' and 'Earligold' cantaloupes.

'Minnesota Midget' ripens a vineload of soft-ball-sized muskmelons.

The watermelon cultivar we keep coming back to is 'Yellow Baby,' a green-and-cream mottled melon that grows to coconut size; spiciness underlies the sweetness of its lemon-yellow flesh. 'Sweet Favorite,' a red watermelon, ripens in the traditional oblong shape, but earlier than most. 'Sunshine,' a medium-sized yellow watermelon growing on compact vines, is on our list for a trial, as is 'Passport,' a green-fleshed melon, recently bred in New Hampshire and said to be "widely adapted."

Southern gardeners may get away with seeding melons directly outdoors, but the rest of us must be prepared to coax them along if we hope for a worthwhile return. Their tropical origins give us clues about making the heat-lovers at home in cooler climes. For healthy and fruitful growth, melons require dawn-to-dusk sun, warm soil, steady moisture and enough time to ripen.

Indoors and Out

To get a head start, we seed melons indoors sometime during the first ten days of May, about a month before we plan to transplant outdoors, a week or so after our frost-free date. Some plants are forgiving about being crowded together at the start and then wrenched apart for planting; lettuce, for instance, bounces back from such treatment. Melons, however, are so sensitive to root stress that they may "up and die on you" if their roots are disturbed. The solution is to sow seeds in individual containers, three seeds in a 4-inch (10-cm) pot.

To germinate, melon seeds need the extra warmth provided by heating cables, a radiator or proximity to the stove during a baking session; ordinary room temperatures leave them cold and dormant. On sunny days our seeded pots, covered with clear plastic or a glass pane, sit in front of a south-facing window. The covering traps the sun's heat like a greenhouse. Once the seeds have sprouted, melons continue to have priority sun space by the windows. (With lettuce and broccoli already in the ground and tomato seedlings "hardening" in the cold frame, window space has been freed up for melon seedlings.) When the young vines are working on a second leaf, we snip away all but the strongest one per pot. Pulling up unwanted seedlings may damage roots of the one left to grow.

Turn Up the Heat

Melons are the most cold-sensitive crop we grow. With an ear to the long-range forecast, we delay transplanting until summery weather has settled in for sure, usually a week or two after tomatoes and peppers are in the ground. A chilly spell may stress the vines beyond recovery.

The ideal melon soil is light, warm, well drained and fertile. Sandy loam is a good start; all that may be needed is a dressing of compost. Whenever possible, we add soil amendments in fall and again in early spring. A balance of natural fertilizer, turned in before transplanting, keeps the hungry vines well fed. Soil that tests below 6.5 on the pH scale needs a measured amount of ground limestone to sweeten it to 7 plus.

Many melon growers resort to artificial means to boost the soil and air temperature. Very effective is the bottom-sheet, top-sheet method: Cover the melon bed with a sheet of dark or clear plastic anchored with sticks, soil or stones; transplant melons carefully through X-slits cut in the plastic at 2-foot (60-cm) intervals; cover plants with a top-sheet of floating row cover, a translucent spun-fiber fabric that lies lightly over the seedlings. Vines run riot under the cloth, which must be lifted when yellow blossoms appear to let in pollinators.

On warm sandy soil, a plastic bottom cover may be redundant—we're glad to avoid it, in any case, because it soon becomes bulky garbage. If I gardened on clay soil, I would experiment with a surface layer of heat-holding sand spread on a melon bed, in addition to the sand turned into the bed. Remember how hot a beach can be underfoot.

Most seasons we grow our melons in a long cold frame that sits over a prepared raised bed. Sometime in late May or early June, seedlings are transplanted, 2 feet (60 cm) apart, in the middle of the frame. With recycled storm windows fitted on top, the frames create a tropical microclimate as June bounces between spring and summer. By July, when melon leaves are pushing at the glass, we remove the windows; the liberated vines soon trail over the frame sides, and, before long, flowers appear.

Sex Among Melons

Melon flowers are either male or female. Female flowers are backed by a small swelling, a tiny embryonic fruit; male flowers are attached to the vine by a thin stem. Melons will develop only if pollen is transferred from male to female, a task usually performed by bees and other flying insects. In short-season areas it is important that the first female flowers are, in fact, pollinated, since these will be the melons most likely to ripen before frost. Flowers stay open for only one day, and if no bees happen by, you can say good-bye to that fruit.

Sometimes one has to play matchmaker, using a small watercolor brush—the kind that comes with a child's paintbox set—to transfer pollen. A random flight with the brush from male to female blossoms should do it, even though melon pollen is so fine you may wonder if you are accomplishing anything. With luck, bees will discover the flowering vines and return on a daily pollen run—and you can let nature take its course.

Once pollinated, the little pea-sized melons begin to swell quickly under the summer sun. Thirsty melon vines need a lot of water to plump their fruit. A deep weekly drink is better than frequent shallow showers; sun-warmed water preferable to icy cold. To reduce the risk of fungus, water in the morning so that vines are dry by nightfall.

Melons are one crop we never mulch; a moisture-holding layer of hay or grass may keep the earth too cool for them. Vine growth is usually dense enough to shade the ground from the sun's full drying force.

Trouble

Both watermelon and cantaloupe vines sometimes fall prey to various wilts, blight and fungae. Fusarium wilt, a disease spread by the yellow-and-black striped cucumber beetle, can cause vines to collapse almost overnight. The floating row cover does double duty by excluding beetles from young plants; the pests are less interested in older vines.

Catnip and nasturtiums are said to deter cucumber beetles, as are onion skins strewn through the patch. Whenever I pull onions or garlic for the kitchen in summer, I twist off the unusable green tops and toss them around the garden, among the melon vines or over the cabbages. Handpicking beetles is always a possibility, and a selective dusting of rotenone may be a last resort, but I'd worry about killing bees.

As always, prevention is better than cure. Breeders have not overlooked the health of melon vines. Look for cultivars with built-in tolerance or resistance to one or more maladies—anthracnose, fusarium wilt, powdery and downy mildew. If any plants do succumb, take them up for burning or disposal. Cleaning up all debris at season's end should be standard practice, along with rotating melons around the garden from year to year. As a further preventive step, space vines at least 2 or 3 feet (60 or 90 cm) apart for good air flow and avoid watering past noon.

Slipping Cantaloupes and Inscrutable Watermelons

The harvest approaches—but when? Picked too early, melons will not be their flavorful best. Watermelons sit there, fat and inscrutable. Cantaloupes, at least, give you some clues. As it matures, a cantaloupe gradually changes from gray-green to buff-yellow. When ripe, it begins a process called "slipping," detaching itself from the vine

In short season areas, melon plants must be started indoors about three weeks before spring's frost-free date and set in the garden about a week afterward when the weather is warm and settled.

(and, one presumes, rolling off on a seed-scattering life of its own). Where stem meets melon, a circular crack appears. A gentle tug and the melon comes away. Sometimes we find melons lying there, unattached. A day or two indoors will bring a cantaloupe to fuller flavor and aroma. The nose will know when the melon is ready to eat.

Mark Twain, watermelon aficionado, once instructed gardeners in a game of musical melons to test for maturity. Pink, pank,

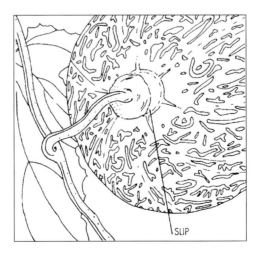

SLIP

As cantaloupes approach maturity, a circular crack appears where the fruit is attached to the vine, a sign that melons are ready to "slip."

Smaller icebox watermelons, such as 'Yellow Baby,' are the choice in areas where the big southern blimps may not mature.

punk: tapped gently, a watermelon will sing a descending scale as it ripens. Punk—low-toned, somewhat hollow—is the sound of ripeness. If you are tone-deaf, a watermelon normally has a light-colored patch on the rind where it touches the ground, and as the fruit ripens, the patch changes from white to creamy yellow—another sign. Or look to see if the tendril nearest the melon has shriveled and browned. If the melon's stem has withered altogether, you might as well pick it; no more juice will flow to that fruit. Some gardeners remove a sample plug from a watermelon to test for ripeness, but the gash invites ants, earwigs and rot. As a rule: If all signs and sounds say "ripe," wait a day or two more. Watermelons, unlike bananas, apples, pears and cantaloupes, do not manufacture any more sugar after they are picked.

All home-grown food is good, but garden fruit is extraordinarily good. After years of growing melons, we are still pleasantly surprised by each one that completes the race to ripeness in our frost-pocket garden. We still gather the fragrant globes with a little wonder, crack them open with the same anticipation felt that first August, grateful for the small miracle that is a melon from a northern garden.

CUCUMBERS

A garden links its maker in an active, cooperative way with nature's cycles. After growing vegetables and fruit for a season or two, you began to appreciate the wonderful match between season and supply. In spring, when a body needs a lift, we gather tonic greens and roots that mine the earth for minerals: spinach and dandelion leaves, spring onions, radishes, Jerusalem artichokes and parsnips all provide concentrated nourishment to cleanse and revitalize. Fall's apples, pears, beets and carrots store up earth-and-sun energy for the cold days. In dark December, a golden buttercup squash, baked to melting sweetness, or a bowl of leek-and-potato soup feels like reserve solar power from the garden.

In the same way, cucumbers seem made for warm-weather eating. If lettuces start to peter out in July, we can always count on cucumbers for salads. In hot eastern lands, cooks combine cucumbers and yogurt for refreshing side dishes: a creamy Indian raita, cumin-and-cayenne spiked, cools a fiery curry, and from Greece comes tsatziki, a tangy cucumber-and-yogurt dish redolent of garlic, olive oil and fresh dill. A basil-flecked salad of cucumbers, tomatoes and Spanish onions is a summer treat.

Roman Baskets

Wild cucumbers, like melons, come originally from Africa. India, however, has been a hotbed of cucumber cultivation since at least 1000 B.C. The vine traveled from east to west, meeting with an enthusiastic reception in ancient Rome. In summer, Roman gardeners grew their cucumbers in baskets rolled around from place to place to catch every drop of sun. In winter, cultivation shifted under cover, into frames or mica-glazed houses, perhaps to please the likes of Emperor Tiberius and court, who called for cucumbers every day of the year. What has changed? Even in the north today, hothouse cucumbers are available throughout the winter, catering to a taste for a vegetable second only to tomatoes in popularity.

Cucumber Cultivars

Gardeners can thank hybridists for cucumbers that are gratifyingly easy to grow. For years, they have been breeding in greater disease resistance and the resulting vines are generally healthy, vigorous, and productive. Every season we grow the same two varieties. Very prolific, 'Marketmore' yields a succession of dark green fruit from plants that resist four common cucumber ailments—scab, mosaic and two mildews. Plants are described as "bitter-free," a trait that, curiously enough, makes them less palatable to cucumber beetles, spreaders of the dread wilt. The cultivar's "uniform green genes" reduce the chance of "yellow bellies," a cosmetic detail of more concern to commercial growers than to gardeners.

According to one catalog, 'Sweet Slice' cucumbers are "tolerant to just about every disease you can think of"—good news for organic gardeners. Long, straight and thin-skinned, with a core of tiny, tender seed, the crisp fruits are remarkably mild and sweet. If pressed to choose, I'd take 'Marketmore' for its unfailing bumper crop.

Cucumber Culture

Up to a point, we grow cucumbers exactly like melons, seeding both indoors in the same way, on the same day in early May. A month later, we transfer seedlings to the garden, again being extra careful with their roots. In the interval, we prepare a bed of extra-fertile earth.

Our best cucumbers to date grew one summer beside a concrete water-lily pool, in soil enriched with cow manure to a depth of 12 inches (30 cm). Sprawling over a stone path, in full sun, the vines were treated to frequent floods of warmed water from the pool. You could almost see the growth. And what a crop—cucumbers "stacking up like cordwood" as a neighbor would say. That summer taught us a lesson in cucumber culture: give them manure, water, sunshine and lots of it.

Currently we grow cucumbers along the south-facing wall of a garden shed. To prepare the soil, we dig a series of holes, about two hand-spans across and 12 inches (30 cm) deep; holes are spaced at 2-foot (60-cm) intervals. Into each excavation we dump five spades of crumbly cow manure or finished compost, and a palmful of natural fertilizer. The amendments are topped with several spades of earth, and the mixture is turned and stirred together. After treading lightly to compress the soil/humus blend, we then sculpt the loose soil over each zone by hand, leaving a raised rim around a slightly concave bowl. As a neighbor once said, after watching us do this, "It's not your fault if the cukes don't grow."

A foundation of organic matter provides a reservoir of moisture and food for vines all season. In the center of each circle, we transplant one seedling. Water poured into the earth-bowls goes directly to roots. If cutworms are active, we protect young vines with collars made from 3-inch (8-cm) pressed-fiber pots with bottoms cut away. At this stage, when temperatures are apt to swing, a blanket of floating row cover mellows the climate underneath.

Cucumber seeds may also be sown directly in the garden, in either rows or hills. Note that hills are not necessarily mounds; indeed, in drought-prone or sandy gardens, they are best made level with the surrounding soil. Where the earth is heavy and damp, a raised area tends to be warmer and drier. Raised or level, think of a hill as a 2-foot (60-cm) circle of soil intensively and deeply enriched, in the manner just described. Gardeners with room to spare might space such hills 3 feet (90 cm) apart and mulch the ground between to hold moisture and suppress weeds. Sow six or eight seeds, a few inches apart, in each hill. As seedlings grow and touch, pinch out all but three of the strongest.

Beetle-Proofing

The same row cover fabric that shelters seedlings from cool spring winds offers renewed hope wherever droves of cucumber beetles appear the moment you turn your back after transplanting, or as soon as seedlings break through. Beetles and larvae not only chew vines and roots, they also spread a devastating wilt disease. If your cucumbers have been menaced by beetles, whether you seed or transplant, don't leave the patch without first tucking it under cover. Drape the cloth loosely over a bed and secure the edges against determined beetles; we keep a bundle of warped one-by-two lumber on hand to batten down the cloth. When flowering starts, vines must be uncovered to let in pollinating insects. By then, the beetles (let's hope) have run their course, moved on for lack of food, or otherwise ceased to pose a threat. Older vines withstand the onslaught better than fragile seedlings.

Send Them Up

When the cloth comes off, we aim vines at their supports, a network of strings tacked to the shed wall. Cucumbers will hoist themselves upward by means of strong, springy tendrils. Trained to climb, they occupy very little space; fruit will be straighter, too. Trellising can be as elaborate and permanent as chicken wire fastened to wooden frames, or as seasonal and compostable as a web of untreated twine torn down with the vines at season's end. I find it fascinating to see how the thin, fragile-looking tendrils get a quick and tenacious grip on anything thin within reach. See that supports are at least 6 feet (1.8 m) high, or vines will be waving around in the air with no place to climb. You may have to encourage cukes on their ascending journey by tying them to supports with soft cloth at the start. Where there is space, cucmber can sprawl over the ground, and you are spared the work of trellising.

Food and Water

As much as cucumber vines appreciate the sun, their roots revel in cool, moist earth. We often pack very old manure, compost or other mulch into those water-catching bowls, or over the entire bed if enough material is on hand. With each rain or watering, the pampered plants get yet another helping of quickly available food. Soaking the cucumber patch every three or four days is not too often in hot dry weather. Liquid manure or fish emulsion also spurs fruitful growth.

If all this feeding sounds excessive, consider that cucumber and melon vines are stretching quickly—several inches a day—at the height of summer. Remember, too, that we are working with gentle, natural ingredients, not concentrated chemicals. It is hardly possible to overdo the humus. An organic gardener looks at the long-term view, taking care of the future in the present. Compost turned in and mulch spread now are part of the slow, steady creation of lively, balanced, fertile soil, a process that in nature never ceases. What we do for cucumbers this summer benefits the garden next season and the next.

It is important to pick cucumbers when they are still slim and dark green; fruit left to grow fat, pale and seedy signal the vines to quit producing.

TSATZIKI

Cucumber and Yogurt Salad

2 cups	plain yogurt	500 mL
3 tbsp	olive oil	50 mL
3	garlic cloves, pressed	3
½ cup	fresh dillweed, minced	125 mL
1 tsp	fresh spearmint, minced	5 mL
1 tsp	fresh basil or tarragon, minced	5 mL
	Cayenne pepper to taste	
3	cucumbers, halved lengthwise and thinly sliced	3
	Salt to taste	

Stir together all ingredients except cucumbers and salt. Add the cucumber to the yogurt mixture. Let stand for half an hour in a cool place. Salt to taste just before serving. Serves eight.

TABOULI SALAD WITH CUCUMBER AND TOMATO

Light but hearty, this summer salad is made with bulgur wheat (cracked wheat that has been partially cooked and then dried). Added to boiling water, it plumps up quickly as a base for a Middle Eastern salad, traditionally served with pita bread and hummus.

For the salad:

½ tsp	salt	2 mL
2 cups	water	500 mL
1 cup	raw bulgur wheat	250 mL
1 or 2	cucumbers, peeled and chopped (remove seeds from larger cucumbers)	1 or 2
1	tomato, chopped	1
1	small red or Spanish onion, chopped	1
½ cup	minced parsley	125 mL
¼ cup	minced spearmint	60 mL

Bring salted water to boil in a saucepan. Remove from heat, pour in bulgur wheat, stir and cover. Let stand until water is completely absorbed and bulgur is tender. Allow bulgur to cool in the saucepan, then transfer to a large bowl. Add cucumber, tomato, onion, parsley and spearmint and mix well.

For the dressing:
¼ cup fresh lemon juice
¼ cup olive oil
salt to taste

Wisk the dressing ingredients together, pour over bulgur and mix well. Allow tabouli salad to stand for an hour or two before serving.

Second Season
Midsummer Seeding for Fall Eating

In February, when seeds arrive in the mail, we gather together six or eight packets, mark them "second season," and put them away until July. These are the seeds that will renew parts of the vegetable garden in midsummer, that will keep beds productive into the fall. It will be a treat in September, season of frosts and farewells, to see bands of green coming along—a double treat to gather fresh salads and roots until the snow flies.

Spring's last frost-free date—May 24 or its equivalent in another region—is too early for the vegetables that come into their own from September onward: Chinese cabbage, endive, turnips, rutabagas, bok choy and Chinese radishes. All are candidates for midsummer planting and fall picking. Sown in spring, they invariably bolt to seed about two months later.

July is not a month traditionally associated with seeding and transplanting, but consider nature's rhythm. By midsummer the first phase of the kitchen garden is coming to a close. April-seeded pea vines are thoroughly picked over and shriveling from the heat. Seedy lettuces are fit only for compost. The first beets grow woodier by the day, and early cabbages are done. The season is ripe for renewal. One July morning we haul the remnants of early crops to the compost heap. Soon after, their spaces are filled with new seeds or fresh transplants that have been waiting in a shaded cold frame. A nice bit of synchronicity starts the garden's second phase, a phase that will continue for three months or more.

Just as in spring, the midsummer garden begins with either seeds or transplants. Seeds present a challenge: In the hot, dry conditions common in July and August, they may sprout halfheartedly, if at all. The solution? First, sow a bit deeper than usual to get seeds below the dusty or crusty surface into cooler ground. Second, cover seeds with sifted compost (if you have it), a medium that stays moist and porous; this practice is especially helpful in clay gardens. Third, cover newly seeded spaces with a very light scattering of grass clippings, enough to provide some shade without impeding sprouts. Finally, water every day or two—most midsummer seeds will show through in four or five days—and continue on a regular schedule until seedlings have extended roots out of drought's way.

Best vegetables for seeding directly into the ground during the first week in July are beets, baby carrots, endive, radicchio and chicory, Florence fennel, fall lettuce, rutabaga and turnips, kohlrabi and various Oriental greens. Long white Oriental radishes such as daikon can wait another month.

A number of second season things are started from seed indoors in early July, and go into the ground as transplants about three weeks later. At this stage, transplants are treated the same as those set out in spring. Here are the steps:

1. Prepare the soil by incorporating compost and/or old manure and natural fertilizer into the whole bed, or spot-enrich to create a zone of fertility for each transplant.
2. Transplant firmly and somewhat deeper than plants were previously growing.
3. Sculpt the earth around each transplant to form a water-catching basin.
4. Water with dilute fish emulsion or other natural liquid fertilizer.
5. Spread a cooling, weed-suppressing layer of mulch.
6. Failing rain, water frequently during the first two weeks after transplanting.

OPPOSITE: A July seeding renews the garden in midsummer and yields a fresh fall harvest of Chinese cabbage, curled and flat-leaved endive, large white Oriental radishes and young carrots. Crisp 'Russet' apples round out the fixings for a wonderful salad.

Chinese cabbage responds to root disturbance by bolting to seed. To prevent this, start seedlings in 3-inch (8-cm) pots and transplant carefully. A spadeful of crumbly compost and a little fertilizer stirred into the soil for each plant concentrates nutrients in the root zone.

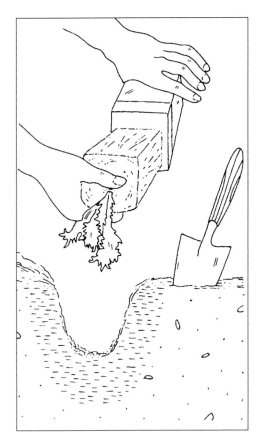

CHINESE CABBAGE

At the head of the second-season class stands Chinese cabbage, a delicious multi-use vegetable that can sometimes challenge a gardener's skill. A member of the Brassica band, it is also called celery cabbage or wong bok. Mature heads may be barrel-shaped or cylindrical, like a stocky Romaine lettuce, packed with juicy pale green leaves that are mild. The fat barrels are known as Napa types; the slimmer cylinders are called Michili types. We frequently grow a Chinese cabbage named simply 'Lettucy Type'; tall and more open-topped than others, it is especially tender and sweet.

Moisture and Fertility

Chinese cabbage is not one of those accommodating crops that make the most of a starved, dry situation and give a decent harvest, crowded together in any old dirt. On the contrary: it asks for moisture and organic fertility. It is also fussy about timing.

"Do not sow before July 10," warns one seed catalog. "The gradually decreasing day length and temperatures of late summer encourage beautiful heads," says another. Under stress of long, hot days, this vegetable goes to seed before forming proper heads. A hint of root disturbance, too, is enough to trigger seeding.

All things considered, July 10 to July 25 is a useful range for starting Chinese cabbage, with the earlier date applicable to more northerly gardens and the later date to those farther south or on the mild West Coast. Individual containers make for root-friendly transplanting later on.

Fill 4-inch (10-cm) pots with a good seeding mix, homemade or store-bought. Into each pot drop three or four seeds, a quarter-inch deep and cover lightly. Water pots, and, once seeds poke through, set them in a sunny window (left open to admit a breeze) or in an open cold frame situated in very light shade if possible—an old window screen, or a length of floating row cover, gives some shade and keeps flea beetles from getting at the seedlings. For the next three weeks, water as necessary and give one drink of fish emulsion, mixed to half the recommended strength.

In our garden, Chinese cabbage usually follows peas or lettuce in the scheme of things. By early August, the shriveled pea vines have been pulled up, leaving a band of ground open for replanting. At this point, it is worth taking time to prepare a special zone of fertility for each Chinese cabbage. A half-hour spent enriching the soil may mean the difference between mediocrity and excellence. You'll need a quantity of fine-textured compost and/or very old crumbly manure, and a balanced natural fertilizer. I like to use a half-sized shovel—sometimes called a border (or ladies') spade to dig a series of small holes, every 2 feet (60 cm) along the length of an intensive bed. The distance may seem excessive, but Chinese cabbage grows a lot of broad outer leaves that soon fill the space. Into each hole toss in a measured amount of fertilizer (usually a tablespoon) and two or three double handfuls of compost/manure.

The organics are then stirred thoroughly into the bottom of the hole—the little spade plunged in and turned from side to side (a washing-machine action) mixes everything without raising subsoil. After stepping lightly into the hole to compress the soil, tip seedlings out of their containers and set them firmly in the ground. Sculpt the soil around each seedling into a "soup bowl," and flooding the basin with water. Later in the day, fluff the soil to leave a loose, drier surface layer. The job is done—for now.

An organic mulch of compost, chopped straw or grass clippings, laid down when Chinese cabbages are taller, is a boon to this hungry, thirsty plant. Given organic fertility and ample moisture, this vegetable grows with astonishing speed in the heat of August. However, there may be bugs in the Brassicas: slugs, cabbage worms and flea beetles. Controls for these are detailed on pages 68–69. Earwigs, too, like to set up house in Chinese cabbage. A squirt of insecticidal soap stops them in their late-night meal.

Harvest Chinese cabbages when they look full and feel dense to the touch. Trim away outer leaves—it may seem as if half the plant ends up on the compost—to reveal the clean, pale central head. In an earwig-infested garden, be careful where you trim up Chinese cabbage (and other vegetables) that may house an earwig colony. I usually carry the whole plant to the middle of a hard flat path, or to an outlying corner of the lawn—not into the house or by the compost pile or near a garden bed. As earwigs drop out and start to scurry away, I scrunch them underfoot or by hand—careful, they pinch!—or spray them with soap.

Fall Feast

Traditionally Chinese cabbage is an ingredient in stir-fries and soups, but in our house it makes a favorite fall salad. Crisp, tender and juicy, the leaves taste mildly of both cabbage and mustard greens. To thinly sliced Chinese cabbage, add grated carrots and apples, fresh herbs—chives, lemon thyme, and tarragon are good—and dress the salad with oil and cider vinegar, yogurt and mayonnaise. Chinese cabbage will store for a month in a very cool place.

ORIENTAL RADISHES

A fine addition to a Chinese cabbage salad is grated Oriental radish, an easy root vegetable ready only in fall from a late July or later sowing. Unlike familiar red radishes, Asian radishes—either mild 'Lo Bok,' the Chinese radish, or the more pungent daikon favored by the Japanese—are white inside and out, oblong, and larger than big carrots. Daikon is so popular in Japan, it accounts for a quarter of all vegetables grown. The difference between daikon and Chinese radish may appear slight, but definite preferences prevail. "Never sell daikon to Chinese chefs," one catalog advises commercial growers. Compared to hot, long-rooted daikon, lo bok is sweeter, shorter, fatter, and not as tapered. Other "winter" radishes such as 'China Rose' and 'Black Spanish' are as big and round as a softball. All mature in less than two months from a midsummer sowing and are grown alike. Crisp in texture, these radishes may be grated and dressed with soy sauce and sesame oil, or cut into rounds for crudités—do a taste test for hotness before setting them out for guests. Radishes can also be stir-fried, added to soup or turned into pickles.

Thriving in loose, open soil, Oriental radishes can reach an impressive size. Where heavy clay is the medium, dig deeply and loosen the soil with sand or compost, being carefully not to trample on the bed after digging. Sow seeds from mid-July until the beginning of August, one inch (2.5 cm) apart, ¼ inch (0.6 cm) deep, in rows or beds. Once plants begin to touch, thin them to 6 inches (15 cm) apart. For milder roots, water every couple of days. By the end of September, radishes will be ready to pull. The fun comes at harvest time. Holding the radish by its "shoulders" (which usually poke out of the ground), wiggle and twist until it is as loose as a six-year-old's tooth, then, pop, up comes a radish that may be as big as your forearm. Like carrots, beets and rutabaga, Oriental radishes stores nicely into winter if kept just above freezing in a fairly humid environment—a traditional cold cellar, a bucket of sand in an unheated shed or the crisper in the fridge. The roots withstand light frost, and may be left in the ground through October. Pull any that are left, for use or storage, before a hard freeze hits.

ENDIVE AND ESCAROLE

Still close to their wild roots, endive and escarole usually display the best of health and vigor when seeded or transplanted in midsummer for fall maturity. Native to Asia and northern China, the original wild endive (*Cichorium endivia*) is closely related to the pretty blue-flowered chicory that decorates roadsides in Canada and the northern United States. Several garden-worthy variations are commonly available. Broad-leaved types are commonly called escarole or Batavian endive; 'Full Heart Batavian' is a standard cultivar, while 'Nuvol' is said to be "somewhat sweeter," a description to be taken with a grain of salt when it comes to naturally bitter escarole. Finely cut and curled leaves characterize 'Salad King,' 'Frisan,' 'Traviata' and others. From Europe comes *chicorée frisée* or *très fine* endive, the most cut and curly of all; 'Tosca,' 'Fin des Louvier' and 'Nina' are three. For the sake of simplicity we'll refer to all three—escarole, endive and *frisée*—as endive.

In France and Italy, endive is to salad what head lettuce is here—an everyday staple. North American palates are beginning to wake up to the pleasure of slightly bitter greens such as chicory, witloof, radicchio, dandelion, escarole and endive. If your taste in salad runs to iceberg tossed with a sweet dressing, be warned: a hint of the wild lingers in endive's pungent leaves. Their full flavor invites a hearty dressing of olive oil, balsamic or cider vinegar, garlicky croutons, fresh basil and Parmesan cheese. With a texture that cannot be described as melt-in-the-mouth, endive also stands up to warm-salad treatment. Simmered in water until tender, then baked briefly with a topping of Parmesan cheese, olive oil and bread crumbs, endive is turned into a side vegetable with Mediterranean tastes.

A hint of bitterness is welcome, but let's face it: poorly grown endive can be as tough and strong-tasting as any old dandelion. The secrets to mellowing its bite are fourfold. First, provide fertile organic soil. Second, time planting so that endive comes to maturity during the cool, damp days of early fall. Third, water often for quick, steady growth. And, finally, blanch your endive by excluding light from their centers to foster pale creamy hearts that are mild and tender compared to the green outer leaves.

ENDIVE
From Seed to Salad Bowl

Endive is an ideal crop to follow quick-growing spring spinach, lettuce, radishes and green onions. In 1885, M. Vilmorin-Andrieux wrote of endive in *The Vegetable Garden*, "The gardeners about Paris...make successional sowings up to the end of August." Endive takes about three months to develop. Since the heads are fairly frost hardy, determine its approximate starting date like this: add two or three weeks to the average date of your first fall frost and then count back three months. Here, where the growing season winds down by the end of October, we seed endive during the first half of July, using one of two methods.

The easiest way to grow endive is to seed directly in the ground, in a space left vacant by earlier vegetables. If sentiment or laziness keeps you from thinning vegetables, it is better to sow with some precision at the outset. Rather than sprinkling thickly in a furrow, sow several seeds in a close group, every 6 inches (15 cm) or so along a row. In time, all but the strongest single young plant is removed from each group. As the adolescent endives fill out to touch each other, take every other one for salads, leaving the rest to mature, nicely spaced about a foot (30 cm) apart.

As an alternative, when endive's future space is still occupied, we start seeds in 3-inch (8-cm) pots. Seedlings are handled in the manner described for Chinese cabbage. In the scheme of things, endive seedlings, spaced a foot apart, often replace passé pea vines. Being a legume, peas take in airborne nitrogen, a free fertilizer, and return it through their roots to the soil. Being a leafy plant, endive responds to nitrogen with lush growth—a compatible succession.

The usual menu of organics prepares the earth for endive in either an entire row or individual zones. A side-dressing of blood meal sprinkled around half-grown plants boosts nitrogen, as does a mulch of compost. Twice-weekly waterings in a dry spell keep endive growing, and a mid-growth drink of fish emulsion makes for fine full heads. Insects, it seems, have yet to acquire a taste for bitter greens.

There remains only blanching (literally, whitening), a process that blocks sun from the hearts of endive. Sunlight turns leaves dark green—and in endive's case, somewhat bitter; blanching keeps endive pale and mild. The process takes place during the last couple of weeks of maturity. Traditional methods tend to be tedious and time-consuming: placing whitewashed glass cloches over the plants or building inverted Vs of boards over them. In French markets you see broad, flat heads of creamy endives that have been blanched with weighted boards laid on top of them, a method that sounds more like setting a trap for earwigs and slugs. A simple, effective blanching technique is to gather up the outer leaves and tie them together with strips of soft cloth. The plant's centers must be dry at the time or they may rot. Endive will endure some frost, but the hearts are better protected from damage if the heads are tied.

TURNIPS AND RUTABAGAS

Native to northern Russia and Scandinavia, turnips thrive under cool, moist conditions, and pine when it's hot and dry. Quick growth in moist soil makes for crisp, mellow roots; turnips that poke along in hot, dry ground grow strong-tasting and woody. Fall, then, is the preferred season—fewer bugs, better weather. Seed outdoors six to eight weeks before you anticipate fall's first frost. A little compost and natural fertilizer should be

A mulch of half-decayed hay keeps the roots of tiny endive seedlings cool and damp during hot, late summer days.

adequate to feed this spartan root vegetable. If turnips follow spring lettuce or peas in soil nicely enriched for the earlier crops, simply loosen the earth before seeding. Sow seeds singly, one per inch, in a furrow as deep as the distance between fingertip and first knuckle joint. Thin seedlings as they touch to stand 3 or 4 inches (8 to 10 cm) apart.

Rutabagas or swedes—big yellow turnips—are planted only in midsummer for fall and winter eating. The plant's blue-green leaves, like those of broccoli, show its connection to the Brassica family. Native to Siberia, rutabagas can cope with cold. Fall frosts, in fact, help sweeten your swedes. Rutabaga are seeded outdoors from mid-June to mid-July, or started indoors in an uncovered cold frame, one plant per 2-inch (5-cm) pot. The timing and treatment described for Chinese cabbage is appropriate for rutabagas as well. Seed ten weeks before fall's first expected frost and transplant three weeks later. Set seedlings 10 inches (25 cm) apart. With a root system that may extend down as far as 3 feet (90 cm) in search of nutrients,

Endive crops up in several variations. The broad-leaved type is often called escarole; curly endive is known in France as frisée.

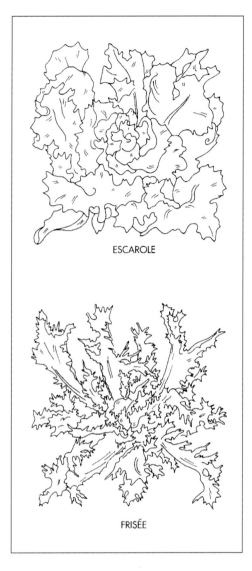

ESCAROLE

FRISÉE

roots to mature at a comfortable 10-inch (25-cm) spacing. In a dry spell, seedlings will need watering until their taproots have burrowed into the ground.

Flea beetles can be murder on tiny rutabagas, but a light dusting of rotenone should prevent damage; the tiny, shiny black hoppers are less interested in older plants. For other cole-crop insects, refer to pages 68–69. Fall rains usually see the swedes through to harvest. If rutabagas look rather skinny in September, don't worry. I'm always surprised how they continue to put on the pounds after most other things have stopped growing. Harvest rutabagas after a few light frosts have mellowed them, but before they are spoiled by a heavy freeze. An old-fashioned root cellar, cold and humid, is ideal for storage. Lacking that, we heap lots of leaves or hay around rutabagas in the garden. Thus protected, they keep beautifully until December and beyond.

MIDSUMMER MISCELLANY

There is no reason why the garden season should end abruptly on the night of fall's first frost. Fall is like a spring encore in reverse, and many of the early season vegetables thrive again as days grow cooler, shorter, damper. A bit of planning, and some timely seeding, keeps beds lush and full almost until the snow flies. Candidates for resowing in July and early August for fall picking include: beets, carrots, leaf lettuce, spinach, snow peas, radishes, mustard and turnip greens and leafy Oriental vegetables such as bok choy. All are quite quick growing and hardy enough to sail unscathed through the first round of frosts and on into Indian summer.

Gardeners soon develop an intuitive sense about when the growing season in their area winds down completely. In October, here, we revel in glorious warm interludes between spells of increasingly chilly winds and rains. By mid-November trees are bare, winds are tinged with winter and dark clouds may obscure the sun for days. Hardy vegetables continue to grow until the going gets very rough, indeed; but, like gardeners,

the big turnips usually find what they need even in less-than-ideal ground. That said, a few inches of compost turned in before transplanting or seeding helps them along.

To sow rutabagas directly in the ground, ten to twelve weeks before fall's first expected frost, open a furrow a scant inch (2.5 cm) deep. If the soil is dry, soak the little trench, and let water drain away before dropping seed in singly, one seed per inch (2.5 cm). Fill in the furrow about halfway with earth, tamping lightly with the back of a rake. When the small plants have a leaf or two, thin them to stand 5 inches (12 cm) apart; in a few weeks thin again, leaving they move slower as the days turn dark and cold.

Think for a moment: when is the season well and truly over, when are the chrysanthemums ashen and "wet flurries" in the forecast? In our area, frost can hit in mid-September, but hardy vegetables continue to grow all through October. To determine when to seed in mid-summer, we refer to the number of days to maturity on the seed package or in a catalog, count back that many days from November 1, and add several weeks to compensate for fall slowdown. For example, lettuce take about 55 to 60 days to mature. Counting back from November 1, and adding two weeks, puts the sowing date in mid- to late July.

Larkwhistle's kitchen garden is not a one-shot affair: our first outdoor seeding takes place early in April, the last in early August. Gardeners accustomed to getting everything in and over with all at once in late spring, may resist the notion of spreading the seeding and transplanting over four months or more. It takes some getting used to, some organizing of seeds, schedules and garden space. The simplest approach would be to sow a few more seeds wherever and whenever garden space becomes free. It's a short step from there to planning a full second phase around the crops that are naturally adapted to thrive in fall. When you're cutting a fresh Chinese cabbage or nicely blanched endive on a chilly late October day, you'll be glad you made the effort to start the season over again in midsummer.

CHINESE CABBAGE SALAD

For the salad:

1 head	Chinese cabbage, well trimmed	1 head
1	carrot	1
1	Oriental radish	1
1	apple, quartered, peeled and cored	1

For the dressing:

2 tbsp	mayonnaise	25 mL
5 tbsp	plain yogurt	75 mL
2 tbsp	olive (or vegetable) oil	25 mL
1 tbsp	cider (or other) vinegar	15 mL
1 tsp	lime juice	5 mL
1 tbsp each	chives and parsley, minced	15 mL each
	Salt to taste	

Cut the Chinese cabbage lengthwise from the top down, about ¾ of the way to the base. Then cut Chinese cabbage crosswise into thin shreds, stopping where it becomes more stalks than leaves. (Reserve lower portion for stir-frying.) Place Chinese cabbage in a salad bowl. Grate carrot and Oriental radish and add; grate or slice apple thinly and add.

In a large bowl whisk together dressing ingredients. Pour dressing over salad and toss well to coat.

RUTABAGA AND POTATO MASH

4–5	potatoes, scrubbed, peeled and quartered	4–5
½	rutabaga, scrubbed, peeled and cubed	½
2 cloves	garlic, peeled	2 cloves
1 tbsp	butter	15 mL
1 tbsp each	fresh chives and parsley, minced	15 mL each
pinch	nutmeg, freshly grated	pinch
	Salt and pepper to taste	

Boil potatoes and rutabaga with garlic in salted water until potatoes are cooked through. Drain well. Mash vegetables with butter, salt, pepper, nutmeg and herbs.

Green Exotica

Arugula, Corn Salad, Florence Fennel, Mustard Greens, Radicchio, Chicory and Swiss Chard

Larkwhistle's kitchen garden is well stocked with the basics. But here and there, among the tomatoes, cucumbers, lettuce, carrots, beans and onions are small plots of oddball vegetables. Visitors scratch their heads trying to identify "that leafy plant with the red stalks—it looks like rhubarb, but not quite"; and wonder out loud why on earth we'd want to plant dandelions when they can't get rid of the darn things. As the arugula, unpicked for months, goes from peppery to incendiary, we may wonder the same thing. Perhaps an old-time writer was on to something when he described gardeners as "insatiable seekers after outlandish things."

ARUGULA

Strong and peppery, with a mustardy bite, arugula has become an acquired taste for many. A recent cookbook suggests getting acquainted with it by tossing "a little to start with in your next salad," adding, "You will soon find you can't do without this pungent counterpoint in your greens." The next recipe, which I mean to try once I get past the salad stage, starts with "4 cups fresh arugula leaves" as a base for a pesto sauce. An all-arugula salad is for those who appreciate the sharp flavor—one friend thinks it tastes "kind of skunky." But there is a vast taste difference between small, young arugula leaves and overgrown older ones.

An easily grown member of the Cruciferae (or Mustard) family, arugula is also known as roquette or garden rocket. Growing in loose, low rosettes, the dark-green leaves are lobed on the bottom half and spoon-shaped above. Seldom found in markets, arugula is exceedingly easy to grow, responding to the minimal attention you'd expect to give a half-wild plant. This is a cool weather green thriving best in spring and again in fall; its compact growth makes it a natural for a square-foot corner of the garden—and that may be all you need. For an extended harvest of tender young leaves, sow a few short rows every two or three weeks.

As soon as the melting snow exposes a patch of bare ground, we set up a cold frame and seed a first round of arugula, along with mustard greens, radishes and leaf lettuce. The frame's storm-window lid holds spring's elusive warmth and excludes flea beetles, arugula's principal pest. To plant arugula, whether in a frame or in the open ground, open a shallow, 4-inch-wide (10-cm) furrow with a hand cultivator, then scatter seed thinly along the band, aiming for a seed every inch or so. A light covering of earth and a gentle watering complete the job. Thin seedlings as they touch to 2 to 3 inches (5 to 8 cm) apart at first, and eventually to twice that distance. Within a few weeks, young leaves are ready to pick, and soon after, whole plants may be cut.

Spring sowings in the open air do better under a remnant of floating row cover. Left unprotected, arugula leaves may be so riddled with flea-beetle bites they lose their appeal. Arugula is naturally strong-tasting, but it can turn unpleasant if grown slowly in hot, dry soil. Frequent drinks and possibly a light mulch help keep the leaves as tender and mild as they'll ever be.

For fall pickings, seed again one month before your anticipated first fall frost—in our garden a mid-August sowing supplies salad greens through fall. Hardy roquette sails through light frosts and continues into Indian summer and beyond. At this season insects seldom pose a problem. Looking forward to next spring, try sowing arugula the day after your first fall frost. The ensuing small plants should be tough enough to

OPPOSITE: Among the kitchen garden's more exotic offerings are dark green arugula, red and white Swiss chard, pale Florence fennel and the dramatic wine-and-white leaves of radicchio.

survive most winters, especially under snow. Come spring, they start to grow at the first warm nudge and are ready to pick well before anything else.

CORN SALAD

While traveling in France, we often bought a half-kilo of *mâche* in the outdoor markets; sold washed and trimmed, the small emerald rosettes became an instant salad course for a parkbench picnic of baguette, olives, and cheese. Better known as *Feldsalat* in Switzerland, lamb's lettuce in Britain, and corn salad in North America, the oval leaves are as delicate in taste and texture as arugula is robust.

In *The English Gardener* of 1883, William Cobbett wrote of *mâche*: "it is, indeed, a weed, and can be of no real use where lettuces are to be had." While I would never trade lettuce for corn salad, the little wilding is a nice touch in salads. In 1693, Scottish gardener John Reid wrote that lamb's lettuce was often teamed with cooked, cooled beets; modern gardener Shepard Ogden agrees and suggests dressing such a salad with walnut oil.

As hardy as arugula, corn salad can also be sown a number of times throughout the season. Seed first in a cold frame, then in the open air around the spring frost-free date and every few weeks thereafter, ending with a late-summer seeding for fall picking—a schedule that supposes an unusual passion for this small salad plant. In hot locales, growth is better in spring and late summer. Sow in bands (4 inches [10 cm] wide), one seed per inch, and thin plants to 3 inches (8 cm) apart. In nineteenth-century Britain, according to one writer, lamb's lettuce was rarely grown by itself, but rather as "useful things to sow between rows of more valuable crops." This interplanting treatment works as well today, with the quick-growing greens filling space between peppers or eggplant until they have stretched to shade the ground. Harvest whole plants when the rosettes are a few inches across and wash carefully to get out the grit. Greenhouse gardeners might experiment with a winter crop of corn salad. The shallow-rooted plants grow well in wooden flats filled with 3 or 4 inches (8 or 10 cm) of a fertile potting mix; seed in February, as the days are getting long enough to foster growth.

FLORENCE FENNEL

In the Italian city that gives this vegetable its name, I once saw mounds of pale-green finocchio heaped high beside the fava beans, peppers, and tomatoes. A familiar vegetable in Europe, Florence fennel seems to be catching on here with cooks and gardeners who appreciate its celery crunch and mild anise flavor. Although the dill-like foliage is useful for flavoring salads and fish dishes, Florence fennel is grown mainly for its "bulb," which is formed above ground where the base of leaf-stalks overlap in a tightly clasped bunch. The plant looks like celery with a wide, flat bottom, thin stalks and wispy leaves.

Related to celery but much easier to grow, Florence fennel thrives in moist, fertile soil. Like celery, the plants have a tendency to bolt to seed if subjected to root disturbance, the stress of temperature fluctuations, or the sudden onset of hot weather. Spring-planted fennel is especially prone to bolting, and may turn tough and fibrous during July's long, hot days. In any case, the bulbs are easily overlooked amid summer's abundance. All things considered, Florence fennel is a prime candidate for midsummer planting and fall maturity. September weather encourages tender growth, and light frost poses no threat to this hardy vegetable.

We grow Florence fennel almost exactly like Chinese cabbage. Start seeds in individual 2- or 3-inch (5- or 8-cm) pots in early July, and transplant carefully to the garden about three weeks later, in ground that has been enriched with compost, old manure, and natural fertilizer. In a row, each Florence fennel stands 8 inches (20 cm) from the next. An excellent follow-up vegetable, finocchio usually fills in space previously given to snow peas, lettuce or early cabbages.

In a dry August, young fennel grow much better when watered every other day—abundant moisture translates into crisp, succulent bulbs with fewer fibers. A drink of fish emulsion provides a surge of available nutrients. When bulbs are half-grown (about an inch wide) we sometimes pull loose soil up around them with a hand cultivator, or mound the row with sifted compost. This earthing-up shields bulbs from the sun for greater tenderness. In our garden, fennel seems to attract few serious predators. Earwigs take a few chews out of new transplants, but, with proper care and feeding, the feathery shoots soon outgrow their unwelcome attention.

Maturing in fall, Florence fennel retains its excellent eating quality much longer than it would in summer. When the bulbs have grown a few inches across, the harvest starts. Pull whole plants; trim away most of the top growth, leaving about an inch of stalk above the bulb. Cut off roots so that the bulb remains intact with all the segments joined at the base like a bunch of celery.

Florence fennel lends a hint of licorice to many dishes, from pasta sauces to fish soups and hearty minestrones—for all three, start by sautéeing thin strips or chunks of fennel with onion and garlic until soft, and go from there. You may find, though, that folks enjoy this unusual vegetable raw, on its own or mixed with other greens as a salad or added to a plate of veggies and dips. I usually just quarter the bulbs and set them out unadorned as an appetizer.

MUSTARD GREENS

A gardening friend once lived in a small town on the edge of agricultural land. One day the weed inspector came to check her garden for noxious plants that might infest neighboring fields. "Everything's fine," he said after looking around, "but you'll have to get rid of that mustard." "Get rid of it?" our friend countered. "I planted it." One person's weed is, indeed, another's flower—or, in this case, vegetable.

Traditionally popular in the southern States as boiling greens, the various leafy mustards are much less familiar to northern gardeners, an odd state of affairs considering that they are among the most cold-tolerant of

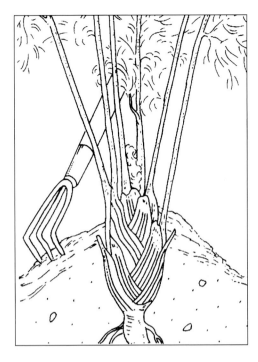

When Florence fennel is half grown, you can draw earth up over the developing bulb for greater tenderness.

plants. The term "mustard greens" applies to an array of leafy plants belonging to the Brassica (or cabbage) family. Most grow into loose, open-topped clusters of broad leaves with thick central ribs. The shape, shade and size of leaves vary with the type. 'Florida Broad Leaf' is self descriptive; 'Green Wave' mustard is curled, frilly and bitingly hot, with the same sinus-clearing sting as the related horseradish. 'Osaka Purple' grows up to a foot tall; at that stage it is fine for steaming or stir-frying, but we pick the white-ribbed, purple-shaded leaves at half that size for salads. 'Green-in-Snow,' also known simply as 'Chinese Leaf Mustard,' stays in the garden until the freezing end. 'Tokyo Beau' and 'Mizuna' are aromatic, cut-leaf mustards, mild enough to toss by the handful into mixed salads. Scattered thickly over an open square of ground in August, 'Mizuna' can be left unthinned and harvested with scissors for many weeks in fall; a friend kept a large pot of this easily grown green in a sunny window indoors all winter as an ornamental edible.

Still close to their wild roots, mustard greens usually display the best of health and vigor. Quick-growing, many are ready in little over a month. Mustard is perhaps most

Looking like a leafy red rose, radicchio 'Giulio' gradually folds into a compact head.

thin shreds, the burgundy leaves add color and bite to a salad. With white veins prominent against the red, whole leaves make a beautiful bed for smoked fish, herbed potato salad and grated carrots as a sweet counterpoint to the sharp radicchio.

Radicchio was once tricky to grow, needing careful timing, cutting back, overwintering, and indoor forcing. But that has changed with the introduction of new cultivars bred to form heads, like any lettuce, when seeded outdoors. That said, spring seeded radicchios may well run to seed in the heat of summer without heading up. Better to wait until late June or early July to sow. And search out varieties described as "sure-heading," among them 'Fiero,' 'Chiogga Red' and 'Inferno.' With luck, they will mature during the cooler days of fall.

We have also had encouraging results with 'Giulio,' a slow-bolting sort developed for spring seeding. Started indoors in April, alongside lettuce and broccoli, in small pots, this slow-poke radicchio gradually folds its burgundy leaves into grapefruit-sized heads that are ready to cut from July onward.

Seed catalogs admit that the heading radicchios are not "very uniform or completely predictable" in their growth habits; and warn us to expect "only 60% firm heads." Such uneven growth may dismay commercial growers who want to bring in the whole crop all at once, but home gardeners can live with 60 percent and, if they mature at different times, so much the better. Still, we're encouraged when a variety is touted to be "the first nearly uniform red radicchio—for all cropping periods," which is to say the plants should do well spring, summer and fall.

In May, as the lilacs are blooming, we transplant April's seedlings to a small bed, fertilized as for lettuces, spacing them a hand-span apart in a staggered grid. After that they are on their own, except for routine watering and weeding. A top-dressing of compost pushes the heads to perfection, but the near-wild plants seem to thrive without the extra attention. Bugs? None. (Ah, it felt good to say that!)

appreciated in spring and fall, when there is not much competition for the salad bowl or stir-fry pan. Our first pickings come from the same cold frames that are seeded with arugula, radishes and other quick greens as early as possible in spring. Sow one seed per inch, cover lightly, and pat the earth down over the rows; thin seedlings to 4 to 6 inches (10 to 15 cm) apart before they get too far along. The next sowing is mid-August, or about a month before we expect our first fall frost. How encouraging it is to see a stand of greens coming into their prime at a time when almost everything else is winding down.

In some gardens flea beetles find spring-sown mustard irresistible; plants grown in the open air are best protected under a floating row cover. Not fussy about soil, the pungent greens respond to any decent loam fed with a little manure or compost. Fast, steady growth results in much milder mustard. Mulch and moisture both help.

RADICCHIO, CHICORY, AND DANDELIONS
Radicchio
Closely related to chicory and dandelions, radicchio (pronounced rah-deek-ee-oh) shares their robust bitter taste. Sliced into

Radicchio can also be seeded in the garden directly either a few weeks before the spring frost-free date, or in midsummer. Plant several seeds in a close group, spacing the clusters 12 inches (30 cm) apart. Thin to the strongest seedling in each place after a few leaves have formed. Successive sowings at three-week intervals until two months before the fall frost date ensure a steady supply. If you have been reluctant to pay the price for radicchio in the market, consider that 2 square feet (0.2 m²) of ground will grow nine red heads or more.

Chicory

When I was growing up in Toronto, many of my Italian relatives would take to the city's ravines and wilder places every spring to dig *cicoria* for salads, soups and pasta with greens. Nobody gave pollution a second thought then. What they were after was the same plant that just about everyone else was trying to get rid of—the lowly dandelion. Since the wild-dandelion season is so short, Italian gardeners often cultivate their favorite *verdura* in the garden; I have one old relative who grows nothing else. Compared to your average lawn specimen, a cultivated dandelion is grand indeed. Look for 'Catalogna Special' or 'Cicoria Catalogna' (a.k.a 'Radichetta'), 'Dentarella' or simply 'Italian Dandelion.' Quite literally big improvements on wild dandelions, these fancy "weeds" are grown like lettuce, their not-too-distant cousin, except that dandelions are spaced 8 inches (20 cm) apart in all directions. Spring seeding or transplanting is possible, but dandelions do better if sown about two months before your average fall frost date. You'll have to keep your weeds weed-free, watered and fed for milder flavor, but nothing removes the bitterness altogether. Harvest any time after leaves are 4 inches (10 cm) tall by snipping individual shoots or cutting whole plants, leaving the crowns to sprout again. Left to develop, Italian dandelions can reach heights that may have the neighbors looking askance.

Very satisfying to grow and eat are the "sugar loaf" chicories that grow much like romaine lettuces—upright, conical heads within a swirl of broad outer leaves. Look for seeds of 'Pan de Zucchero' or 'Sugar Loaf.' Their nicely blanched centers are as close as we get to those lovely pale-yellow Belgian endives that are so expensive to buy and so hard to grow at home. 'Sugar Loaf' chicory is seeded soon after the summer solstice (June 21), sowing three or four seeds ¼ inch (5 mm) deep, in close clusters, 12 inches (30 cm) between the groups. When seedlings are a few inches tall, we thin to the strongest one in each spot. Growing slowly all summer, the heads fill out nicely by September and stand unharmed in the garden through fall's first few light frosts. Before a hard freeze, we cut any remaining heads and store them in a cold, moderately damp place, where they'll keep for several weeks.

SWISS CHARD

I can't imagine the garden without Swiss chard, a lovely, leafy plant that is always there when you hanker for a feed of greens. A slow and steady grower, chard stands in the garden from June until late October, without turning tough and bitter, seedy, or overripe. While corn rushes past its prime and all the beans need picking at once, chard waits for you.

Still found growing wild in the Canary Islands and around the Mediterranean, chard is (as one old book notes) "the beet as it was grown by the Greeks and Romans." The ancient plant was thin-stemmed and smooth-leaved, more like today's "spinach beet." Through centuries of breeding and selection, this simple green has been transformed into Swiss chard, a robust biennial distinguished by wide fleshy stalks, either white or red, and broad, dark green, crumpled leaves.

Few edibles are as ornamental; few keep their looks for so long. With dark glossy leaves and brilliant stalks, red-stemmed chards such as 'Ruby' and 'Charlotte' are dramatic accents anywhere in the garden, all the more striking contrasted with green-and-white 'Fordhook Giant' or 'White King.' For a row of many colors, the new 'Bright Lights' grows chard of pink, purple, orange,

A half-dozen pots of Swiss chard, both the red-stemmed 'Ruby' chard and the glossy green type, start a family off on a long harvest of tasty, nutritious greens.

yellow and red. Every spring we plant a small but prominent bed with both red and green chard next to blue-green curly kale. Once the textured leaves fill out, the corner remains lush and fresh-looking for the next four months, all the while supplying a perpetual harvest of tasty, vitamin-rich greens. A bonus: Chard is one of the few food plants that does well in light shade.

In the past, we used to seed Swiss chard in the garden, like beets and carrots, toward the end of May. The results were uneven. One year would see a thriving row, more chard than we could ever use; the next, a patch that can only be described as patchy. Earwigs, slugs and flea beetles are all partial to newly sprouted chard. Since a dozen well-grown plants keep us in greens, it seemed a simple matter to add that many more pots to the windowsill season.

We now start chard indoors, or in a cold frame, about a month before our spring frost-free date. Four-inch (10-cm) containers give the quick-growing roots some space to roam. An indoor start gives us hefty young plants that are much less appealing to insects. It also allows us to prepare a deep fertile bed by turning under spadesful of compost and/or old manure boosted with natural fertilizer. Because we want Swiss chard to expand to its full decorative potential, we space them a generous foot apart. That said, I know many gardeners who seed Swiss chard directly in the ground toward the end of May with excellent results.

As a leafy crop, chard responds to an extra helping of nitrogen fertilizer—a palmful of blood meal stirred into the soil around each plant, and/or a mulch of compost or strawy old manure. Fish emulsion, applied once a month, works wonders, as does a deep weekly soaking. But note: Wetting leaves in the evening is a sure way to encourage fungus. Chard's principal insect pest is the leaf miner, a small, squishy, pale-green maggot that burrows between a leaf's thin layers. Its tunneling shows up as squiggly white trails or blotchy areas. Unless miners arrive in great numbers, the damage may be merely cosmetic. Having trapped themselves in a leaf, miners can be crushed by hand. Look for the clusters of tiny white eggs on the undersurface of leaves at the same time. It is best to collect badly infested foliage for burning or disposal, and to shift the patch around the garden. Garden fabric or netting protects chard, but you lose its decorative value.

Earwigs, too, lodge between the stalks of chard, nibbling the new growth which then grows up full of holes. Spraying down into the crowns with soap solution—a teaspoon of dish soap to a liter/quart of water send the pincered pest scurrying (and kills them, too). I always follow the soap treatment with a rinse of clear water from the hose or watering can.

Sometimes recommended for salads, raw chard has (to my taste) a certain throat-catching harshness, like raw beet greens, probably due to its oxalic acid content. All that changes, however, when chard is simmered until tender; stalks are especially savory. Much milder than spinach or beet tops, steamed chard, seasoned simply with butter or olive oil and a touch of garlic, is a favorite dish of garden greens. Since stalks take a longer time to cook than leaves, slice them diagonally into one-inch pieces and put them on to steam or simmer for a few minutes before adding the torn leaves. A rich source of vitamins A, C, B_1 and B_2, a serving of chard contains a walloping 15,000 units of vitamin A, and goodly amounts of iron, calcium and phosphorus. Nutritious, practical, easy to grow, prolific and ornamental: After one season, Swiss chard moved from the realms of exotica to our list of basics.

ARUGULA AND ROQUEFORT SALAD

For the salad:

2 handfuls	arugula, washed and dried	2 handfuls
	Grated carrots	
	Cooked new potatoes, sliced	
	Beets, sliced	

For the dressing, mix together:

¾ cup	plain yogurt	175 mL
⅓ cup	olive oil	75 mL
⅓ cup	crumbled Roquefort	75 mL
1	garlic clove, pressed	1
1 tbsp	fresh chives, minced	15 mL
1 tsp	lemon juice	5 mL
1 tsp	honey	5 mL
1 tbsp	fresh basil, minced	15 mL
	Freshly ground pepper to taste	

On a plate, arrange the arugula, carrots, potatoes and beets. Pour on the dressing. Serves two to four.

PASTA FINOCCHIO

The tarragon enhances the licorice taste of fennel in this quick pasta sauce.

2	medium fennel bulbs	2
3 tbsp	olive oil	50 mL
1 tbsp	sweet butter	15 mL
2	garlic cloves, minced	2
1 tbsp	fresh French tarragon, minced	15 mL
pinch	fresh nutmeg	pinch
3 tbsp	bread crumbs	45 mL
1 cup	milk or soy milk	250 mL
	Salt and pepper to taste	
	Fusili or other pasta	
	Grated Parmesan cheese	

Quarter the fennel bulb and slice thinly crosswise. Sauté fennel in oil and butter over medium heat until translucent and just soft. Add the garlic, shallots, tarragon and nutmeg, and sauté for a few minutes longer. Stir in bread crumbs, then add milk or soy milk and simmer until the sauce thickens slightly. Add salt and pepper to taste and serve the sauce over freshly cooked fusili or other pasta. Pass the grated Parmesan and garnish, if desired, with strips of roasted peppers. Serves four.

FENNEL, CARROT AND SQUASH SOUP

Fennel bulbs give a mild anise flavor, while tomatoes balance the sweetness of carrots and squash in this easy low-fat fall soup. For richer taste, add a little butter, milk or cream during the final reheating.

1 tbsp	butter	15 mL
1 tbsp	vegetable oil	15 mL
1	onion, diced	1
1 stalk	celery	1 stalk
2 bulbs	Florence fennel, diced	2 bulbs
2	carrots, diced	2
2 cups	winter squash, cubed	500 mL
1 cup	tomatoes, puréed	250 mL
4 cups	water or stock (vegetable or chicken)	1 L
½ tsp	mild curry powder	2 mL
½ tsp	salt (or to taste)	2 mL
	Pepper to taste	

In a large soup pot, sauté onion and celery with salt for a few minutes. Add diced fennel and carrot and sauté for several minutes more. Add curry powder and stir to coat vegetables. Add puréed tomatoes, squash and water or stock. Bring soup to a boil, then turn heat down to simmer. Simmer soup gently for 40 minutes. Purée soup to a thick, smooth consistency. Reheat, correct seasonings and serve.

All about Alliums
Garlic, Shallots, Egyptian Onions and Wild Leeks

Allium is the botanical name for a group of bulbous plants that includes not only some lovely flowering perennials known as ornamental onions, but also every cook's standby, the indispensable onion itself. Branching out, there is a lot of flavor to be found in several easily grown alliums: garlic, shallots, chives, garlic chives and Egyptian onions; and from the woods come wild leeks, a favorite of foragers. All sprout a sheaf of flat or round leaves that gradually mature, in the process storing food for next year in underground bulbs.

GARLIC

At Larkwhistle, planting the garlic is one of fall's most enjoyable rites. Sometime in late September, we take an hour to "seed" one of the wide kitchen-garden beds with garlic cloves. Next July (with luck), we'll pull enough full-sized bulbs, or heads, to see us through a year. I'm always surprised by garlic's generous return for so little work—plant one clove, harvest a nicely wrapped cluster of ten.

Garlic is associated with the Mediterranean, with hot southern lands such as Italy, Spain and Greece. It might grow in California, too, but for years I had assumed that it couldn't be grown here in our central Canadian Zone 5 frost-pocket. The assumption was shattered one September day, when a friend arrived with a basket of big, beautiful, organic garlic that had come, not from way down south, but from a nearby garden. On her advice, we planted a small experimental patch the next day—and we have been reveling in the "reeking rose" ever since.

Visitors often ask if they can start a patch with store-bought garlic. I wouldn't. Usually imported from China, commercial garlic is often sprayed with a sprout and root inhibitor that confuses its natural growth cycle; bulbs may rot before they root. And having come from the south, store-bought garlic may not be suitable for our harsher climate. Much better to start with locally grown stock of proven hardiness, and lately there is quite a bit around. If we need new planting stock, we can almost count on finding it at a local farmer's market in October.

Garlic is as hardy and easy to grow as any lily; in fact, the two are distant cousins related under the family name Liliaceae. Like lilies, garlic is best planted in the fall. Sometime in September, after frost has blackened beans, tomatoes and peppers, we choose one of the garden beds for garlic. To prepare the earth, we whiten the surface with bone meal (or a balanced natural fertilizer) before spreading an inch of fine-textured compost or crumbly old manure. After turning in the soil amendments, we rake the ground to a fine tilth. If the garlic bed-to-be is weedy or stony, you'd do well to pick out the largest rocks and make an effort to turf out as many weed roots as possible.

Every year, at harvest time, we reserve some of our finest bulbs for replanting. When the bed is ready, we break the heads into individual cloves, being careful to retain their protective papery covering. Very small cloves are set aside for kitchen use. We then space the cloves, at 6-inch (15-cm) intervals, in short rows across the bed, with rows spaced 10 inches (25 cm) apart. In freshly dug, fluffy, sandy soil you may be able to push the cloves in by hand, as deep as your index finger is long. Otherwise, trowel out little planting holes. A warm, drawn out fall will often induce thin blades of garlic grass to emerge and continue growing until

OPPOSITE: *Pest-free and easy to grow, a bed of garlic starts from single cloves planted the previous fall. In less than a year, one garlic clove yields a cluster of eight or ten.*

checked by severe cold. In regions where snow is here today, gone tomorrow, it is wise to mulch beds with straw, hay, or leaves in late fall to prevent freeze-and-thaw cycles from heaving the cloves out of the ground.

Come spring, the receding snow uncovers a bed studded with sprouting garlic that begins to grow with remarkable vigor at the first hint of warmth. By June the arching gray-green leaves, a foot tall or more, are conspicuous in a garden full of small seedlings. More than one visitor has looked at the garlic bed then, and wondered why the "corn" was so far ahead. The day after a June downpour, we do a once-over weeding before mulching the garlic bed with old hay to conserve moisture and suppress weeds. But mulching is not an absolute must— many growers harvest excellent garlic from unmulched plots.

Mulched or not, garlic generally takes care of itself. In a dry season, soak the bed occasionally. Needless to say, insects give the garlic (which has built-in insecticidal properties) a wide berth.

By midsummer, a sort of curled pigtail, topped with a small papery "bulb," emerges from the center of each plant. Peel back the thin husk to reveal a tight cluster of small green garlics, ideal for use, whole, chopped, or blended, in pickles, pesto, sauces, salad dressings and roasted dishes. Some gardeners pick off these "seed heads" in order to divert all of the plant's juice to the underground garlic. One summer, as an experiment, we snapped the top bulbs off some plants, and left others on. At harvest, there was no discernible difference between the two. Use the top bulbs and stalks—now sold as a gourmet item, scapes—to extend the fresh garlic season. Do not, however, plant the small bulbs, which take at least two seasons to grow to full size.

By late July, or when roughly half of the leaves have withered and turned yellow, we dig the garlic. If bulbs are left in the ground much longer, especially in wet weather, they continue to plump up and may split their skins. Garlic bulbs keep much better if properly cured, a process that dries and sets their skins. To do that, we lay out the whole plants—bulbs, shrivelling tops and roots—in a single layer on a slatted bench in an airy garden shed, and roll them around once or twice over the course of the next two weeks. By then the tops are dry and crackling, and bulbs are encased in crisp papery skins. Finish the bulbs by rubbing off caked earth and loose flakes of husk. Snip off roots close to the bulbs' base and cut off tops, leaving a stub of an inch or so. Put aside for immediate use any bulbs that have split their skins or are a touch moldy. The rest are ready to store in open baskets or mesh bags, in a dry, cool spot, where they should keep firm and fresh for months. Some day I'll learn how to turn out those decorative garlic braids.

Garlic breath? Eating lots of fresh green herbs, especially lovage, parsley and celery, with a garlic-laced dish helps mute the "sulphorous stink" that is garlic's chief virtue in the kitchen but a liability in some company. But the surest cure is to feed it to family and friends so you can all breathe easier.

Elephant Garlic

When elephant garlic suddenly appeared in catalogs, I was suspicious. If this were such a splendid allium—"produces huge bulbs… flavor is milder than regular garlic"—where had it been hiding until now? Of course, we had to try it. But after one season we knew we would never trade our patch of the real thing for this disappointing novelty. Planted next to regular garlic, the supposed giant failed to reach mammoth proportions—not that we'd know what to do with a one-pound garlic clove. Worse, a hint of bitterness underlies the mild flavor. The off-putting taste disappears with cooking, but then the bulbs are bland. We keep a small patch going perennially at one end of a vegetable bed for the sake of the handsome flat leaves and decorative pale lilac flowers—an ornamental allium.

SHALLOTS

Rosy-skinned shallots are so often linked with gourmet cooking that ordinary gardeners might assume that they are as tricky to grow as white asparagus. Scarcity and high price adds to the illusion that shallots are for specialists. Not so: just push single bulbs up to their necks, about 6 inches (15 cm) apart, into any good garden soil. Shallots are often planted in early spring, but they are hardy enough to go into the ground in fall like garlic. Under cover of snow or a fluffy mulch, the bulbs will come through winter and begin to grow first thing in spring. One shallot turns into an aggregate of six or more by midsummer. When tops have died back, lift the clusters, curing and storing the shallots precisely as you would garlic. Shallots become perennial if you choose some of this season's bulbs for replanting, thus perpetuating your own from year to year.

EGYPTIAN ONIONS

"A vegetable triffid" is how one visitor described our Egyptian onions, a gangling perennial allium that looks ready to take giant steps across the garden. No other plant gets around in quite the same way. In place of flowers, this onion sports a cluster of bulblets atop its fat hollow stalk, and often another cluster above. One day the whole thing collapses from sheer weight and down comes the stalk, top onions and all. The little bulbs waste no time putting down roots where they land, often several feet from the parent, and then raising a new family that moves on from there. The "walking onion" is an apt alias.

Plant Egyptian onions where they have room to roam, and leave them alone; or, if you are a more orderly gardener, collect the top bulbs in mid-summer and line them out in a row like onion sets. Either way, this allium provides the season's first green onions without any further intervention. Later the bulblets can be peeled and pickled like pearl onions, popped into a ratatouille or roasted vegetable dish or chopped for cold summer soups. You can begin a perennial plantation of Egyptian onions in spring, summer or fall—anytime a handful of bulblets comes your way. If they start to traipse

too far, surplus bulbs are easily dug up and re-positioned, or given away. Tossed on the compost heap, they are sure to sprout.

WILD LEEKS

In his guide to wild food, Roger Tory Peterson describes wild leeks, *Allium tricoccum*, as "our best wild onion." Not only is this woodland native the only wild onion I know, it is also one of the strongest-tasting alliums, wild or tame—not even raw garlic packs such a kick. Also known as ramps, wild leeks ramp in great profusion under the maples and beech trees of our local woods, and (says Peterson) throughout southern Canada and the northeastern United States. As hepaticas and spring beauties fade and trilliums light up the forest, the wide, dark-green leek leaves emerge so thickly that they cover the ground in many places. After attempting to pull the bulbs from the ground, and coming up with handfuls of leaves, we have learned to take a strong trowel along on our woodland walk to pry leeks out of the dense, root-ridden woodland soil.

To prepare this best of wild foods, wash soil from the leeks, peel back a layer or two of onion skin to reveal the clean white bulbs, pare off roots, trim the leaves and rinse again.

There is nothing subtle about the flavor of wild leeks, but after a winter of stored vegetables, we welcome their pungency in May's robust salads along with young dandelion leaves, cold-frame-grown mustard greens and radishes, young asparagus, snippets of lovage and chives—a tonic mixture of whatever is fresh, green and growing. A hearty, healthful soup begins with lots of chopped wild leeks sautéed in oil or butter. Add water or stock and cubed potatoes; season with fresh lovage (or celery), sorrel, caraway seed and any other spring herbs that take your fancy. Add salt and pepper to taste, and simmer until the potatoes are tender. Serve as is, or purée the soup, adding some milk or soy milk (if you like) before reheating.

ROASTED SUMMER VEGETABLE PASTA SAUCE

Garlic, onions and tomatoes are essential in this easy-to-make sauce. Add zucchini and/or eggplant as available. Oven roasting saves standing over the stove and stirring. Start the pasta 10 minutes before the herb-infused sauce is done.

2–3	onions, red or yellow	2–3
5–10 cloves	garlic	5–10 cloves
1	eggplant and/or	1
1	zucchini	1
3–5	ripe tomatoes	3–5
handful	rosemary, oregano, thyme, marjoram, finely chopped Whole basil leaves	handful
10–15	cured black olives, pitted and halved (optional) Olive oil, salt, pepper	10–15

Preheat the oven to 350°F (180°C). Peel and cut onions into quarters or sixths. Peel garlic cloves and leave whole. Cut eggplant, if using, into chunks; cut zucchini into thick rounds. Leaving aside tomatoes and basil, toss the vegetables with a liberal amount of olive oil to coat thoroughly; add a generous amount of salt and pepper, and a handful of minced herbs and toss again. Herbs will adhere to the oil-coated vegetables. Turn vegetables into a casserole dish large enough to hold them in (more or less) a single layer. Cover and roast vegetables for 45 minutes. Uncover and add tomatoes, cored and quartered, whole basil leaves and olives, stirring them into the other vegetables. Continue to roast, uncovered, for 30 minutes or more, or until the tomatoes are partially "melted" down—sauce may look a little watery. Correct seasonings and spoon sauce over cooked pasta. Drizzle on a little olive oil if desired. Serve without Parmesan to let herb flavors shine through.

ROASTED GARLIC PASTE

Make this versatile pesto variation with fresh garlic bulbs in mid-summer, or dried bulbs in fall or winter. At any season, roasting sweetens this pungent and healthful allium. Fresh basil is ready in summer, while parsley stays green until the snow flies. Garlic paste may be spread over toasted bread and topped with diced tomatoes to make bruschetta, or spread over thick slabs of tomatoes before broiling. Dollop into rice or mashed potatoes, or mix with Parmesan cheese and add to pastas or vegetable soup. Keep for up to two days, tightly covered, in the refrigerator.

5 whole bulbs	garlic	5 whole bulbs
¼ cup	olive oil	50 mL
3 tbsp	fresh basil or parsley, finely chopped Salt to taste	50 mL

Peel away the loose papery skin from garlic bulbs, leaving the whole bulb, or head, intact. Oil a roasting dish small enough to hold garlic heads in one layer. Cover the bottom of the dish with water. Roast garlic in a 350° (180°C) oven until soft, about 45 minutes, adding a bit more water if needed. Remove garlic and allow to cool. Separate and peel cloves, then squeeze out the garlic. Mash garlic with oil, salt and herbs until blended and creamy.

Kitchen-Garden Perennials
Asparagus, Jerusalem Artichokes and Sorrel

Most vegetable plants are annuals, growing from seed to maturity in one season. Tender annuals such as tomatoes are stopped in their tracks by frost. Hardy annuals grow on into fall, and the very hardiest—kale, parsley, and Brussels sprouts—are usable even after they have been frozen solid. But all finish up within a year. Perennial food plants, like flowers, come back year after year; but unlike the plethora of perennial flowers, only a handful of edibles are hardy enough to survive even one winter, let alone many.

ASPARAGUS

Alphabetically, and in every other way, asparagus is the pre-eminent perennial vegetable. Short season and high prices have contributed to asparagus's reputation as a gourmet vegetable. At one time I thought it must be a frail and fussy plant, a specialty crop beyond the skills of an ordinary gardener. On the contrary, the delicate spears rise from one tough and hardy plant, a perennial that survives winters far into the north and returns for as long as most of us will tend a garden.

Our first asparagus bed, in ground freshly broken for the purpose, was an unqualified failure. We thought we had done everything by the book—careful trenching, fertilizing and planting— but weeds got the best of us. After three seasons, when (according to the book) we should have been cutting fat spears, only a few stringy shoots managed to push through a jungle of perennial weeds. Serious weeding ensued, but there was no hope of obliterating the quack grass, goldenrod and bindweed that infected the asparagus bed. Trying to release the asparagus from their grip proved a losing battle. In the end, we decided to start over, this time in a space that had already been cultivated for several seasons.

The moral: Before you plant any perennial vegetable (or flower, for that matter), see that the roots of persistent weeds have been thoroughly turfed out. A once-over digging may not do it. Missed roots will begin to rise again as lusty thistles or many-tentacled grasses the moment you turn your back. Tilling only multiplies the problem by chopping roots into lots of lively pieces. There is a compelling reason for making a thorough job of the preliminary groundwork: Once planted, asparagus stays in place for decades—indeed, some well-tended plots have grown on productively for over a century.

An asparagus bed should be situated in full sun, and in a place where the ferny asparagus fronds, often reaching over 6 feet (1.8 m), will not cast a shadow on other vegetables. With the site chosen, digging is next: a slow, deep and careful removal of sod, rocks and all traces of perennial weeds. This is best done in fall or early spring. Then you wait. After the next rain, the patch will green-up again as missed roots and weed seeds, brought to the surface in the first round of digging, begin to sprout. If you can tell perennial weeds from annuals, do some spot digging to round up the former, before hoeing (or tilling) the annuals. If not, you had better redig the whole patch.

At this point, you have two choices: Either repeat the digging process several times over the course of one season, or use the space for summer vegetables. Potatoes are excellent for the purpose since there is a lot of earth-moving—opening trenches, hilling-up, digging the tubers—involved in their culture. The goal is a clean bed ready to receive asparagus next spring. Of course, if you are starting with a tame, relatively weedless lawn, you may get away with removing

OPPOSITE: Week after week, from mid-May until well into November, Larkwhistle's kitchen garden yields a marvelous bounty of fresh, lively food filled with flavor and nutrition.

Asparagus, the garden's first vegetable, is a welcome treat. If you do the groundwork thoroughly at the start, you can expect to gather this delicious perennial every spring for decades.

the sod in fall, and digging the patch over before planting in spring.

In most areas, April, or just as soon as the soil is workable, is the time to make a new asparagus bed. Traditionally, roots are set in fairly deep trenches, well enriched with compost and manure. It's a tradition worth keeping. Although asparagus can be grown from seed, a much better start is made with two-year-old roots. Ours came through the mail, but they are often available at well-stocked garden centers in spring. It is a good idea to buy a few more roots than you need to fill a bed because some are bound to be weak or rotten. Mail-order sources should send stock at the right time for planting. Keep roots moist, but not sodden, covered with damp earth, until you are ready to plant.

Asparagus for Four

With careful soil preparation, asparagus can grow much closer together than the usual recommendation—that is, roots 2 feet (60 cm) apart in rows 4 feet (120 cm) apart. Planted intensively, a 5 foot (1.5 m) by 30 foot (9 m) bed will hold forty roots—two rows of twenty—enough to provide an

abundant harvest for a family of four. The following steps for creating such a bed are adaptable to any size or shape. I'm assuming the bed is part of a larger cleared space, but you could have an island of asparagus surrounded by lawn, if you were willing to edge it twice a year. The same instructions and spacing of roots apply to smaller beds.

To Make an Asparagus Bed

1. Once the ground has been thoroughly cleared of perennial weeds and grass roots, use stakes and string to mark out the sides of the bed, 30 feet long (9 m) by 5 feet (1.5 m) wide. Use two more lengths of string to define a 2-foot (60-cm) path on either side of the bed.
2. With a shovel and/or rake, scrape up several inches of topsoil from each path and put onto the bed itself, spreading it around evenly. Rake the bed to a smooth, level surface. Level pathways with a rake, clearly defining the edges of the raised bed.
3. Measuring in 12 inches (30 cm) from either edge of the bed, reposition the strings to mark off two 12-inch-wide bands as shown in the diagram; these will be the trenches.
4. Using a square-blade spade (rather than a rounded shovel), dig out a spade's depth of soil from the marked bands, piling it carefully on either side. This layer of earth will be primarily topsoil.
5. See that the sides of the trenches are as straight as possible and then square off the bottom, scraping away soil until you see a change in color, which marks the transition to subsoil.
6. Remove subsoil, piling it into a wheelbarrow (or buckets) as you go, until the trenches measure about 14 inches (35 cm) deep. Rich in minerals (if low in humus), the subsoil can be added in thin layers to the compost heap.
7. What is needed, at this point, is finetextured compost, and/or crumbly aged cattle or horse manure, and/or finished leaf mold—your basic "muck," as

Gogh, the Jerusalem artichoke is a hardy, self-sufficient food plant that can be tucked in a sunny, out-of-the-way corner of the garden and forgotten—that is, unless it threatens to grow out of bounds. Once planted, it will be with you perennially. Our introduction to this unusual vegetable came when a gardening friend brought us three sprouting tubers one April day. With the gift came some advice and a warning: "They're tall and they spread like crazy; plant them where they won't be in the way or shade the garden. You might enjoy them next spring when there's nothing else in the garden—just leave them in the ground until then."

The tubers were planted in an otherwise wasted space against a cedar-rail fence, between the garden shed and a mulberry bush where the compost pile used to be. Except for a leftover layer of compost, the sandy ground was unimproved. Over the summer, sturdy stalks of heart-shaped leaves rose up until they were waving above our heads—all without watering, weeding or fussing on our part. By October the plants were blooming nicely, a flurry of yellow-petaled, sweetly scented daisies. As winter approached, we piled leaves around to protect the tubers; stalks were left standing all winter to mark the spot. When the snow began to fade in March, we pulled back the leaves and found (as hoped) soft, unfrozen earth. Digging in at the base of the stalks, we came up with six or more tubers for every one we had planted. Over the next few weeks, we dug 'chokes as needed until we had harvested the lot, or so we thought. In early May we replanted five reserved tubers to perpetuate the patch. By mid-June, however, a dozen or more sunflower stalks were pushing strongly out of the ground.

The warning: Jerusalem artichokes will sprout from every fragment of broken tuber. Needless to say, if you rip through a patch with a tiller, you'll be coping with the scattered volunteers forever after. Even as early as 1833, one William Cobbett was complaining, "This plant…to the great misfortune of the human race, is everywhere but too well known." With a little care, it is not too

difficult to keep a patch under control: a dig in time saves a lot of work later on. Every spring we make an effort to dig up every last tuber. If we uncover more than we can use or give away, we dump the surplus in a back field, well away from the garden, for the wild creatures to munch. Never put Jerusalem artichokes in the compost. We still replant the usual five tubers every May, but now we're not so shocked when quite a few more pop up on their own.

There is no trick to growing Jerusalem artichokes: For an average family, three to five plants should be enough. Plant whole or cut tubers in early spring or fall, setting them 4 inches (10 cm) deep and 1 to 2 feet (30 to 60 cm) apart in a sunny spot, in reasonably good, well-drained soil. Sandy ground enables the tuber to fill out better. At over 6 feet (1.8 m) tall, the plants are well placed along the sunny side of an outbuilding or shed, where they have genuine decorative value. Harvest some tubers in fall. Mulch the patch to protect tubers over winter for another harvest in early spring. Tubers keep much better in the ground than out, so dig only what you need for a feed. Keep an eye on the patch for signs of expansionism. That done, you can count on a perennial supply of nutritious, tasty root when they are most appreciated.

At the tail end of winter a body craves something fresh and lively; and what better spring tonic than root vegetables and greens that come straight from earth to table. Eaten

Looking like over-grown dill, asparagus fronds form a feathery hedge that blends in decoratively with the mix of vegetables, herbs, and flowers in the kitchen garden.

One of our gardening goals is to eat fresh from the garden as early and as late in the season as possible. The first harvest— spinach, asparagus, leaf lettuce, green onions and various herbs—are ready for the table in mid-May, the time when gardeners who follow tradition may be just getting around to planting seeds.

raw, steamed, baked and in soups, Jerusalem artichokes are a welcome addition to the garden's early menu of wintered-over parsnips and carrots, tangy sorrel and dandelion greens, wild leeks and watercress, asparagus and the new shoots of perennial onions and herbs. Considered an excellent substitute for potatoes in a diabetic's diet, the tubers contain no starch; instead, they store sweetness as levulose, a form tolerated by the sugar-sensitive. As well, they are one of the few vegetable sources of vitamin B_{12}, or pantothenic acid.

The lack of starch means that an overboiled 'choke is soggy, bland and unappealing. Steamed just to the point of tenderness, their mild nutty sweetness comes through. Raw 'chokes have a refreshing crispness reminiscent of Chinese water chestnuts. A simple spring salad combines grated carrots and artichokes with watercress and minced wild leeks (or chives); dress with a lemon-and-oil vinaigrette seasoned with sorrel, lovage, lemon thyme or whatever garden-fresh herbs you have.

We couldn't get a hold of the Queen's recipe, but how about a sweet and creamy soup featuring a trio of spring roots— parsnips, carrots and artichokes.

SORREL

At spring's first softening, light-green, puckered sorrel leaves begin to sprout. Growing unattended for many years in the dappled shade of an open-topped apple tree, our single clump provides all the sorrel we need for many months. I'm never sure whether to call this plant herb or a vegetable. Like any herb, the sharp, lemony leaves season salads, omelets and soup. Finely minced with chives, lemon thyme and chervil, sorrel turns plain cream cheese into a special spread. I like the suggestion of adding pureed sorrel to mayonnaise as a sauce for fish, hot or cold; and using a little chopped sorrel instead of a lot of salt in a sodium-restricted diet. Then again, like carrots or broccoli, sorrel is featured as a solo vegetable in a creamy soup. Steamed with a bit of butter, a potful of leaves cooks down like spinach; garlic, grated Parmesan, and bread crumbs mellow the acidic bite. Then there is the simple pleasure of munching the refreshing vinegary leaves as you work in the garden.

Native to Britain, the original skinny-leaved sorrel, *Rumex acetosa*, was adopted by enthusiastic French cooks as *l'oseille* and transformed by French gardeners into fancy, broad-leaved cultivars such as 'Blond de Lyon' and 'Nobel.' Seeds or small nursery plants will get you started. The surest way with seeds is to start them in early spring in small pots set in a sunny window or cold frame. Sow a half-dozen seeds in each container, and thin eventually to the strongest single seedling in each. Transfer the young plants to the garden when they look large enough to fend for themselves. I can't imagine any household needing more than three sorrel plants, but a single clump can be turned into several more by dividing the roots just as new growth resumes in spring. Pry the plant out of the soil with a spading fork; bounce it a few times on the ground to shake away some of the earth, the better to see the natural dividing lines. Use a sharp knife and pruning shears to sever the ties that bind, and replant divisions.

Like all plants cultivated for their leaves, sorrel responds to moist, organically fertile soil with lush, tender growth. To that end, we turn under several shovels of compost or aged manure for each plant, and surround the clumps with a moisture-holding mulch of straw, leaves or compost. With a preference for cooler weather, sorrel is at its tart best for weeks in spring. The long hot days around the summer solstice trigger the formation of seed stalks and tough, harsh leaves. No matter: We never miss sorrel when the garden is full of other food. Experts suggest cutting off seed stalks, but we've found that there is no way to prevent the plants from heeding nature's call sooner or later. We let sorrel go until midsummer, cutting it back before seeds ripen and scatter—no point encouraging yet another self-inflicted weed. Once trimmed, sorrel starts growing fresh, tender leaves again and continues into fall. I like what one garden book has to say about pests and disease that might afflict sorrel: "None of note."

Sorrel may strike a sour note on the tongue, but, according to folk medicine, its acidic property acts as a "general tonic for the liver." I like to think that it is no coincidence that sorrel sprouts so early in spring, just when a tonic is most needed to remedy the winter blahs. What better way to take your tonic/medicine than as a hot bowl of sorrel and wild leek soup?

It's curious how the pendulum of fashion swings. Until the seventeenth century, sorrel was a popular kitchen-garden inhabitant in Britain. It then began to fall from favor, until, by the nineteenth century, it was found "only on fashionable tables." Nowadays, sorrel seems to be more trendy than commonplace, but there is no reason why this stalwart perennial shouldn't return to kitchen gardens everywhere.

SESAME STIR-FRIED ASPARAGUS

Green onions are ready in the garden at the same time as asparagus. This is a quick dish for those who like sesame, and may be elaborated with chunks of tofu or chicken. Serve with rice or pasta.

2 handfuls	asparagus	2 handfuls
1 clove	garlic (optional)	1 clove
1–2 tbsp	sesame oil	15–25 mL
1 tbsp	sesame seeds, toasted	15 mL
1 tbsp	tamari sauce	15 mL
2	green onions, slivered	2

Cut off the bottom ¼ of asparagus stalks. Slice remaining asparagus tops on the diagonal into pieces about ½ inch (1.25 cm) wide. Heat sesame oil in a skillet or wok and sauté garlic briefly if using. Add asparagus and stir fry over medium heat for 4 minutes. Add slivered green onions and stir fry for another minute. Add tamari sauce and cook asparagus for another minute. Sprinkle with sesame seeds and serve.

CREAM OF SORREL SOUP

The acidity of sorrel comes through sharply in this simple pale green soup. A relative of spinach (but with a very different taste), sorrel melts almost to a purée with little cooking. Allowed to self-sow, chervil will be ready to pick with sorrel in early spring.

2 tbsp	butter	25 mL
1	onion, minced	1
2 cups	sorrel leaves, washed and very finely chopped	500 mL
3 tbsp	fresh chervil, minced (optional)	50 mL
1 tbsp	flour	15 mL
1½ cups	milk	375 mL
1½ cups	chicken stock (or water)	375 mL
pinch	nutmeg, freshly grated	pinch
½ tsp	salt (or to taste)	2 mL
	Pepper to taste	
	Fresh chives, snipped as a garnish	

In a soup pot, sauté onion with the salt in butter until onion is translucent and soft. Add sorrel (and chervil if using), and cook with the onion a minute or two. Sprinkle in flour and nutmeg, and stir to coat vegetables. Add milk, stock, salt and pepper, and simmer soup gently for about 20 to 30 minutes. Serve as is or blend for a smoother consistency.

The Fruitful Season
Strawberries and Raspberries

Is there a gardener who doesn't yearn to grow fruit? I wonder if it has something to do with images of the mythic Eden garden, a peaceful paradise shaded by fruit-laden trees growing beside a sparkling stream. Bright colors, tastes bordering on the heavenly: fruit seems to be nature at her most extravagant and generous, playful almost.

When my friend and I came to the country, we looked over the wide sunny field that we hoped to transform into a down-to-earth paradise and, in imagination, we filled the space with fruiting plants. With the enthusiasm of new gardeners—and visions of sugar plums, peaches, pears, apricots and cherries dancing in our heads—we cleared circles of grass, dug holes and planted a dozen dwarf fruit trees. Setting out a line of dry sticks with roots along a new post-and-wire fence, we pictured the future grapevines, precisely pruned, heavy with purple, red and green clusters. We planted brambles, currant bushes and strawberries.

Our innocent notion that we could have fruit for the planting soon came a cropper at the hand of reality. Out in that wind-swept field, all the grapevines died the first winter. The few trees that survived failed (as they say) to thrive. Gradually, however, we discovered what tree fruit would "do" here—apples, sour cherries, certain plums and pears—how to prune, what to spray and when. We learned that fruit plants fared much better within the bounds of the kitchen garden where we could keep an eye on them; that heat-loving grapes did better in the shelter at the south-facing, stone house wall. Fruit takes time, attention, skill, study and patience—not to forget that unavoidable aspect of all post-paradise gardening, the "sweat of your brow," which is no reason to throw up your hands and say forget it.

STRAWBERRIES

An encouraging note in all that early fruitlessness was the strawberry patch. In June the kitchen garden yields lettuce, spinach, scallions and radishes, but most of the beds are showing more promise than produce. With one notable exception: A heady fragrance rises from the place where strawberries—the season's first fruit and, some would say, its best—are ripening. Sunrise finds us in the patch, searching for ripe berries. Early botanists were so smitten with the scent of strawberries that they named the genus *Fragaria*, the fragrant ones.

Strawberries recommend themselves to home gardeners as the best choice of fruit for several reasons. First, the small plants are well suited to culture in wide, raised beds alongside other vegetables. Indeed, as one expert (from Britain's Royal Horticultural Society) notes, "strawberries are best grown in the kitchen garden" where they can be shifted from one bed to another every few years. Strawberries are quick to grow: plant dormant nursery stock in early spring and you can expect a fulsome harvest about fourteen months later; move some of your own best plants to a new bed in August, and you'll be picking next June. And they are productive: according to one study, four 25-foot (7.5-m) rows should yield "3 quarts of berries a day over a period of 3 weeks."

Strawberries are possibly the easiest of fruit to grow. Given a modicum of attention, they usually flourish and spread. Like a green octopus, each plant sends out a criss-crossing network of wiry runners. Some end in a single new rosette; others trail on to sprout a string of plants. The most puzzling aspect of strawberry culture is what to do with the surplus. Left alone, they eventually

OPPOSITE: Sweet rewards from the home garden: a bowl of perfectly ripe, pesticide-free strawberries. What could be better for a snack right in the garden?

Early spring is the time to set out new strawberry plants. Over the summer, runners will fill in the bare spaces with young daughter plants.

form a dense groundcover showing more leaves and less fruit.

Nursery Stock

Once started with strawberries—and assuming the patch stays healthy—a gardener can perpetuate them indefinitely by periodic renewal. First-time growers, however, must avail themselves of nursery stock, either through the mail or from a garden center. What you'll receive are tight bundles of 25 or 50 dryish, small tufts with withered leaves attached to limp, pale roots—not very promising. If you cannot get plants into the ground the day they arrive, you're advised to keep the unopened bags in the refrigerator for no more than three days. To store the plants any longer, hoe open a shallow, V-shaped trench in the garden, separate the bundle into individual plants and line them out, side by side, with roots pressed flat against one side of the trench, and crowns above ground. Pull earth over the roots, covering them completely, and tamp by hand or with the back of a rake for firm root/soil contact; water well. The same process, called heeling-in, is used to hold any bare-root nursery stock, from raspberries to roses, for a week or two before they are moved to a permanent home.

Ground Work

If you are breaking new ground for a strawberry bed, give yourself a full season to dig and redig the space, rounding up every scrap of quack grass, bindweed, thistle and such as you go. Once perennial weeds have crept in among the berry plants, you'll be hard-pressed to root them out totally. The steps outlined for preparing a new asparagus bed apply here. Better yet, use an established kitchen-garden bed that has had the benefit of years of weed clearing and organic improvement.

Any soil short of dry sand or water-logged clay will grow strawberries. Keep in mind, though, that the small plants have a ravenous appetite for organic matter, and what they relish most is barnyard manure, compost and rotted leaves. A slightly acidic soil pH of between 5 and 6.5 is best, so lime is not needed, unless the site is very sour. New strawberries are planted in early spring, traditionally "when the deciduous trees are beginning to leaf out." I like to prepare a bed the fall before, digging or tilling in at least 3 inches (8 cm) of year-old cattle or horse manure, which continues to mellow and decay over winter, leaving the earth in fine shape by planting time. Compost, spent mushroom medium, and partially decayed leaves are excellent alternatives (or additions) to manure. Abundant organic matter translates directly into a more bountiful crop. Before planting in spring, we may broadcast a measured amount of balanced natural fertilizer and scuffle it into the top few inches—strawberries are shallow rooted compared to many plants—before raking the bed level and smooth.

Planting

Having endured a trip through the mail or weeks on a garden-center shelf, strawberry plants are revived by an hour-long soak in a bucket of water prior to planting. Strawberries are extremely sensitive to the depth at which they are set in the earth. As one expert warns, "Half an inch either way will seriously restrict future growth." Look for the point where leaves sprout, and position plants so that this point, the crown, is level with the soil surface. See, too, that all roots extend down into the ground without bunching or bending upward; you may have to trim the odd root. I have a pint-sized digger, halfway between a trowel and a spade, that makes short work of strawberry holes, which I excavate all at once, assembly-line style, before starting to plant. Cover roots completely, firm soil around them, and drench. Once the water has drained, go over the patch and gently ease up any plants that have been sucked too deep by the draining water. After a few hours, or the next day, scratch lightly around each plant, leaving a thin layer of loose soil.

Pinching Blossoms

Now comes the hard job. Newly set strawberry plants usually start to flower within a few weeks. For their own good, and to stimulate the growth of runners that will bear heavily next summer, we're told to nip all first-season blossoms in the bud. Note, however, that this applies only to June bearers, by far the most widely grown type of strawberry. If you have planted everbearers or day-neutral strawberries (see below), stop pinching buds toward the end of June; chances are you'll reap a modest late-summer harvest. Nipping of strawberry flowers is uneasy work; it seems so manipulative and counter productive—a rule meant to be broken? I have to say that most of the time we miss this step, and the plants do just fine.

Mulching and Weeding

No one knows for sure where the strawberry got its name, whether originally strew- or stray-berry from its wandering ways, or whether straw refers to the tradition of spreading barley or wheat straw beneath the plants to cushion the delicate fruit. In any case, a permanent mulch of straw, leaves, old sawdust, pine needles, even shredded cornstalks saves a fair bit of weeding and watering, and keeps the berries off the ground. But even when we don't mulch, we make a point of pulling or digging weeds

An everbearing strawberry shows every stage from flowers to ripe fruit all at once.

whenever we are training runners, or picking blossoms or berries—especially in a young patch. Weeds soon crowd new berry plants, stealing food, water and sunlight. If you're the kind of gardener who thinks weeds are part of the garden's natural balance, merely innocent wildflowers growing in the "wrong place," think twice before planting strawberries. Thistles, lamb's quarters, goldenrod and such may well be wildflowers, but a strawberry patch (to my mind) is no place for them. That said, a neighbor grows abundant crops of succulent strawberries in a field swamped with weeds, so it may be more a matter of aesthetics than culture.

The Hill System

The most impressive strawberry bed I've ever seen belongs to a neighbor who sets her original plants 1 foot (30 cm) apart in compost-rich soil, mulches them heavily with maple leaves and conscientiously cuts off all runners before they roam too far. This practice, called the hill system, sends all of the juice to the mother plants, which grow into robust clumps loaded with fruit. As soon as the last berry is picked, she shears off all of the leafy top growth, replenishes the mulch with compost or more leaves and continues

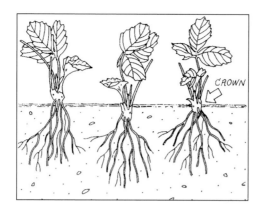

Strawberry plants are very sensitive to depth of planting. See that plants are positioned so that crowns—the point where leaves sprout—are level with the soil surface, not too high nor too deep.

to watch for stray runners. To extend or renew the planting, she allows the required number of runners to root down in 3-inch (8-cm) earth-filled flower pots sunk in the ground up to their rims. Rooting accomplished, she severs the cord linking mother and daughter and transplants the young one elsewhere.

Strawberry Geometry (or Spaced Matted Row)

Needing almost daily attention, this strict scheme is not for laissez-faire gardeners—or lazy-fair-weather ones either. The opposite approach, called the matted-row system, is to let all the runners root, but what you gain in time you lose in berries. We've settled, at least in theory, on a compromise between nipping every runner and total hands-off. The result is a modified or spaced matted row, once called a hedgerow.

Starting with a typical 4 foot (1.2 m) by 25 foot (7.5 m) kitchen-garden bed, we set out two rows of strawberry plants. The rows are measured 1 foot (30 cm) in from the edge of the bed, 2 feet (60 cm) apart. Within the rows, plants are spaced 2 feet apart. During their first season, we allow each mother to produce four runners. Two are trained to fill the gaps along the rows; the other two are stretched out to either side to start two more lines parallel to the original rows. The next year, as the original mothers and their daughters are fruiting, new runners are coaxed into empty spaces, leaving plants 8 to 10 inches (20 to 25 cm) apart over the whole bed. All unwanted

runners are cut away. After the mother plants have fruited for a year or two, we dig them out and encourage new ones to take their place.

That's the theory. In practice, the strawberry bed usually falls into chaos and congestion after three or four years, and we are left scratching our heads, wondering "who's offa who" (as an old neighbor says when trying to sort out the family ties of folks around him), which are the mother plants, grandmothers, daughters, and how on earth we'll get rid of all that bindweed. When that happens, it's time for a fresh start, and that, alas, means tearing up the old patch.

Renewal

Rooting out and composting hundreds of healthy strawberry plants feels like the opposite of gardening, but when we remember how bounteous the patch used to be, the big luscious berries compared to the current small crop of undersized fruit, we're motivated to dig. Not, however, before we carefully pry up as many young plants as needed to start over someplace else. Keeping a ball of earth intact around their roots, we set the plants, as before, in a fresh weedless bed that has been generously enriched with compost, manure and natural fertilizer. The job can be done anytime from July to September, always remembering that newly set plants respond to frequent waterings in the heat and drought of summer. At any season, a cooling mulch is very much to their liking, but mulch is a must for strawberries shifted in September to keep them in the ground during the coming cycles of freeze-and-thaw.

Aftercare and Renovation

When our friend shears back her plants after they have fruited, she is following the most drastic method of strawberry renovation—and, by all accounts, the most effective. Here goes, drastic measures: The day after you pick the last berry—time is of the essence, here—set the lawn mower to its highest cut and run it over the patch, cutting off all foliage. In a small patch use a sickle or shears. Rake up the leaves for compost. Now is the time to dig out all unwanted plants, leaving the remainder no more than a handspan apart. Pull up overgrown older clumps rather than vigorous younger plants. You may need to position stakes and string to bring the berry patch into line; fork out any runners that have strayed beyond the boundaries of the bed or row. I always feel like an ogre tearing through the strawberries like that, but if I think of the excess plants as compost fodder, it's not so bad.

Thinning completed, spread the required amount of natural fertilizer for the size of the patch. We use either a commercial fertilizer with a balance of nutrients, or rich compost or rotted manure—sometimes all three! A newly renovated bed looks bald and patchy. But soak it thoroughly, spread more mulch if you have it, and you'll be pleasantly surprised at how quickly things green up. Before long, the strawberries are off and running again.

The dramatic makeover just described applies only to June-bearing strawberries, those that ripen all their fruit over a few weeks in late spring. Everbearers, which yield a light first harvest in June and a smattering of berries throughout the summer, respond nicely to the hill system of culture; set the plants a foot apart and remove the few runners that form unless they are needed to increase or renew a patch. Although we grow a small bed of everbearers, we would never trade their on-again, off-again habit for the June-bearers that bring in a satisfying bumper crop at a time when garden fruit is most appreciated.

Because new cultivars are always being introduced and some do better in one region than in another, I hesitate to recommend specific strawberry varieties. Local fruit experts, whether at a university, county extension office or garden center, as well as current gardening magazines, make it their business to keep abreast. We make our choice from catalogs that originate in a climate zone similar to our own. What we look for can be summed up as disease resist-

As soon as fruiting is over, cut away all strawberry foliage, thin the patch, fertilize and renew the mulch. The comeback will be dramatic.

ance—no point in tempting fate—and excellent flavor. Commercial growers can have the firm, flawless beauties, all glossy red surface and little taste, that travel the continent with never a bruise. But give this gardener melt-in-the-mouth, close-your-eyes strawberries that ooze juice and recall the intense essence of tiny wild strawberries in the meadow beyond.

Frost Warning

Strawberries should be in the sun, and if possible, in an area where late-spring frosts are not known to settle. It happens every year: just when the strawberries are full of flowers, the wind shifts into the north, bringing a last blast of arctic air. By evening all is calm and you can almost smell the impending frost. Out come blankets, sheets, big towels, anything to throw over the blooming berry bed. It's time well spent. Frost does no harm to the plants, but it strikes at the heart of strawberry blossoms, leaving them black—and a blackened blossom means no fruit.

Strawberries of all kind fare better with some protection over winter wherever the temperature falls into the frigid digits (below 20°F/–7°C) and the snow comes and goes. The goal is to keep extreme cold from blasting the buds that are hidden in the plants' heart. Mid-November or later, after a freeze or two has triggered dormancy, is soon enough to cover the patch; the delay allows plants time to form a few extra flower buds during the warmth of Indian summer. At this point, we spread mulch not just around plants, but over them. Choose pine needles, straw, evergreen boughs, armloads of leaves or any other fluffy organic matter laid on about 3 inches (8 cm) deep. We have a neighbor with a barn full of ten-year-old hay, free for the taking; the old stuff seems to harbor very few weed seeds compared to newly cut.

Come spring, when the first snowdrops and early crocuses are out, we rearrange the hay, snugging it around the plants and piling the leftover on the pathways. A strawberry, they say, should be picked with its green cap attached. This is one rule we feel free to ignore as we breakfast in the strawberry bed, reclining on the hay-cushioned path. Decadent? Not at all. The gentle June sun, the mingled scents of hay and berries and earth, the sweet-tart taste of ripe fruit are innocent pleasures all.

RASPBERRIES

Raspberries are among the most delicate and delicious of fruit. Never abundant in markets, they are almost always expensive. Anyone considering growing their own ought to know two more things. First, while raspberries' roots are perennial, the canes—the part you see above ground—are biennial. This means that, each summer, raspberries send up a number of new shoots, called primocanes; but it is not until the following year that these canes, now called floricanes, branch out, flower and set fruit. Their mission accomplished, they gradually die back. All of this is happening at once: In a given year, some canes will be shooting upward, others fruiting, and—unless you step in with pruning shears—still others will be dying back.

The second thing to know about raspberries is that their roots have no intention of staying where you put them. In our garden, suckers routinely travel more than 5 feet (1.5 m) under a well-trodden path to get into the rich soil of a perennial flowerbed across the way. If it weren't for its berries, this prickly, invasive bramble would be classed as a bad weed.

The big pricetag on a small box of raspberries reflects not only the fragility of the fruit but also the work involved in raising canes. Low-maintenance they are not. And yet, we persist in pruning, pulling up suckers, and protecting the canes over the winter for the pleasure of grazing on the aromatic berries for a few weeks in July.

Ground Work

The most fruitful approach to raspberry culture—thorough soil preparation—is also the most time-consuming at the start. Consider, however, that a patch may be in place for ten years or more. A good start not only pays off handsomely in berries, it also reduces care and maintenance in years to come. As with asparagus and strawberries, it is crucial that the future raspberry bed be completely free of perennial weeds. Dig the space over once, and remove all the roots you unearth; wait a few weeks to see what sprouts, then dig again to catch the strays. Repeat.

Once the land is clean, it's time to add as much organic matter as you can spare. Raspberries thrive in slightly acidic soil (pH 6.0 to 6.7) that retains ample moisture but drains well; standing water can injure or kill roots. All soil, whether light and sandy or dense with clay, responds to an organic menu of decayed manures, compost, rotted leaves, extra-old sawdust and such, applied with a generous hand. One expert recommends 1 ton of well-rotted manure, and a heavy application of rock phosphate, tilled into a 4-foot (1.2-m) by 100-foot (30-m) bed.

On a smaller scale, I like the traditional English method of preparing a raspberry bed. First, mark off a 2-foot-wide (60-cm) band with stakes and string. The length depends on your garden space, but consider that an established 25-foot (7.5-m) row—a mere dozen plants to start—should yield berries enough for four in a good year. Remove the soil, down to the depth of a spade, along the band and pile it to one side. Fork into the trench a 3- to 4-inch (8- to 10-cm) layer of old manure and/or compost. Whiten the surface of the organic stuff with

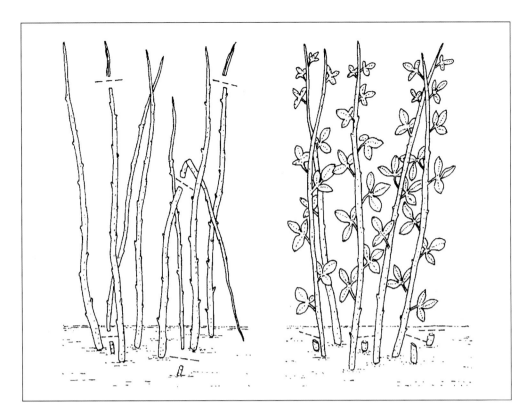

In spring, prune away broken and winter-killed canes or tips. Thin the remainder to stand about 4 inches (10 cm) apart, cutting out the weak and spindly canes. In summer, after all berries have been picked, cut at ground level all canes that have borne fruit.

bone meal and/or rock phosphate and stir the works into the bottom of the trench, mixing it thoroughly with the soil. Return the topsoil, mixed with additional fine-textured organic matter if you have it. Before raking, sprinkle on a measured amount of a balanced natural fertilizer. Parallel rows should be spaced 6 to 8 feet (1.8 to 3 m) apart, center to center, and should, if possible, run north and south so as not to shade each other. But note: If your soil is in fairly good shape already, either naturally fertile (you lucky gardener) or improved over the years with organic matter, you may well get away with simply planting raspberries and feeding them later on from the top with a constant mulch.

Planting

New raspberry canes are best planted in early spring. Ours usually arrive in the mail, a bundle of prickly, dead-looking sticks with a beard of dry roots looking the worse for the trip. To revive them, soak the roots in a pail of cool water for several hours prior to planting. Never leave plants lying around uncovered in the sun; one good drying could weaken them beyond recovery. For speed's sake, dig all the holes at once, spacing them 2 feet (60 cm) apart, and making them wide enough so that roots can be spread out naturally, and deep enough so that the canes will be a little lower than had previously been growing—you'll see a line on the cane. This slightly deeper planting is said to inhibit the rise of suckers—and raspberries can stand a little slowing down. Firm soil around roots with gloved fingers or a blunt stick, then pour on the water to saturate the root zone. Trim any long canes back to 4-inch (10-cm) stubs. Once new shoots sprout, cut these stubs right to the ground.

Mulch, and More Mulch

The next step, mulching, is the best thing you can do for a raspberry patch over the long term. See that mulch does not touch newly planted canes, but lay it on thickly as the patch gets established. A permanent deep mulch might be as much as 5 to

10 inches (12 to 25 cm) of old straw or last fall's leaves; or half that amount of strawy manure, well-aged sawdust, shredded bark, or wood chips. Fresh wood byproducts steal more nutrients than they supply in the process of breaking down, so let raw sawdust sit in a heap and mellow for at least a year. If all talk of sawdust and manure makes raspberries seem impractical, bear in mind that a permanent mulch of deciduous leaves, usually abundant and always free, supplies all the nutrients that raspberries need. Well-mulched raspberries may get by nicely on rainfall alone. Water is especially necessary during blossoming and fruit formation. If rains fail then, soak the ground every five days or so.

PRUNING
Spring and Summer
There is no way around it. Twice a year, raspberries must be pruned, a task we approach with impenetrable gloves and strong shears. In spring, as canes are leafing out, cut away dead canes and any winter-killed tips, as well as weak, spindly, and damaged shoots. We then thin the remainder, leaving the strongest canes standing about 4 inches (10 cm) apart. It's not easy to cut out fine-looking canes, but steel yourself and thin them. Don't cut back the tops of live canes unless they are waving around in the air out of reach. Given enough moisture and fertility, raspberries will flower and fruit right to their tips.

The next major pruning comes in July, immediately after the berries have been picked. This is the time to cut all canes that have finished fruiting right back to ground level; do not leave stubs, an inviting breeding ground for bugs and blights. For the health of the patch, the cut-away canes should be burned or disposed of at some distance—they are not compost material. This second pruning is crucial. Dying canes are easy targets for diseases that are then spread to the rest. Of course, suckers that have strayed beyond the allotted raspberry row must be yanked out as weeds.

Fall Pruning
Like strawberries, various raspberry cultivars bear fruit at different times. The pruning methods detailed above apply to the so-called June-bearers, which actually fruit in July in most areas. These are the most widely planted type of raspberry.

Fall-bearers, in contrast, yield a modest crop from August to October at the tops of first-year canes and more berries on the same canes next year. There are two possible approaches to pruning fall-bearing raspberries. Once they have fruited, you can shorten the tops, leaving the rest of the cane to flower and fruit the following July like a "normal" raspberry. Alternatively treat the canes as annuals, cutting them right to the ground in late fall or early winter—there will be no prickly shoots to protect and nothing but stubble showing in the patch over winter. In spring, new canes will rise up vigorously and, by late summer, you're in the berries again. 'Heritage' is a popular fall raspberry; fruiting rather late in the season, it is not suited to regions where cold summers are the rule and frost strikes in September. Both 'August Red' and 'Fall Red' are earlier. A lovely sweet amber berry, 'Fall Gold' is vigorous and early but must have winter protection in cold areas; it is also apt to be slowed by viruses. As with strawberries, choose varieties that are adapted to your area. I doubt that any of our raspberry growing neighbors could name the varieties they grow—canes are often passed around. But where wilt, mold or diseases pose a problem, avoid starting with suckers from a patch down the road, or propagating your own raspberries. Plants from an established nursery should be certified disease-free.

Untrained Canes
Books abound with elaborate methods of training and supporting raspberries: single or double fences, Scandinavian style, the single-post system. The various setups of posts and wire look neat and professional—and we mean to try them one of these days—but until then, we'll grow raspberries, as we have

for years, without support. We have many neighbors, too, who grow long rows of free-standing canes to one side of their big farm gardens. Raspberry canes, properly pruned and thinned, are sturdy enough to hold themselves up; if they do loll over a pathway, a temporary arrangement of stakes and strong string is enough to hold them back. Truth is, the only place I've seen those tidy trellised raspberries is in books—to which I refer you.

Down for the Winter

Where winters are bitter—and especially in places where cold drying winds howl across the land—raspberries come through in better condition if the pliable canes are bent gently as close to the ground as possible in late fall. We hold them down with lengths of two-by-four; some growers heap soil over the cane tops, or ease the canes over in bun-dles and secure them with stout wire hoops pushed deeply into the ground. The arched interlaced shoots catch the snow, the best insulation for any perennial. When the snow melts in March, we remove the boards and watch the canes spring back upright. But note: in most areas such time consuming protection is not necessary. These are steps to take if canes are consistently killed back every winter.

Raspberries may not be for every garden or every gardener. The canes take up a fair bit of space and, left unattended, they soon grow into a tangled briar patch. If I had but one bed for berries, I'd grow strawberries instead. But if you have the room, and the inclination to prune and train, the rewards are sweet. Most of our raspberries never make it to the kitchen.

Appendix
North American Seed Sources

UNITED STATES SEED SOURCES

Abundant Life Seed Foundation
Box 772
Port Townsend, Washington 98368-0772
360-385-5660; fax 360-385-7455
www.abundantlifeseed.org
abundant@olypen.com
A non-profit seed foundation and preservation project. Seed catalog, book list and periodic newsletters. Non-hybrid varieties with a number of heirlooms, some of which are noted as such. Write for membership information. Catalog $2 or on-line.

Baker Creek Heirloom Seeds
2278 Baker Creek Rd.
Mansfield, Missouri 65704
417-924-8917
www.rareseeds.com
seeds@rareseeds.com
This company sells only non-hybrid vegetables, flowers and herbs. Catalog free.

Bountiful Gardens
18001 Shafer Ranch Rd.
Willits, California 95490-9626
707-459-6410; fax 707-459-1925
www.bountiful gardens.org
bountiful@sonic.net
Interesting selection of non-hybrid seeds, as well as books, tools and organic gardening supplies. Catalog free to U.S.; $2. to Canada.

Burpee & Co.
300 Park Ave.
Warminster, Pennsylvania 18974
800-333-5808; fax 800-487-5530
www.burpee.com
custserv@burpee.com
Large listing. Catalog free.

Cook's Garden
Box 535
Londonderry, Vermont 05148
802-824-3400; fax 802-824-3027
Cook's Garden is committed to ecological and sustainable farming methods. All seeds are untreated and time tested. Claims to have the largest selection of lettuce and salad greens in the world. Catalog free.

Donna's Heirloom Tomatoes
5423 Princess Drive
Rosedale, Maryland 21237
www.heirloomtomatoes.net
Heirloom seeds of tomatoes and other vegetables. Catalog free,

Down on the Farm Seed
P.O. Box 184
Hiram, Ohio 44234
Offers a full line of untreated, open-pollinated, heirloom vegetable, herb and flower seeds. All seed packets except corn are $1. Catalog free.

Ed Hume Seeds
P.O. Box 73160
Puyallup, Washington 98373
www.humeseeds.com
jeff@humeseeds.com
Small company with seed for cooler climates. Catalog free.

Fedco Seeds
P.O. Box 520-A
Waterville, Maine 04903
fax 207-872-8317
www.fedcoseeds.com
Organic products and vegetable seeds. Catalog $2, refundable, or on-line.

Fox Hollow Seed Co.
204 Arch St.
Kittanning, Pennsylvania 16201-1501
724-548-7333; fax 724-548-7333
www.foxhollowseed.com
seeds@alltel.net
Organic products and seeds, including heirloom. Catalog free.

Franklin Hill Garden Seeds
2430 Rochester Rd.
Sewickly, Pennsylvania 15143
412-367-6202; fax 412-367-6202
www.nb.net/~franklin/
Small but interesting selection. Catalog free or on-line.

Garden City Seeds
Box 307
Thorp, Washington 98946
877-733-3001; fax 800-964-910
www.gardencityseeds.com
potatoes@irish-eyes.com
Specializes in varieties adapted to northern climates. Offers a number of heirlooms, marked as such. Catalog free.

Heirloom Seeds
P.O. Box 245
West Elizabeth, Pennsylvania 15088-0245
412-384-0852
www.heirloomseeds.com
Vegetable seeds, onion and garlic bulbs. Catalog $1, refundable, or on-line.

High Mowing Organic Seed Farm
813 Brook Road
Wolcott, Vermont 05680
802-888-1800; fax 802-888-8446
www.highmowingseeds.com
Open-pollinated and heirloom varieties for New England. Catalog free.

J.L. Hudson Seedsman
Star Route 2, Box 337
La Honda, California 94020
www.JLHudsonseeds.net
All seeds are open-pollinated, public domain and biodiversity. Catalog $1.

Johnny's Selected Seeds
184 Foss Hill Road, RR#1, Box 2580
Albion, Maine 04910-9731
207-437-4301; fax 207-437-2165
www.johnnyseeds.com
homegarden@johnnyseeds.com
An excellent selection of varieties regionally adapted to New England. Johnny's does plant breeding and thoroughly tests the varieties it offers. Catalog free.

Le Jardin du Gourmet
P.O. Box 75I, Dept. 1
St. Johnsburg Ctr., Vermont 05863-0075
802-748-1446; fax 802-748-1446
www.artisticgardens.com
orderdesk@artisticgardens.com
Catalog free.

Marianna's Heirloom Seed
1955 CCC Rd.
Dickson, Tennessee 37055
www.mariseeds.com
Specializes in heirloom vegetables, tomatoes and peppers. Catalog free or on-line.

The Natural Gardening Company
P.O. Box 750776
Petaluma, California 94975-0776
707-766-9303; fax 707-766-9747
www.naturalgardening.com
Organic products, plants, seeds. Catalog free.

Nichols Garden Nursery
1190 Old Salem Rd. NE
Albany, Oregon 97321-4580
541-928-9280; fax 541-967-8406
www.nicholsgardennursery.com
Organic, non-GMO seeds, onion and garlic bulbs. Catalog free.

Park Seed Company
1 Parkton Ave.
Greenwood, South Carolina 29649
800-213-0076
www.parkseed.com
info@parkseed.com
Large established seed firm with extensive selection. Catalog free.

Pinetree Garden Seeds
P.O. Box 300
New Gloucester, Maine 04260
207-926-3400; fax 888-527-3337
www.superseeds.com
superseeds@superseeds.com
Excellent prices on seed packets sized for home gardeners. Catalog free.

Redwood City Seed Co.
Box 361
Redwood City, California 94064
www.ecoseeds.com
Ancient varieties of vegetables and culinary and medicinal herbs. Catalog free.

Seed Savers Exchange
3076 North Winn Rd.
Decorah, Iowa 52101
563-382-5990; fax 563-382-5872
www.seedsavers.org
A grassroots seed exchange. Members receive two information-filled issues and a huge seed listing. A free heirloom and products catalog published for the general public.

Seeds from Italy
P.O. Box 149
Winchester, Massachusetts 01890
781-721-5904; fax 612-435-4020
www.growitalian.com
seeds@growitalian.com
Non-hybrid, non-GMO European varieties. Catalog free.

Sow Organic Seed
P.O. Box 527
Williams, Oregon 97544
888-709-7333
www.organicseed.com
organic@organicseed.com
Organic products and untreated seeds. Catalog free or on-line.

Stokes Seeds
P.O. Box 548
Buffalo, New York 14240-0548
800-396-9238; fax 888-834-3334
www.stokeseeds.com
An old standby company of excellent reputation; very helpful growing instructions on seed packets. Catalog free.

Territorial Seed Company
P.O. Box 158
Cottage Grove, Oregon 97424-0061
541-942-9547; fax 888-657-3131
www.territorial-seed.com
tertrl@territorial-seed.com
Large selection of organic products, seeds, fruit and berry plants. Catalog free.

Thompson and Morgan
Box 1308
Jackson, New Jersey 08527-0308
800-274-7333; fax 888-466-4769
www.thompson-morgan.com
tminc@thompson-morgan.com
Catalog has a huge variety of seeds with in-depth information. Catalog free.

Underwood Gardens
4N381 Maple Ave.
Bensenville, IL 60106
630-616-0268; fax 630-616-0232
www.underwoodgardens.com
info@underwoodgardens.com
Many hard to find or endangered, untreated, open-pollinated seeds of heirloom vegetables, herbs and flowers. Catalog $3.

Victory Seed Company
P.O. Box 192
Molalla, Oregon 97038
503-829-3126; fax 503-829-3126
www.victoryseeds.com
Inquiries@VictorySeeds.com
The Victory Seed company is a family-owned and operated garden packet seed company specializing in open-pollinated and heirloom seeds, with many heirloom tomatoes. Catalog $2, refundable, or on-line.

CANADIAN SEED SOURCES

Alberta Nurseries & Seeds Ltd.
Box 20
Bowden, Alberta T0M 0K0
403-224-3544; fax 403-224-2455
www.gardenersweb.com
seed@telusplanet.net
Flowers, vegetables, perennials, seeds, bulbs and fruit. Catalog $2 to U.S., free in Canada.

Allan, Ken
61 South Barlett St.
Kingston, Ontario K7K 1X3
allan@kingston.net
Organic and open-pollinated. Hardy sweet potatoes, climbing peas, tomatoes, peppers, etc. SASE or international reply coupon for a price list.

Along the Garden Path
P.O. Box 1222
Cobourg, Ontario K9A 5A4
www.eagle.ca/~akeenan/Gardenpath
akeenan@eagle.ca
Catalog online or by request. Committed to preserving Heritage varieties of vegetables.

Aurora Biodynamic Farm
3492 Phillips Rd.
Creston, B.C. V0B 1G2
250-428-4404; fax 250-428-4404
www.kootenay.com/~aurora
aurora@kootenay.com
Organic and open-pollinated herbs vegetables and flowers. Catalog U.S. or Can $3 or on-line. U.S. address is P. O. Box 697, Porthill, ID 83853

Beckers Seed Potatoes
RR#1
Trout Creek, Ontario P0H 2L0
705-724-2305; fax 705-724-1392
beckers@vianet.ca
A large selection of elite seed potatoes many heirlooms Catalog gives descriptions places and dates of introduction. Catalog free.

Circle Dance Seeds
RR#3, 84354 McNabb Line
Brussels, Ontario N0G 1H0
905-887-9793
circledanceseeds@scsinternet.com
New company aiming to inform on health, whole foods, organic sustainability and self-sufficiency. Offers medicinal herbs and heirloom vegetables. Canadian postage stamps. Catalog $2, refundable with first order.

The Cottage Gardener
4199 Gilmore Rd., RR#1
Newtonville, Ontario L0A 1J0
905-786-2388
www.cottagegardener.com
heirlooms@cottagegardener.com
Heirloom plant nursery in Southern Ontario specializes in growing plants from the past using organic methods. They offer plants, bulbs and seeds. Catalog $2 or on-line.

Dominion Seed House
Box 2500
Georgetown, Ontario L7G 5L6
800-784-3037; fax 800-282-5746
www.dominion-seed-house.com
mail@dominion-seed-house.com
Mail order catalog of seeds, plants and bulbs for gardeners. Catalog free and on-line.

Early's Farm & Garden Centre Inc.
2615 Lorne Ave.
Saskatoon, Saskatchewan S7J 0S5
800-667-1159; fax 306-931-7110
www.earlysgarden.com
earlys@sk.sympatico.ca
Early's has been in business since 1907 offering a large variety of seeds and garden accessories. Catalog $2 to U.S., free in Canada.

Ecogenesis Inc.
1267-2384 Yonge St.
Toronto, Ontario M4P 3E5
416-485-8333; fax 416-489-0288
www.ecogenesis.ca
Ecogenesis offers early, heirloom and certified organic seeds to gardeners. They do not sell hybrid or genetically engineered seeds. Ecogenesis also donates seeds to charities. Catalog $5.

Eternal Seed
657 Pritchard Rd.
Farrellton, Quebec J0X 1T0
819-827-8881
edecas@travel-net.com
Ellen de Casemaker offers seeds of heirloom herbs, flowers and vegetables of more than fifty years ago. Catalog free.

Fish Lake Garlic Man
RR#2
Demorestville, Ontario K0K 1W0
613-476-8030
Ted Maczka offers several selected cultivars, all organically grown, and a list packed with informative tidbits. Catalog $3 with SASE.

Florabunda Seeds
Box 3
Indian River, Ontario K0L 2B0
705-295-6440; fax 705-295-4035
www.florabundaseeds.com
contact@florabundaseeds.com
Jeri-Lynne Rushton and Dirk Berghout offer untreated seeds for heirloom and unusual flowers, medicinal herbs and black, white and fragrant flower collections. Catalog free and on-line.

Full Circle Seeds
P.O. Box 807
Sooke, B.C. V0S 1N0
250-642-3671; fax 250-642-3671
fullcircleseeds@yahoo.com
Offers open-pollinated, untreated seed grown without herbicides, pesticides or synthetic fertilizers on Vancouver Island. Catalog is free for an SASE or as a listing by e-mail.

Greta's Organic Gardens
399 River Rd.
Ottawa, Ontario K1G 3N3
613-521-8648
www.seeds-organic.com
greta@seeds-organic.com
Greta's catalog is full of open-pollinated seeds, especially grown for short season. Catalog $2, refundable with first order.

Halifax Seed Company Inc.
Box 8026, Stn A, 5860 Kane St.
Halifax, Nova Scotia B3K 5L8
902-454-7456; fax 902-455-5271
www.halifaxseed.ca
info@halifaxseed.ca
Canada's oldest seed company offers a wide variety of vegetable, flower and herb seeds, gardening supplies, roses, perennials and bulbs. Catalog free or on-line.

Hole's Greenhouses & Garden Ltd.
101 Bellerose Dr.
St. Albert, Alberta T8N 8N8
888-884-6537; fax 780-459-6042
www.holesonline.com
info@holesonline.com
The Holes specializes in seeds for northern gardeners. The visual color reference catalog is a mine of information, and because the price list comes separately the catalog can be used for years. Catalog on-line.

Hope Seeds and Perennials
9 Apple Lane
Keswick Ridge, New Brunswick E6L 1P5
506-353-4450
www.hopeseed.com
hopeseed@nbnet.nb.ca
Dedicated to preserving Maritime heritage and other zone 4–5 varieties. All seed produced using environmentally friendly practices. Catalog free.

Howe Sound Seeds
Box 109
Bowen Island, B.C. V0N 1G0
604-947-0016; fax 604-947-0945
Specializes in open-pollinated late Victorian (1885–1901) vegetables. Descriptions and dates are given.

Island Seed Co.
Box 4278, Depot 3
Victoria, B.C. V8X 3X8
250-744-3677; fax 250-479-0221
The company provides a broad range of culinary herbs, heirloom vegetables and old-fashioned flowers. Catalog $2, refundable.

Les Jardins du Grand-Portage
800 Chemin du Portage
Saint-Didace, Quebec J0K 2G0
450 835-5813; fax 450 835-5813
www.intermonde.net/colloidales
colloidales@pandore.qc.ca
Canada only. All seeds are organic. Catalog free.

Lindenberg Seeds Ltd.
803 Princess Ave.
Brandon, Manitoba R7A 0P5
204-727-0575; fax 204-727-2832
www.lindenbergseeds.mb.ca
lindenbergr@lindenbergseeds.mb.ca
Specializing in seeds for northern climates. Catalog free to Canadians.

Mapple Farm
129 Beech Hill Rd.
Weldon, New Brunswick E4H 4N5
506-734-3361
wingate@nbnet.nb.ca
Unusual but useful certified organic (OCIA) seed
& plant stock: short-season sweet potato slips, a
select list of distinctive tomatoes, Jerusalem and
Chinese artichokes, Egyptian onions, French shal-
lots, horseradish. Catalog free with SASE or by
e-mail.

McFayden Seed Co. Ltd.
30–9th St.
Brandon, Manitoba R7A 6N4
800-205-7111; fax 204-725-1888
www.mcfayden.com
Mails everything, but specializes in prairie-hardy
nursery stock. Catalog free.

OSC Seeds (Ontario Seed Company)
Box 7, 330 Phillip St.
Waterloo, Ontario N2J 3Z6
519-886-0557; fax 519-886-0605
www.oscseeds.com
seeds@oscseeds.com
For over 100 years the Ontario Seed Company
has been serving gardeners with the finest quality
flower, vegetable and herb seeds. Catalog free.

Prairie Garden Seeds
Box 118
Cochin, Saskatchewan S0M 0L0
306-386-2737
www.prseeds.ca
prairie.seeds@sk.sympatico.ca
Organically grown open-pollinated seed for short
season, dryland growing. Many heirloom varieties
with historical backgrounds supplied. On-line
catalog or obtain printed catalog for $2.

Rawlinson Garden Seed
1979 Rte 105, Hwy 2
Sheffield, New Brunswick E3A 8H9
506-446-3882; fax 506-357-2256
rawlinson@fundy.net
The Hatt family specializes in cultivars that can
be successfully grown in a short season with many
heritage and open-pollinated species on hand.
Catalog free.

Richters Herbs
357 Hwy 47
Goodwood, Ontario L0C 1A0
905-640-6677; fax 905-640-6641
www.richters.com
orderdesk@richters.com
An enormous selection of unique seeds and plants.
On-line catalog gives descriptions and uses for
plants. Catalog free.

Salt Spring Seeds
Box 444, Ganges P.O.
Salt Spring Island, B.C. V8K 2W1
250-537-5269
www.saltspringseeds.com
Dedicated to sustainable agriculture. Organically
grown open-pollinated seeds. Specializes in beans.
A large and interesting variety of vegetables,
grains and garlic. Catalog $2 or on-line.

Seeds of Distinction
PO Box 86, Station A
Etobicoke, Ontario M9C 4V2
416-255-3060; fax 416-255-0633
www.seedsofdistinction.com
seeds@seedsofdistinction.com
Full-color on-line catalog that is searchable,
sortable and downloadable. Printed version by
request only. Catalog free.

Seeds of Diversity Canada
(Semences du patrimoine Canada)
Box 36, Stn Q
Toronto, Ontario M4T 2L7
905-623-0353
www.seeds.ca; www.semences.ca
mail@seeds.ca
A grassroots seed exchange whose members offer
seeds and bulbs of heirloom and scarce varieties of
vegetables, fruits, grains, herbs and flowers.

Seeds of Victoria
395 Conway Rd.,
Victoria, B.C. V9E 2B9
250-881-1555; fax 250-881-1304
www.earthfuture.com/gardenpath
Organic vegetable, flower, herb seeds: Heritage
plants, old-fashioned flowers; open-pollinated,
heirloom vegetables. Catalog $2.

Siloam Orchards
RR#1, 7300 3rd Concession
Uxbridge, Ontario L9P 1R1
905-852-9418; fax 905-852-3182
www.siloamorchards.com
mail@siloamorchards.com
Heritage disease-resistant fruit trees, including
apples, plums, pears, peach and cherry. Small
fruits include gooseberries,cherry plums, blue-
berries, currants, asparagus and horseradish.
Catalog $2.

Stellar Seeds
S6 C38, RR#1
Sorrento, B.C. V0E 2W0
250-675-3309; fax 250-675-6849
www.stellarseeds.com
info@stellarseeds.com
All seeds offered are high quality organically
grown by Stellar Seeds. Catalog $2, or download
for free from Web site.

Stokes Seeds Ltd.
296 Collier Rd., Box 10
Thorold, Ontario L2V 5E9
800-396-9238; fax 888-834-3334
www.stokeseeds.com
stokes@stokeseeds.com
Catalog has enormous information for the starting
and growing of flowers, herbs and vegetables.
Offers untreated seeds in many varieties. Catalog
free.

T & T Seeds Ltd.
Box 1710
Winnipeg, Manitoba R3C 3P6
204-895-9962; fax 204-895-9967
www.ttseeds.mb.ca
orders@ttseeds.mb.ca
Wide variety of excellent quality seeds and plants
offered. Also offers herbal and health products.
Catalog $3.

Terra Edibles
Box 164
Foxboro, Ontario K0K 2B0
613-961-0654; fax 613-968-6369
www.terraedibles.ca
karyn@magma.ca
Organically grown vegetable and flower seeds
including uncommon rare and heirloom varieties.
Catalog free or can be downloaded on-line.

Terra Viva Organics
505-1009 Expo Blvd.
Vancouver, B.C. V6Z 2V9
888-350-2847; fax 604-899-9374
www.tvorganics.com
info@tvorganics.com
Terra Viva is an on-line company offering envi-
ronmentally friendly gardening products. They
also produce weekly tips, feature products and a
monthly newsletter. Catalog free.

Tomatoes Etc.
63 Nelson
Outremont, Quebec H2V 3Z8
514 272-5185; fax 514 272-5185
tomatoesetc@yahoo.ca
Offering over 50 varieties of heirloom tomato
seedlings. Catalog by e-mail request.

Upper Canada Seeds
8 Royal Doulton Dr.
Don Mills, Ontario M3A 1N4
416-447-5321
uppercanadaseeds@rogers.com
Organic open-pollinated heirloom varieties of vegetables herbs and fruit. Catalog free.

Vesey's Seeds Ltd.
Box 9000
Charlottetown, P.E.I. C1A 8K6
800-363-7333; fax 800-686-0329
www.veseys.com
veseys@veseys.com
A large selection of seeds, plants and gardening supplies. Spring and fall bulb catalogs for Canadian customers only. Catalog free.

West Coast Seeds Ltd.
3925 64th St., RR#1
Vancouver, B.C. V4K 3N2
604-952-8820; fax 877 482-8822
www.westcoastseeds.com
info@westcoastseeds.com
Many excellent organic varieties. On-line catalog also includes growing information and planning for year-round harvesting. Catalog free.

William Dam Seeds
Box 8400
Dundas, Ontario L9H 6M1
905-628-6641; fax 905-627-1729
www.damseeds.com
willdam@damseeds.ca
Untreated seeds; more than 900 varieties of vegetables, flowers and herbs. Many European and heirloom, but not marked as such. Catalog free.

Windmill Point Farm and Nursery
2103 Boul. Perrot, N.D.
l'Ile Perrot, Quebec J7V 8P4
514-453-9757; 514-425-2728
www.windmillfarmorganics.com
windmillfarmorganics@qc.aibn.com
An OCIA-certified organic source for open-pollinated vegetable seeds and hardy seedlings of standard and unusual fruit and nut trees. The catalog also acts as a planning and planting guide. Catalog $5.

The sources above have been expanded and revised from the excellent resources list compiled by Seeds of Diversity Canada, available on their Web site, **www.seeds.ca.** Used with permission. For further information, contact Seeds of Diversity Canada, P.O. Box 36, Station Q, Toronto, Ontario M4T 2L7.

Index